TRANSNATIONAL BUILDINGS IN LOCAL ENVIRONMENTS

Transnational Buildings in Local Environments

LUCIANA MELCHERT SAGUAS PRESAS

ASHGATE

Published by
Ashgate Publishing Limited
Gower House
Croft Road
Aldershot
Hants GU11 3HR
England

Ashgate Publishing Company
Suite 420
101 Cherry Street
Burlington, VT 05401-4405
USA

Ashgate website: http://www.ashgate.com

British Library Cataloguing in Publication Data
Presas, Luciana Melchert Saguas
    Transnational buildings in local environments. - (Design
    and the built environment series)
    1. Office buildings - Design and construction 2. Sustainable
    architecture 3. City planning - Environmental aspects
    4. Globalization 5. Office buildings - Design and
    construction - Case studies 6. Sustainable architecture -
    Case studies 7. City planning - Environmental aspects - Case
    studies
    I. Title
    720.4'7

Library of Congress Cataloging-in-Publication Data
Presas, Luciana Melchert Saguas, 1973-
    Transnational buildings in local environments / by Luciana Melchert Saguas Presas.
        p. cm. -- (Design and the built environment)
    Includes bibliographical references and index.
    ISBN 0-7546-4316-6
    1. Urban ecology. 2. City planning--Environmental aspects. 3. Office buildings--
Environmental aspects. 4. International business enterprises--Environmental aspects.
    I. Title. II. Series: Design and the built environment series

    HT241.P74 2005
    307.76--dc22

                                                                        2004020410

ISBN 0 7546 4316 6

Typeset by Saxon Graphics Ltd, Derby
Printed and bound in Great Britain by T. J. International, Padstow

Contents

List of Figures, Tables and Charts

List of Figures

List of Tables

List of Charts

Preface and Acknowledgements

The office building is the most intriguing type of building in the contemporary world. It synthesizes the current post-industrial era of late modernity, an era that has introduced a new, globally interconnected social system based on information technology. The office building displays the power of the modern corporation while centralizing the command-and-control activities of the globalized economy. It is an internationally oriented commodity present in almost every nation; a visible symbol of local economic wealth, social, technological and economic progress, which rules – and yet transcends – the skyline of the contemporary global city. More than a local structure, the office building is now a transnational building, part of a broader socio-spatial matrix where key cities now meet. Probably few other building types depict so clearly what Castells calls a 'node and hub' of the network society: the crossroads between the highly dynamic world of global economic exchanges, governed by worldwide information-based flows, and local realities and (environmental) problems, governed by the dynamics of the place. My aim with this book is to explore how the transnational building may turn into a green building.

Several individuals and organizations provided generous financial and intellectual support without which this study would have not been completed. I would like in the first place to express my deep gratitude to Wageningen University and Research Centre, particularly to the Environmental Policy Group, for enabling the research and its field studies financially. I am more than indebted to Professor Arthur Mol and Professor Gert Spaargaren for all the exchanges we have had, which indeed built up the foundation for the material presented in this study; I honestly do not know where their ideas finish and where mine begin. It has been a privilege to work with them and other colleagues in Wageningen. Thank you Zhang Lei, Susan Martens, Corry Rothuizen, Dick Legger, Peter Oosterveer, Peter Ho, Kris van Koppen, Bas van Vliet and many others for a close collaboration all these years.

This study has also benefited enormously from the support of the Institute for Housing and Urban Development Studies (IHS) in Rotterdam, particularly at its beginning. I am very grateful to Professor Isa Baud, Dr Okke Braadbaart, Dr Jaap de Vries and the students of the first International Training Programme on Sustainable Building and Urban Development for broadening my understanding of the social dynamics of technological change in different local realities.

Many thanks are of course due to the persons interviewed for the research, who provided the information that forms the empirical body of this work. Many of these interviews were indeed inspiring. Among these, much gratitude goes to Architect Roemer van Toorn, Professor Peter Schmid, Architect Max van Huut and Dr Juriaan van Meel (in the Netherlands); Architect Jorge Wilheim and Architect Renato Siqueira (in Brazil); and Architect Zhaohui Wu, Architect Cui Kai and Patricia

Lamberts (in China) for their special attention in receiving me. Thanks are also due to Dr Song Yehao from Tsinghua University for providing helpful comments on my chapter on Beijing and David Coles for revising my English.

   In closing, I would like to express my gratitude to my family, particularly to my sister Roberta. I would like to dedicate this work to them and also to Michel for always intriguing and inspiring me in so many different ways.

São Paulo

Chapter 1

Overview

Figure 1.1   Commerzbank headquarters, Frankfurt

In 1997 Europe's tallest skyscraper was inaugurated in the centre of Frankfurt to serve as the headquarters of a major German bank. Beyond its technical innovations, this building also marked a major step in the urban policy field: it was the first skyscraper constructed to comply with ecological conditions. These conditions represented the outcome of a long decision-making process, involving the bank's directors, local politicians and utility managers. After years of negotiations, they became the basis of a covenant signed by the bank and Frankfurt's urban planning department.

The first ideas for the Commerzbank headquarters (see Figure 1.1) had in fact come forward in the 1980s, when the bank's directors decided to construct a large office tower in the city centre with the goal of relocating the staff, at that time scattered throughout different office units in Frankfurt. While several feasibility studies were then carried out and various options considered, the project was time and again opposed by strict municipal policies aiming to outlaw high-rise developments. Among other drawbacks, such a building would pose a burden to the local infrastructure and environment, worsen traffic congestion and clash with the local architectural style.

A more flexible approach seeking to balance such interests would only be made possible some years later when, paradoxically, the Green Party became the local authority. Its proposal was to subject the construction permit to a series of criteria that would benefit the city, and which would be negotiated between the different stakeholders. These criteria comprised a range of ecological prescriptions, including the reduction of energy consumption.

These prescriptions, too, represented a major development in the energy policy field. Since the 1970s, German policies had mainly insisted on end-of-pipe strategies, such as targeting the energy use of air conditioning and other energy-intensive equipment. With this project, urban planners aimed to go one step forward and introduce clean technological approaches, creating the first naturally lit and ventilated skyscraper in the world.

The architecture of the Commerzbank was thereby developed around an equilateral triangular plan surrounding a central atrium, with a cladding system based on a triple glazed layer allowing natural ventilation in the tower, hence decreasing its cooling load. As a result, the building achieved a high level of energy efficiency, consuming around 60 per cent less energy than a regular building constructed in a similar climate for the same purpose in the same period. In addition, it achieved a high degree of environmental performance overall by incorporating a water efficiency system, considerations for the use of materials and indoor micro-environmental quality and minimum parking facilities so as to encourage the use of public transport.

And it also turned out to be a good investment, at least in terms of marketing, despite the high costs involved. The bank's directors claim that, with its new headquarters, the Commerzbank produced a global icon sealing the image of a solid and innovative multinational company seriously committed to its social and environmental responsibilities.

But to what extent are such environmental responsibilities also applied to the design and operation of the bank's offices elsewhere? While this building attracted much publicity for the bank's environmental concerns, questions as to whether the Commerzbank fulfils the same environmental standards in its premises in other cities have not yet been raised. If it does, how far are the environmental innovations deployed in the Commerzbank building in Frankfurt contributing to the greening of other buildings, in other cities? Is there a transnational network of urban environmental management emerging?

Transnational Buildings in Local Environments

Urban environmental management is a relatively new field of study. For this reason, it is still methodologically and theoretically unsettled. As we enter the new millennium, this field has been turning into a highly complex one, so complicated by growing local challenges, so influenced by new ideas and approaches, so permeated by new stakeholders. This complexity is particularly evidenced – and this is the challenge this book proposes to explore – in the case of metropolitan cities.

Ever since the term 'urban environment' came to the fore some 30 years ago, most such cities were mainly industrial or regional trade centres. Approaches to reducing their traditional environmental problems – such as tackling industrial and automotive emissions into the air, contamination of waterways and lands, and the disruption of ecosystems – then relied largely on local and place-bound environmental politics and discourses for the articulation of environmental interests and their incorporation by different (often local) actors, in different practices. Many initiatives have been successful, such as the control of air pollution in Amsterdam and industrial emissions in Pittsburgh and Tokyo (Cohen, 1996). The case of Curitiba became a by-word for its ability to implement environmental care practices with limited public budgets. Most of these initiatives were elaborated by a centralistic local or national government, usually applying restrictive, command-and-control policy approaches; negotiated approaches, such as those fostered in the Commerzbank building in Frankfurt, were not yet in place. These showed how stringent regulations have at least prompted a growing public sophistication and accountability for managing the urban environment. In most cases, however, their effectiveness remained doubtful as the environmental quality of most metropolitan cities, in both the developed and developing worlds, continues to deteriorate in general. This is due to at least two possible causes.

First, traditional policy approaches such as those fostered by centralistic states through command-and-control instruments mainly have in most cases been incapable of dealing with the thousands of sources of pollution contaminating the city as well as with the related polluters. This has mostly taken place due to the high monitoring costs that such approaches require, leading too often to infractions hence to the impossibility of managing the urban environment properly. Urban environmental management has also been hampered because of the inability of the state in developing necessary expertise and techniques as well as in providing sufficient budgets given their other priorities. This was exacerbated by the oil crisis of the 1970s, during which the slow economic growth experienced worldwide led to a decrease in public investments in urban infrastructure provision – such as water and electricity supply, wastewater treatment, solid waste collection, and so forth – sealing a growing gap between urban growth and environmental planning ever since, particularly in metropolitan cities in the South. As a result, these cities have been facing a growing environmental management deficit, which has now become hard to cope with through such traditional policy approaches. In metropolises located in the North, the state has also failed to establish an adequate, effective set of rules concerning acceptable levels of resources consumption, making their environmental footprint a tremendous one.

The second possible reason why the quality of the urban environment steadily deteriorates is because over these 30 years major changes in the world economy have led nearly all metropolitan cities to undergo marked transformations, bringing new environmental challenges. Globalization and digitization have led to the recentralization of the scattered activities of the world economy into some of these metropolises, such as London, Tokyo, New York, São Paulo and Singapore (Sassen, 1994, 2001). In the process, these cities started to develop new functions beyond being industrial, trade and banking centres, as they began serving as headquarters for multinational companies, producing highly specialized services and innovations. These new functions have been reshaping their socio-economic bases, triggering multiple economic, political, cultural and societal changes. At the same time, these new functions have also been prompting substantial spatial changes accompanied by changes in the character of their environmental problems. In different ways and to differing degrees, most metropolitan cities have been experiencing a verticalization of their urban fabric, as service sector activities require physical concentration and compactness, increasing the land value in specific (often central) areas, thus prompting a massive densification of land use. This results in infrastructure overburden and in changes in the urban microclimate, including the creation of the urban canyon effect, with valleys being formed within corridors of high-rise buildings changing wind and sunlight patterns, thereby disabling the use of natural ventilation and lighting in their interiors. It has also heightened the heat island effect, with the concentration of heat-absorbing and heat-reflecting surfaces increasing inner-city temperatures, requiring in turn more and more cooling energy in buildings and other structures. All in all, this is being added to the increase and concentration of vehicular atmospheric pollution from commuting, the increase in energy and water use as well as waste and wastewater emissions per square metre on the surface, among other impacts.

Against this backdrop, individual buildings are being increasingly decontextualized, as more and more they seek to avoid such external pollution, reproducing global design styles and construction techniques that seal themselves from the external environment. This is mostly done through what came to be known as 'environmentally rejecting' techniques, such as the curtain wall (popularly known as the 'glass box' approach), which all too often do not correspond to the local climatic context, for example, in tropical regions. In this context, whereas in the past buildings had to rely on natural ventilation, heating and lighting systems, curtain wall buildings are more and more dependent on artificial systems of acclimatization and lighting to operate, consuming great amounts of energy and water and posing further burdens on the local environment and infrastructure. A vicious circle of urban environmental problems is thereby arising – where a poor urban environment prompts the construction of resource-intensive buildings, and where such buildings pose more and more burdens on the local environment.

This book departs from the argument that globalization is conversely also unfolding a whole new set of mechanisms, which may contribute to curb the traditional inefficiency of local governments in carrying out urban environmental management in large metropolises. With globalization, not only is the function of major cities changing, leading to these transformation processes, but these changes are also occurring in the very structural organization of the urban space. Certain 'transnational urban spaces' have emerged within their territories, spaces which provide a direct and continuous link between the 'local' and the 'global'. These are, for instance, business districts, export processing zones, offshore banking centres and corporate headquarters, which are creating a link between different localities where a network of innovations (ideas, technologies, management approaches) navigates. A new type of building has emerged – the transnational building – often planned by global developers, designers and investors as well as maintained by multinational companies and banks. More than just a local office building, the transnational building transcends the city's skyline, interconnecting urban spaces via diverse global flows.

The first thesis advanced in this book is that the transnational building, as a nodal point between global flows and local infrastructures, can trigger the ecological restructuring of the urban environment. The transnational building is a typical illustration of the Castellian notion of node and hub of the network society (Castells, 1996). It intercepts flows of information, capital, goods and people – that circulate in an often virtual 'space of flows' – with the local particularities and specificities of the place, such as the socio-economic-political background of the urban node, referred to as the 'space of place'. From city to city, transterritorial connections of *but how climate ?*

social practices – from 'above' and from 'below' – are now *fusing* in such transnational spaces, bringing to the fore a context of transnational urbanization which is helping homogenize their metabolism and shape, worldwide. We increasingly see how such spaces are growing alike – to the extent that they are now composed and occupied largely by the same global economic agents – as well as suffering from the same kinds of drawbacks.

This study argues that whereas in the past urban environmental management was conceptualized and implemented as local and place-bound processes, now, with globalization, as transnational spaces are being created within urban settings, a new context of urban environmental management is unfolding. Transnational urban spaces lying in between the local and the global are no longer only influenced by the politics of the place, by local utility managers, governmental authorities and urban planners. They are also being influenced by policies emerging from global actors, from the space of flows. This takes place via in-house environmental management concepts diffused by multinational companies that occupy and manage them, via environmental innovations introduced by international designers, developers and manufacturers that frequently create them, via the diffusion of urban environmental policies and programmes worldwide, such as Sustainable Cities Program, Local Agenda 21, in addition to other mechanisms. This new context, I argue, allows isolated green building examples – such as the ABN AMRO in Amsterdam, the Commerzbank in Frankfurt, Reuters and Condé Nast in New York, The Gap in San Francisco, Swiss-Re in London – to transcend the locality where these buildings stand. Via this local-global interface of social action prompted by globalization, these environmental innovations may land into other urban spaces, thus favouring an ecological restructuring of such other localities – or a 'virtuous circle' of environmental reform to counter the vicious circle above described.

This argument brings us then to the second major theme explored in this book, which is about *how* this global-local interplay is taking place in different urban nodes. How is the environmental restructuring of transnational buildings developing at the interface between global environmental strategies and urban environmental policies? Are local urban policies facilitating, stimulating or perhaps overruling the positive effects of globalization in the urban environmental management sphere? How does this local-global interplay vary from city to city? To answer these questions this study is framed around the ecological modernization theory. The ecological modernization theory has been developed since the mid-1980s, originally in Germany, and is now a leading reference in environmental policy discourses. It argues that environmental protection can be achieved within the same framework of (global) modernity, with the same institutions that rule capitalist modes of production and consumption. That is, environmental protection does not need to be hampered by economic rationalities, since ecology and the economy can, in principle, share similar objectives. Its argument, however, is that modern institutions have inherited a structural design fault leading to environmental abuse, which needs to be refined in a process in which ecology gains its own rationality to restore the balance between nature and society. This takes place via a twinning process of ecologizing economy and economizing ecology, in which industrial sectors start developing environmentally sound production processes, in a further modernization process, in which markets start applying environment-oriented criteria, such as eco-labels, environmental auditing, green financing and through concepts such as environmental performance, and in which consumers start opting for more sustainable choices. For ecological modernization theorists, the state remains imperative as an environmental care 'enabler', proactive in the sense of providing adequate incentives and stimuli; however, the dynamics of environmental change takes place within the cycle of production and consumption, eventually leading to the environmental self-regulation of modernity.

Based on these assumptions, this study analyses how far global market actors, as major players in the current phase of modernity, are promoting this ecological modernization in the sphere of the urban environment in different localities. Focusing on the buildings/offices maintained by multinational companies in different metropolitan cities, it explores the diverging interests and concerns of local and global actors – their power relations and decision-making processes in the public-private continuum – and the extent to which global companies such as the Commerzbank may constitute worldwide channels for the consolidation of new approaches, or new rationales, for enhancing the environmental performance of transnational buildings in different cities. Its main hypothesis is that, while migrating to different cities contributing to the spatial and environmental transformation of the urban space, global companies may also bring in positive influences, which one way or another may trigger the environmental reform or the ecological modernization of office buildings from city to city.

These two main themes advanced in this volume intend ultimately to shed additional light on debates on the role of multinational companies in the environmental disruption or reform of different localities. These debates, taking place since the 1970s onwards, have aroused much controversy as to the role of transnational economic agents *vis-à-vis* the environment, whether they contribute to the globalization of environmental problems or to the globalization of environmental reforms. Many environmentalists have argued that gaps in national environmental standards draw the most polluting OECD (Organization for Economic Co-operation and Development) industries to developing countries, creating pollution havens and propelling a 'race to the bottom' in local environmental standards. Conversely, proponents of globalization have claimed that global market forces may also diffuse best management practices with multinational companies, in most cases from OECD countries, creating pollution 'halos' in developing countries. Yet, while international environmental conventions and codes of conduct – such as the International Chamber of Commerce Business Charter for Sustainable Development, Agenda 21 and OECD guidelines – have increasingly pressed multinational companies to homogenize their environmental standards on a global scale, this is not necessarily so obvious with the environmental impacts of their physical premises: buildings, offices, facilities, and so on. Likewise, while environmental innovations are being more and more incorporated into the running of corporate offices at least as far as their home-countries are concerned, the extent to which this is happening on a global scale remains under-investigated.

On the other hand, the urban space has traditionally been dealt with by locally embedded planning and regulatory processes, as well as serviced by local utilities. Approaches in urban/environmental policies adopted by different cities – a product of the different political systems, markets and stakeholder relations – may either facilitate or perhaps inhibit the potential ingress of environmental innovations into the urban space through this transnational corporate network. In this context, evaluating the mechanisms through which multinational companies are introducing in-house environmental management approaches in their different offices worldwide requires an evaluation of the *interface* between the environmental management routines triggered by such companies and the diverse local environmental management routines of the different cities where they operate. As will be shown with practical case studies of corporate buildings in different cities, globalization is in some cases acting autonomously as an urban environmental management trigger. In other cases it needs further stimuli from both sending and receiving localities to be put at work in such a process. This book concludes by suggesting how such stimuli may be steered in different cities, with different economic-political contexts, through different kinds of multinational companies.

*   *   *

A word about the methodological approach used in this volume is in order at this point. In sketching how I intend to investigate such global-local interface of social action I will also outline the structure of the argument.

This book is divided into a theoretical part and an empirical part. Theory-wise, chapters 2, 3 and 4 are reconstitutive of the arguments summarized in this brief introduction. Chapter 2 outlines the debates on globalization, modernity and the environmental transformation of the urban space, drawing parallels between globalization, the rise of transnational urban spaces and their environmental externalities at the local level. Conversely, trends that are currently emerging in the environmental restructuring of urban office-stocks are discussed in chapter 3, taking into account their technical, societal, managerial and political dimensions. These trends are subsequently reviewed by means of a broader sociological perspective on the relationship between technological change and globalizing modernity in chapter 4, following the postulates of ecological modernization theory. At this point the applicability of such a theoretical framework as well as the definition of the empirical research content are outlined.

As will become clear by then, this book presents 12 empirical case studies of city-company interactions in the greening of transnational buildings, comprising the buildings/offices held by the companies ABN AMRO, ING, Andersen and IBM in the cities of Amsterdam, São Paulo and Beijing. These case studies are investigated by means of an intensive, exploratory research strategy, which allows us to conduct a detailed analysis and comparison of the different mechanisms in place in different cities, through different multinational companies. Andersen, in this sense, despite now being extinguished as a company, illustrates an intriguing dynamics of environmental change in place. Such an explorative analysis allows us ultimately to revert to and refine our theoretical arguments. This empirical part of the book is comprised in chapters 5 to 7, which describe the local-global environmental management of transnational buildings in the cities of Amsterdam, São Paulo and Beijing. Each of these chapters begins with an overall description of the 'locality' of the urban setting, including its main characteristics, infrastructure and environmental profile, regulatory framework and local environmental policies. Each chapter subsequently moves on to explore the global environmental strategies that are possibly emerging, by analysing the premises of the four selected companies. In each of these chapters we come to a conclusion as to how the local environmental management meets and interacts with the global environmental management and vice-versa, and how this interface affects the overall environmental restructuring of the office-stock of each of the three cities.

Finally, chapter 8 reverts to such local-global, city-company, public-private inter-actions by exploring the actors at play and analysing the resulting kinds of environ-mental innovations in place. In this chapter, the study explains how the greening of transnational buildings is developing in our 12 case studies, describing and inter-preting the mechanisms through which environmental innovations are emerging, as well as indicating the mechanisms that should be enhanced to activate the ecological modernization of transnational buildings. Based on these conclusions, the chapter also reviews the innovative theoretical propositions elaborated in this book, suggesting directions for future research.

As will become clear in the empirical chapters, this study explores contemporary events, that is, social actions occurring mostly from 1990 onwards. It also explores the operational phase of buildings, which is the most resource intensive phase in a building's life cycle. This corresponds to the phase during which the building is actually being run, consuming numerous resources and emitting substantial wastes, year after year, involving such issues as energy and water use, waste and wastewater emissions, traffic management, indoor environmental quality management, and so forth. In exploring the operational phase, focus is given to the energy and water management of transnational buildings in Amsterdam, São Paulo and Beijing, describing how the local energy and water utilities and environmental policy networks facilitate, if anything, the greening process and, conversely, how global companies are introducing environmental innovations at the energy and water consumption level in their offices in these three cities. In this context, the 12 case studies explored in this volume should be enlightening, given the different back-grounds and approaches adopted by the three cities and the four companies, and their related examples of failures or successes in urban environmental management.

Chapter 2

Globalization and the Environmental Transformation of Metropolitan Cities

Since the early 1960s onwards, information, mass travel and mass communication technologies have started to revolutionize the world economy, changing the means of production and labour relations, and prompting a dispersal of economic activities around the globe. Large companies and financial institutions have thereby internationalized and dispersed their production processes along so-called 'global assembly lines', operating complex information and logistics systems (Sassen, 2001; Hoogvelt, 2001). The indirect result of this has been the recentralization of command and control functions in major cities – such as London, New York, Paris, Bangkok – cities which have started to emerge as nodal points within this globalizing geo-economy, where dispersed production processes are reintegrated, materialized and organized. As a consequence, while these cities have started to play a key role in the dynamics of the global economy, these dynamics have in their turn been reshaping not only their socio-economic order but also their spatial forms.

A sociological analysis of the contemporary major city requires the inclusion of a broader scope of issues, which go beyond the locality. Putting it another way, while urban sociologists and commentators have traditionally analysed the city as a closed space with local problems, today the intersection of global and local social agencies requires an understanding of numerous realities so as to grasp the transformations of the urban space. The aim of this chapter is thus to highlight the implications of such new realities for major cities, focusing on their environmental dimensions. First, an introductory section outlines the most prominent debates about the relationship between globalization and modern societies, exploring such topics as culture, economy and politics, and also discussing some aspects of the environmental question. After this introduction, we analyse how globalization is affecting the composition of the urban space as well as triggering environmental challenges.

Globalization and Modernity

The concept of globalization started to appear in the social sciences vocabulary in the 1980s. Within one decade it established itself as one of the key concepts for analysing and understanding the modern world. The main definition of globalization in the *Oxford Dictionary of Sociology* describes it as a theory that examines the emergence of a global cultural system, which materialized as a consequence of a variety of social and cultural developments, including the consolidation of a global economic system. Modernity, in turn, is a concept that has been applied in various circumstances, often with different connotations. In general terms, modernity can be referred as a new mode of societal organization that started in Europe in the seventeenth century and became influential more or less worldwide (see, for example, Giddens, 1990). As can be noted, modernity and globalization are very closely interlinked concepts and for this reason certain observers introduce the thesis of the 'myth of globalization', refuting the notion of a globalized world order as something new. These observers claim that the current internationalized model of economic practice is not unprecedented, that truly transnational companies are fairly rare, that foreign direct investments remain concentrated in the richer regions of the world and therefore that the world economy is also not global, so to speak, but remains concentrated in the region known as the triad, comprising Europe, Japan and North America, also referred to as the G3 (Hirst and Thompson, 1996). They also argue that the G3 exerts tremendous economic power, putting pressure on financial markets and other fields of business, so that global markets are in fact not global, but follow a logic determined by the triad.

In contrast, various other scholars now share a consensus that certain pronounced transformations started around 30 to 40 years ago, with the emergence of an information society and the growing sense of global interconnectedness and awareness. These theorists claim that such transformations have brought about a new phase in modernity, which can no longer be restricted to the mere internationalization of business practices, but which have also touched other spheres of society and human life. Understanding these transformations, in their view, has become an essential condition for understanding contemporary events, particularly since the early 1990s. Yet, although they agree with the magnitude of such transformations and with the emergence of a new world order, namely of globalization, interpretations of these transformations vary according to different intellectual traditions, where two main theses have dominated.

According to one strand, globalization can be understood as the corollary of the processes of interdependence and interconnectedness that started with capitalism around 400 years ago. In that era, Europe began to exert an influence on the rest of the world, through colonialism and later on imperialism, and to transplant European cultural institutions on all continents. One of the leading advocates of this theory is Immanuel Wallerstein (1990) – followed by authors as Robertson, Gordon, Glyn and Sutcliffe, and Hirst and Thompson – stressing the 'continuity' of the internationalization of the world economy, parallel to the development of capitalism, with globalization being, within this perspective, the aftermath of the process.

The second strand states that globalization can be interpreted as a new phase in modernity, which indeed goes beyond the previous period of internationalization. While most scholars of what came to be known as the 'discontinuity' school do acknowledge that historically global interconnectedness and interdependence did exist, they disagree with the other group that claims that globalization is a by-product of the capitalistic system. These theorists attribute this new phase to certain fundamental technological changes that have been occurring over the last 30 to 40 years, which are irreversibly reshaping the world's societal systems. Authors such as Giddens, Castells, Dicken, Urry and Held emphasize the role of new information technologies that have provided new forms of mass communication, with potentials hugely extended by satellite transmission systems and fibre optic cabling. These new technologies, in addition to the advent of mass travel technologies, have brought about an acceleration and compression of units of space and time, and in turn an 'annihilation of space through time' (Giddens, 1990). As a consequence, the relationship between the individual and the world has been drastically intensified to the extent that individuals can now have a global reach via information technologies. At the same time, a 'network society' has emerged operating on a 'space of flows' (flows of capitals, knowledge, information, images, sounds, symbols, and so forth) and on 'timeless time', in simultaneity and immediacy (Castells, 1996). Giddens summarizes the discontinuity theory by claiming that globalization is a process that enabled a disembedding of social systems, that is, the '"lifting out" of social relations from local contexts of interaction and their restructuring across indefinite spans of time-space' (1990, p. 21); a phenomenon unprecedented in history.[1]

Moving the discussion beyond this continuity/discontinuity duality, sociologist Malcolm Waters (1995) also provides a distinction between 'old' and 'new' theories of globalization. Old theories have developed since about 1975, regarding topics such as modernization and convergence (for example, Parsonian functionalism), world capitalism (such as Wallerstein's world system theory), issues of international relations and the growing interdependence of countries, as well as McLuhan's global village concept. According to him, these theories attempt – arguably unsuccessfully – to identify and explain the prime causes triggering globalization. New theories, conversely, seek pluralistic causality behind the social processes and transformations that are bringing about a globalized world order. Starting in the late 1980s, particularly with the work of Robertson, followed by Giddens, Castells, Urry and others, these new theories are interesting in that they began to provide growing contributions to the debates and controversies revolving around the relationship between globalization and modernity: reflecting on the dynamics of the 'glocal' (the intersection of global and local flows of capital, people, information, among others, and thus the heterogenizing effects of globalization); and also interlinking globalization with the environment. What is interesting, too, in this new context is that a parallel body of scholarly research has started to emerge that explores the relationship between globalization and urban transformation, also in view of such glocal constructions.

The coming sections of this chapter explore these new theories of globalization. First we provide an overview of the social restructuring process following the advent of globalization, analysing the consequences of globalization for the different social subsystems,[2] namely the cultural, the economic and the political, and also bringing some insights to the environmental issues of advanced modernity. This analysis, which is not exhaustive, attempts to provide an impression of the main concepts currently being debated, so as to complement or provide a better understanding for the discussion that will follow. At that point we will shift our focus to the urban dimension and explore the different theses and debates revolving around the transformation and restructuring of major cities in the era of globalization, mostly through the work of scholars such as Friedmann, Sassen, Castells and Cohen. The chapter closes with a number of observations about the urban environment with reference to the spatial transformation being forced onto major cities in the age of globalization.

Social Transformation and Restructuring[3]

It is probably logical to start an analysis of the transformation and restructuring of society in view of the processes brought about by globalization by exploring the cultural dimension, one of the main domains of modernity affected by globalization. This is in addition a relevant debate for the study of urban spatial transformation, which we will return to at another stage in this chapter. The emergence of a global cultural system indicates that a variety of social and cultural developments are creating a globalized culture, through the expansion of mass communication systems, the rise of global consumers with similar standards of consumption, the rise of cosmopolitan citizens, the internationalization of the sports industry, the development of global tourism, and so forth (Marshall, 1998). This suggests that globalization has, at least on the surface, a homogenizing effect on products and places, together with the capacity for introducing cultural evenness.

Exploring this homogenization effect, urban planner Michael Cohen (1996) analyses the transformation of cities in the North and South in the age of globalization. By looking at the growing similarity among major metropolises in North and South, such as New York, Shanghai, São Paulo and London, he raises an 'urban convergence' hypothesis. He claims that similar processes are transforming such metropolises spatially and institutionally, and bringing many types of problems in their wake, including environmental ones. Along the same theoretical line of reasoning, sociologist George Ritzer (2000) explores a thesis of the McDonaldization of society, critiquing the growing homogenization that comes from worldwide restaurant chains, shops, products, and so forth.

More sceptical cultural theorists suggest, in contrast, that globalization has both homogenizing and heterogenizing effects. Roland Robertson (1991, 1992), for instance, claims that it is inadequate to interpret globalization as the mere westernization or the Americanization (or even the McDonaldization) of the world. He explores therefore the notion of 'world compression' – which takes place through the growth of interdependencies, such as those introduced by information technology, mass communication, mass travel, and so on. This has intensified the notion of 'global consciousness', that is to say, the notion that the world is intrinsically interlinked and that events that take place in one corner of the planet inexorably affect another.[4] Consequently, in this increasingly compressed world, nationally constituted societies are also increasingly exposed to internal and external multiculturality, which is due not only to the hypermobility of people but also to the hypermobility of information, images, symbols, products, and so on. Mobility via the different media assaults societies on a global scale, such that the local is intrinsically affected by the global and vice-versa. Curiously, at the local level this exposure to globalization produces both self-enforcing and transforming identities – in other words, people tend to seek their individuality and self-actualization by diverging from global trends, while at the same time making use of such trends as long as they provide them with some type of benefit. This leads in turn, according to Robertson, to both kinds of effects of globalization in different local contexts: particularity and difference, on the one hand, and universalization and homogenization, on the other. The result is the 'interpenetration of the universalization of particularism and the particularization of universalism' (Robertson, 1991, p. 73).

Examples of these effects of homogenization and diversity are numerous. A case in point is, for instance, global cultural producers such as CNN, which, although broadcasting essentially the same news, have to adapt their programmes according to the specificity of each market. The same applies to other producers, particularly multinational companies, whose products need to receive local adjustments to suit local consumers' tastes. A good example here is the case of McDonalds: although it sells the same ranges of products in its branches all over the world, it readapts these ranges (introducing new products, eliminating others) according to the local markets. Similarly, the automobile industry also has to take into consideration such homogenizing effects as the same manufacturer producing the same car must adapt this car for different markets, changing exhaust types, lighting systems, and the like. In this context, trends of homogenization, particularly in the economic sphere of production and consumption, are always challenged to diversify according to local particularities, rendering the McDonaldization or evolutionary convergence theories somehow inappropriate for discussing, at the moment, the implications of globalization to local structures.

Another major debate in line with this global/local interplay is that proposed by Anthony Giddens (1990), who explores the interpenetration of the global and the local from a slightly different perspective.[5] Together with Ulrich Beck (1992, 1999) he interprets globalization as a phenomenon that occurred because the main traits of a first phase of modernity – namely, mass production, mass communication and mass consumption – triumphed, giving birth to certain interlinked processes of globalization, individualization, gender revolution, underemployment and, not least, the environmental crisis. Therefore, *because of* globalization, modernity has now entered a new phase, one he calls 'reflexive modernization'. The term 'reflexive' stands for the constant re-examining or re-evaluation of modern social practices resulting from the massive influx of information that individuals and institutions have to face and absorb everyday, as a result of globalization and its effects. It also explains the fact that modern societies are increasingly challenged to confront the negative consequences of modernization itself, such as violence, environmental problems, poverty, and so forth. Unlike Robertson, who limits himself to a discussion of cultural issues, Giddens analyses this interplay of global/local also in terms of its consequences for social relations. He concludes that, at the level of individuals, at the core of a globalized culture lie feelings of anxiety, fear, uncertainty, which produce in sum a general loss of parameters. This scenario of lack of clarity, he goes on to say, drives people towards a process of 'life politics' or the search for self-fulfilment through the exploration of their own individuality, a search which may manifest itself as divergent consumerist options, new political beliefs, new religions and deviant social practices. Finally, at the institutional level, Giddens suggests that reflexivity triggers a new *modus operandi* involving decision-making, technology and science, management issues, and the like – which confront institutions with the need to constantly incorporate new information and knowledge, re-examine their practices and go forward with the flux.

What the urban environmentalist can learn from these debates is that dealing with local environmental problems is far from simple, even when globalization contributes to enforcing, worldwide, the idea that environmental problems are serious issues of modernity that deserve a prime position in the local institutional agendas. There is not 'one' single logic of environmental reform that would suit all the different situations, problems and locations. This brings the notion of 'glocal environmental regimes' to the fore, as the homogenizing effects of international environmental standards, corporate codes of conduct, and the like will need to cope with differing developmental/technological levels, financial disparities, political priorities, different urban ecosystems and other particularities of each specific place.

Beyond its cultural implications, globalization is most often connected to the dynamics of the world economy, which historically may have started with the Pax Britannica of the nineteenth century or even earlier with mercantilism, events that triggered the growth of international trade activities. In a way, sceptics of globalization are right in linking the activities of the so-called globalized economy with a particular geographic concentration, that is to say, in the triad region (or the above-mentioned G3, composed of the three economic regions which historically were the most advanced ones in terms of economy and industrial development). Following this line of reasoning, globalization still largely remains a process of westernization, a fact borne out by four indicators. The first refers to the role of multinational companies in the globalized economy; of the 100 largest multinational companies of the world, only one – Petróleos de Venezuela SA – does not have its main head-quarters in a country within the triad. What is thus claimed is that the corporate power of the triad has in fact increased during the past decades with the advent of globalization and its neo-liberal variants, for instance, deregulation, demonopolization and privatization of local companies. The second indicator relates to the uneven distribution of foreign direct investments worldwide, as these usually originate in the triad and end in the triad, much more than in developing countries as commonly thought. In the 1980s, for instance, 75 per cent of all foreign direct investment stock remained in the triad, although investments into both developed and developing countries have increased ever since. Similarly, the third and fourth indicators – the expansion of trade flows and the development in financial products and services – also follow the patterns of foreign direct investments in terms of concentrating on the triad. In 1990, for instance, 75 per cent of global trade businesses took place in the triad and throughout the 1990s the circulation of goods and financial capital also concentrated on this region (Mol, 2001).

At the other end of the spectrum, as explored by Ankie Hoogvelt (2001), there are certain developments in the global economy, which clearly did not previously take place. In the first place, globalization has dissipated the traditional classification of primary, secondary and tertiary sectors (agriculture, industry, services), whereas activities are now distinguished as 'real-time' ones (for which distance and location are not relevant), and as 'material' activities (for which the limitations posed by location and transportation are still imperative). In this context, the economics of globalization – and its consequences for the 'real economy' – can be deconstructed according to three strands. The first one evokes the emergence of a 'global market principle', which is distinct from the previous notion of a global marketplace, as countries that used to specialize in a particular product now compete for the exports of the same products; a fact that is increasing competition while also prompting a dominant standard of price, quality and efficiency set forth according to global parameters. The emergence of such global market principle has in turn reordered the way economic activities are organized, that is, it has produced a new global division of labour, as a consequence of the delocalization of the production of goods and services. This has particularly taken place as for the so-called material activities, following the emergence of 'global assembly lines', which of course have been facilitated by the reduction in logistics costs, allowing factories to be installed anywhere in the world. In turn, as the logic of moving factories has followed cost benefit ratios, certain areas of the planet have been undergoing de-industrialization processes, while others are being industrialized. In the same way, while manufacturing employment declines in highly industrialized regions, it augments in industrializing ones, changing the relationship – but also sealing the interdependency – between core and peripheral regions. The last strand of consequences regards the undertaking of real-time activities via a process known as 'global financial deepening'. This means that with globalization money capital has become totally volatile for investment opportunities that may arise in the planet, and therefore move from one location to the other within seconds. This also means that profits have been deterritorialized also affecting the real economy, as in these transactions, to the same proportion that some win, others lose, and these are usually the economically less privileged ones. As a consequence, Hoogvelt finally claims that globalization has also entailed a process of weakening social solidarity worldwide, and, one may add, of increasing the gap between the rich and the poor, between private interests and public interests, in brief: between the capital and the state.

Consequently, in view of such transformations in the economic sphere, major debates have been initiated as to the implications of globalization for the nation-state. These have primarily discussed the notion of the decline of national sovereignty, as the national bureaucratic and decision-making structures are increasingly changing and readapting themselves to the new, globalized world order. As Held (1995) and McMichael (1996) have argued, the political role of individual states has been also significantly reduced due to the emergence of new international forms of political and economic authorities – including, for instance, the United Nations (UN), the European Union (EU), North American Free Trade Agreement (NAFTA), the World Trade Organization (WTO) and multilateral institutions, such as the World Bank (WB) and the International Monetary Fund (IMF). National sovereignty is claimed to have declined insofar as these authorities have started to deploy new instruments of governance that have a global reach, such as international laws, international conventions and universal agreements (for example, for trade, security and environment), among other issues. With such instruments, supranational authorities have also attained an internal logic, in turn with their specific interests and dynamics, trapping all governments into their system, and to some extent also undermining the power of hegemonic states such as the USA.

(Hyperglobalist) theorists as Hardt and Negri (2001) go one step further in this analysis and argue that national sovereignty itself has not declined with globalization, but has rather taken a new shape. For them, national sovereignty is now an interconnection of both national and supranational powers that together exert a new type of authority, which operates the logic of capitalism or capital accumulation. For these authors, the emergence of supranational authorities represents a major shift from traditional international law, defined by conventional contracts and treaties, to the constitution of new supranational world authorities, which may exert totalitarian powers. Therefore, while in this policy-oriented discourse on globalization it is usually accepted that most decisions are still made by national governments, an undeniable context has emerged in which supranational conventions legitimately – and powerfully – overrule domestic conventions.

The role of the nation state is also claimed to have declined due to the emergence of sub-political regimes – such as non-state or non-governmental actors. This argument suggests that these are actors that have also become important stakeholders in national/international decision-making processes. The presence of NGOs implies a new process of negotiation that emerges among the different actors (for instance, interfering between businesses and authorities) so that the state becomes less and less able to dictate regulations on its own (and the market to act as it wishes) and has to mediate conflicting interests. This new approach further reshapes the traditional design of political instruments to control a country, as it implies the incorporation of the interests of these new actors, usually in negotiation processes. In this respect, and while NGOs contribute to the consolidation of life politics, or to the ability of individuals to express their individual opinions politically, they also break down the centralization of power and responsibility within and among the nation-states.

Finally, concerning the rise of an imperative global business culture, a number of authors such as Castells, Hoogvelt, in addition to Hardt and Negri have denounced and condemned the fact that the modern state has lost much of its sovereignty in view of the forces of global networks of wealth, power and information. These authors claim that large companies – such as multinationals and major financial institutions – also increasingly exert a political power, in turn rendering the authority of nation-states more and more insignificant. Here the debate on transnational urban spaces and the role of the local government in managing them has become another focus of debate. In particular, Catalan urban theorists as Jorge Borja and Manuel Castells even admit that major cities are in fact turning into the major 'multinationals' of the 21st century, trying to increase their power to attract investments and technologies, and the multinational companies that may provide them. A question that emerges in this context (and to which we will return later on in this chapter) regards the capacity of the local government in controlling such global flows once they settle on the urban space prompting, among other things, numerous spatial transformations at a certain environmental cost.

But before moving on to the urban dimension, the last aspect of the relationship between globalization and modernity – and the most relevant one for this study at this point – regards the consequences of globalization for the environment. Of course this debate will be carried out in much more detail later in this text and in the following chapters of this study but it seems that at this point it deserves an introduction. The environmental question has appeared only incidentally in the globalization discourse. One of the first contributions in this regard was provided by Giddens, who analysed the current ecological crisis – as well as the growing importance of ecology in the social system, particularly *vis-à-vis* the economic sphere – within the globalization theory. In elaborating on the consequences of modernity, Giddens presented in 1990 the thesis that with globalization an intensification of worldwide social relations links distant localities in such a way that local events are reciprocally influenced by events that occur in other localities. In 1991 he introduced in this reflection the environmental question, arguing that ecological problems contribute to amplifying the notion of global interconnectedness or the notion that global systems are growing increasingly interdependent (see also Beck, 1992). According to him, while environmental problems or environmental degradation may travel far away from their agents of causation, they may also lead to local heterogenizing consequences, as the effects of environmental problems are not distributed equally in the world.

Reflecting on environmental problems and their uneven distribution in the era of globalization, an interesting distinction has been provided by sociologist Michael Redclift (2000), who primarily reproaches transnational actors for the transfer of environmental degradation out of their territories. Of course, the spreading of pollution itself may be caused by risk industries, such as nuclear plants, chemical industries or environmental intensive activities, such as deforestation, which not only lead to local problems of desertification, once in an advanced stage, but also global warming issues. The first variant of his analysis regards the *diffusion of sources* of pollution, which defines the spread of polluting industries especially from North to South. This statement defends the notion of 'pollution haven', as the South, by in general terms having more lax environmental regimes and regulations, and also by having an interest in attracting foreign investments, to a certain extent allows multinational companies to operate in their territories with little attention being assigned to the environment. The problems that may follow can be severe and may also go beyond the national territory. In this sense, Redclift takes this analysis further and elaborates on a second form of global environmental impact that occurs through the *diffusion of impacts*, namely through the mediums of water, soil and the atmosphere, such as the dispersal of hazardous wastes and the threat posed by radioactive leakage and fallout, for instance. Such impacts can be generalized as 'global concerns' affecting the so-called 'global commons', many of which are contained in the texts of international negotiations, such as global warming, ozone depletion and acid deposition. These problems may be interpreted as the negative consequences of globalization (of production and consumption) itself, that arise through the processes of global trade, foreign direct investment, economic decision making, management concepts and increase of transportation for distribution of goods, among others.

This concern for the global commons became, in turn, a transnational trend along with the intensification of environmental awareness around the world. With globalization, it can be argued that while the global economic activity with its unequal distribution of goods and money favours the North, it conversely also makes the North dependent on the South, due to the unequal distribution of resources and environmental space that favours the latter. Thus, while certain scholars advocate the rise of pollution hells in particularly the third world, others stand for the rise of pollution halos with the relocations of industries that may have a positive environmental effect in the South, with multinational firms propagating, worldwide, their trends in environmental management and technological reform. These authors explain that the issue regarding conflicting environmental regimes would only be marginal in the decision making of industrial delocalization; moreover, the economic benefit that might arise would be somewhat irrelevant as compared to the whole cost of the investment.

In the discourse of globalization and the environment, particularly referring to the question of pollution halo, one leading author has been environmental sociologist Arthur Mol (2001), who analyses ecology as an emerging rationality in the social system, which is slowly catching up with the (still) dominant economic one. According to Mol, as the interdependence of North and South in terms of natural resources and technology increasingly intensifies with globalization, it follows that there is plenty of room for positive results to emerge out of the relationship between globalization and the environment. A globalization of environmental reforms can materialize following the worldwide introduction and consolidation of environmental management systems, as well as the intensification of international standards such as the ISO 14000 series.[6] One promising field is the growth of corporate voluntary initiatives, such as the Business Charter for Sustainable Development under the International Chamber of Commerce, the Coalition for Environmentally Responsible Economics (CERES), Agenda 21, OECD guidelines, among others, once sustainable industrial development becomes a common search between North and South. Finally, global economic institutions such as the WTO, IMF, World Bank, OECD, among others, are increasingly being compelled to be transparent regarding the environmental side-effects they should be accountable for, somehow changing global governance concerning environmental issues. These institutions are slowly promoting the harmonization of environmental policies in view of global trade practices and foreign direct investment issues, via, for instance, the Multilateral Agreement on Investment (MAI), promulgated by the OECD, and the Article XX and the various Multilateral Environmental Agreements (MEAs) promulgated by the GATT/WTO regime[7] (Mol, 2001). However, much controversy is arising *against* the worldwide homogenization of environmental policies, reflecting the point that as ecosystems are evidently not equal across countries, simply homogenizing environmental rules on a worldwide basis may create situations of conflict among different nations and organizations, in addition to a decrease in the environmental quality (Vaughan, 2001). On the other hand, however, this does not exclude the possibility of homogenizing environmental policy *rationales*, as the expected target or standard may be achieved through different strategies.

Globalization and Urban Space

Within the framework of the 'new' theories of globalization described above, that arose from the 1980s onwards, a body of scholarly research started to also explore the relationship between globalization and the urban space. Before looking at these studies, a word or two about the concept 'urban space' is in order here to explain why such studies started to emerge. Space, following Castells' reading, can be interpreted as the expression of society – or a material product that relates with other material products which together provide it with a form, a function and a meaning (Castells, 1996). If we see it this way, we can assume that the urban space is the product of social relationships that take place within cities. It is therefore a product that is in itself emblematic of urban societal functions, meanings and values.

According to authors such as Saskia Sassen in addition to Castells, while cities have traditionally been analysed as contiguous urban spaces, or as the 'ecology of urban forms and the distribution of population and institutional centres' (Sassen, 1994, p. xiii), studied in terms of local people, lifestyles and problems, to the extent that (urban) societies started to undergo fundamental transformations with the advent of globalization, the implications of such transformations to the local economy, culture, politics, and so forth, as described above, have induced profound changes also in the urban dynamics at the local level, translating into a new construction of the locality. In this view, analysing cities merely as closed spaces with local problems seems to have now become inadequate or incomplete. This new construction of the locality is prompting the rise of certain 'transterritorial' spaces within the urban territory – such as business districts, airports, export processing zones, offshore banking centres, corporate headquarters, which in this book are referred to as 'transnational urban spaces' – which provide a direct and continuous link between the local and the global; a fact unprecedented in urban history.

It is in this context that a group of urban theorists began to incorporate global-ization processes and dynamics in their discussions to understand the major processes governing urban change. And it is also in this context that a body of scholarly literature emerged pointing to different hypotheses why certain cities such as New York, London and Tokyo – but also São Paulo, Singapore and Frankfurt – have converted into major sites where globalization processes somehow materialize, and subsequently where the urban space is being reshaped in a rather similar way. There are at least three main lines of theory that have dominated this debate – the postmodern city (David Harvey), the global city (John Friedmann and Saskia Sassen) and the informational city (Manuel Castells) – whose claims, though diverging slightly, converge at the idea that globalization has now become a dominant reference point for understanding urban change:

Harvey (1989), to begin with, has produced a comprehensive body of Marxist urban theory in the urban sociology literature, speculating about the impacts of economic globalization on cities. For him, the major economic rules of global capi-talism have subordinated culture to the economic sphere, triggering thereby a new 'urban experience'. Also following the claims of Anthony Giddens, he posits that the notions of space and time have undergone a 'compression' with globalization, also affecting the urban socio-temporal perception, and causing a certain degree of social and psychic malaise and a growing sense of uncertainty. He calls this experience 'the condition of postmodernity'. Harvey contends that such feelings of anxiety and malaise have prompted the pursuit of life politics (cf. above) or local oppositional moves, which he yet believes to be a dead-end solution, because they do not lead to the development of a global political stance to face major global institutions or chal-lenge the rise of globalized problems.

Yet, it is probably John Friedmann that should be seen as the first prominent writer on the relationship between world economy and cities.[8] In his short but influ-ential article *The World City Hypothesis*, published in 1986,[9] Friedmann draws attention to seven interrelated hypotheses to explore (or start exploring) this rela-tionship between cities and globalization. These are summarized as follow. First, the way that cities integrate with the world economy, and the functions it performs, are imperative for the structural changes taking place within them. These functions correspond to the world division of labour, in which different localities perform different tasks, such as the headquarter function, financial centre, and so on. Second, key cities, mostly but not exclusively in core countries, have become centres or 'basing points' for the articulation of the world economy. Exceptions are, for instance, São Paulo and Singapore, which nevertheless follow a complex spatial hierarchy constructed in this system. Third, the dynamics governing production sectors and employment of these cities start to directly reflect their global control functions as they start to absorb corporate headquarters, develop financial products, high level business services, and incorporate into the major international grid of global transport and communication (for example, international airports and the frequency of international flight connections would be an indicator of that). Fourth, and in so doing, these cities start to become major recipients of international capital and therefore to thrive economically at rates strikingly disproportionate as compared to certain neighbouring cities that thrived, for instance, during the industrial age (such as London as compared to Liverpool). Fifth, these cities have thereby become also major recipient centres for both domestic and foreign migrants. Sixth, as a result, these cities are also subjected to social polarization. And seventh, this social polarization is in turn followed by onerous social costs, many times beyond the state's fiscal capacity.

Saskia Sassen has contributed enormously to the world city hypothesis, by complementing and substantiating these hypotheses with empirical evidences, which she first analysed in the case of the three main world or global cities – New York, London, Tokyo (2001) – and subsequently in the case of a number of other important metropolises – such as São Paulo, Hong Kong, Miami, Toronto and Sydney (1994). Sassen's argument, following Friedmann's line of reasoning, is that the globalized economy has been organized around main command-and-control centres, the 'global cities', which mainly serve to coordinate and manage the inter-twined web of activities of networks of firms. She therefore speculates about a major contradiction that emerged with the advance of modern telecommunication systems. The idea that information technology would allow a massive decentralization of economic activities – particularly of information processing services (operating 'real-time' activities) and provided by advanced services firms such as finance, property, auditing, insurance, legal, advertising, management and marketing – with people working from any location in the globe connected to a mainstream network *did happen*, but in a completely unforeseen way. While such activities have been indeed dispersed around the globe, they have simultaneously also been re-centralized in specific locations: in major metropolises. 'Information technologies have not eliminated the importance of massive concentrations of material resources but have, rather, reconfigured the interaction of capital fixity and hypermobility' (Sassen, 2001, p. 96) so that the activities of the globalized economy have indeed been spread all over the world, but at the same time major cities have been given a new competitive edge, in view of the complex management and coordination that this dispersal requires.

To explain this duality of what she defines as 'spatially dispersed, yet globally integrated organization of the economic activity' and its consequences for the metabolism of cities, Sassen also deploys other hypotheses, which she uses to organize a model for the global city research (2001, p. 3). To begin with, these assume that globalization and digitization are processes that have enabled the geo-economic dispersal of corporate enterprise, in which case the more dispersed are these undertakings around the globe, the more complex and strategic are the related management and coordination activities. This of course takes place following mainstream developments in the globalized economy and its internationalization processes, such as the liberalization of financial markets and the growth of foreign direct investments and international transactions (particularly in services), where companies are now spatially organized in a kind of 'global assembly line'. This notion of global assembly is an important one in Sassen's analysis as she contends that it is precisely due to the emergence of such global assembly lines, with the assembly of products and goods in factories and deposits around the globe, that new forms of centralization have become necessary to manage, plan and control complex webs of activities.

Subsequently, as these management and coordination activities become extremely complex, companies also tend to increasingly outsource them to highly specialized firms (for instance, marketing, accounting, legal and auditing, which basically process information). These highly specialized firms, in turn, by turning out highly complex products, need to operate in agglomeration economies, due to the need for face-to-face communication in the service sector. As a consequence, key cities have turned into major 'information industries', generating highly specialized products and operating in highly complex networks. In this context, Sassen explains how major metropolitan areas, beyond their traditional functions as trade and banking centres, now operate new functions as these have developed into the command centres of the globalized economy, in turn concentrating financial and advanced services firms, in turn becoming major sites of production, including the production of innovations, and subsequently becoming the major markets for these products.

As a result, Sassen posits that a context has emerged in which cross-border city-to-city transactions start to take place at unprecedented intensity. Accordingly, a kind of *transnational urban system* is constituted, as such global cities start being subjected to the transterritorial networks of economic activities and their related influences, and function as 'nodal points' where globalization materializes. This means that an urban system may encompass several nation-states and, conversely, one nation-state may encompass several urban systems (2001, p. 171). In line with this, in addition, and in view of the directions of flows of investments from city to city, a context has also emerged in which a new, global *urban hierarchy* has been constituted in this transterritorial kind of urbanism, for which London, New York and Tokyo may be attributed as the core sites of command-and-control. An important question Sassen therefore raises is: what happens to the relationship between the global city, with its new transnational spaces subjected to transnational urban systems and hierarchies, and the national government, with its sovereign rules?

Her answer is that to the extent that national governments play a minimum role on the globalized economic activity, it seems that they also start playing a minor role in such transnational spaces. To explain this, Sassen mentions that the national urban system grows somewhat disarticulated from the global urban system (for instance, the discrepancy between London and former industrial cities such as Liverpool, or New York and Detroit, or even Tokyo and the former Toyota-city, Nagoya, as Toyota transferred its headquarters to Tokyo and moved its production lines to such countries as Thailand, South Korea and the United States). She also mentions that these cities constitute rather a system, in which they do not necessarily compete with each other; nevertheless in which growth that may arise in the system does also not necessarily revert as growth to the respective country.

If we look at it this way, such global cities may indeed be embedded in both global and local spheres although disembedded from the national sphere, but this does not mean that the global city is merely the product of the logics of global capitalism. In this regard, authors such as Harvey and Castells, and particularly – and also more recently – Michael Peter Smith, although recognizing the contributions that Sassen and Friedmann have made to the urban theory, have criticized the rather unilateral view of the global city research in which globalization and transnational practices materialize 'from above'; global cities being the *stasis* of such process. A number of indicators suggest that some practices are also triggered 'from below' in such global cities, which are largely overlooked in the global city discourse, developing along 'different forms and degrees of social and spatial inequality in these cities, and the local, national, and global determinants of these disparities', and expressing in local political particularities (Smith, 2001, p. 59). These are, for instance, transnational migration networks, grassroots social cohesion practices and grassroots politics. According to Smith, these cities do not simply die politically.

In this sense, in view of the numerous connections – from above and below – that now fuse in the urban space, Smith theorizes about the emergence of a context he terms 'transnational urbanism'. This metaphor suggests the conceptualization of the city – and urban space – as a crossroads between diverse networks of social relations that go beyond the local, transcending one or more nation-states. What distinguishes Smith's theory from the global city research is the fact that the latter emphasizes the functionality of global capitalism 'from above', somehow overlooking transnational practices that also emanate 'from below' – 'which now cut across urban landscapes, producing disorderly, unexpected, and irretrievably contingent urban outcomes' (Smith, 2001, p. 12). In short, while the global city research revolves around the restructuring of global capitalism in major command-and-control centres, research into transnational urbanism is also concerned with the local social constructions that emerge with globalization, and how these may be connected across localities so as to produce transnational social spaces.[10] Smith's claim is that the mainstream analysis of the global-local interplay advanced by scholars such as Sassen and Friedmann – representing the 'global' as the site of dynamic flows and economic forces, while the local as the place of stasis or assimilation of such dynamics – is incomplete. For him, the local should also be seen as a 'dynamic source of alternative cosmopolitanism and contestation' (Smith, 2001, p. 167).

Castells has also criticized and complemented the work of Sassen by saying one should see that 'the global city is not a place, but a *process* – a process by which centres of production and consumption of advanced services, and their ancillary local societies, are connected in a global network, while simultaneously downplaying the linkages with their hinterlands, on the basis of information flows' (Castells, 1996, pp. 407–459, italics added). By elaborating a theory on the informational city, and concentrating on the construction of transnational spaces as 'nodes and hubs' of international flows in a network society, particularly of electronic circuitry, Castells emphasizes that crucial to understanding the transformation of major cities is understanding how the flows connecting advanced services, production centres, and global markets operate – 'with different intensity and at different scale depending upon the relative importance of the activities located in each areas *vis-à-vis* the global network' (Ibid.) – and thus how these change over time.

Illustrative of this is his analysis of the largest information flows among American cities (data provided by the Federal Express Corporation, including volumes of letters, packages and boxes), in which he concludes that there is indeed an urban hierarchy, where certain nodes dominate (in the USA these are New York, followed by Los Angeles), and where connections take place in selected national and international circuits, not randomly. However, he also points that this hierarchy is far from being stable or assured, but an ongoing process, where an accentuation of investment flows that certain major cities may experience at a certain point in time may imply economic slumps in others. In the early 1990s, for instance, when cities such as Bangkok, Shanghai, Mexico DF and Taipei exploded economically, Madrid, New York, London and Paris underwent a decline, where the volumes of foreign direct investments reduced, also affecting the prices in property and even halting new constructions. Conversely, by the end of the decade when cities in emerging economies saw an economic downturn, the others saw an economic recovery (Ibid.). It can be concluded, in this context, that *because* major cities now function in a transnational hierarchical system, to a certain degree there exists competition among them. And to secure their position in the hierarchy, such cities will inevitably seek to attract increasingly more foreign direct investments, eventually also into the property sector.

The Internationalization of the Urban Property Market and Spatial Transformation

We have thus far discussed the relationship between globalization and cities in terms of the new functions they assume in view of international flows of capital and investments, leading to the construction of transnational spaces and the constitution of urban hierarchies. At this point we will shift our analysis to the property industry, and explore how this dynamics of securing foreign direct investments is influencing the local property market, internationalizing it, and eventually transforming the urban space. The property market is not only a sector that demonstrates the economic performance of major cities and possible fluctuations in the urban hierarchy, but a segment whose function is to supply such major cities with the required 'built space' so as to support their economic activities. Its products do therefore become part of the investments companies place in these cities. If there is competition or not among global cities, or an urban hierarchy, will be above all manifested in the volumes of local property developments and the directions of investments in property, whose ensemble not only reshapes the urban space but also transforms the urban environment.

Since the beginning of the 1980s, as the activities of the financial sector and other fields of business started to expand in major cities and concentrate high-income workers, so did the demand for top-segment office and residential space. Urban land prices in cities such as London, New York and Paris thus rose sharply and rapidly. Throughout the 1990s, the price of commercial property continued to grow substantially, boosting massive construction projects including developments of speculative building. Sassen (2001), for instance, reports that cities such as New York and Amsterdam saw an increase in property prices of approximately 50 per cent during the period 1995–8, while Madrid had 80 per cent and Dublin almost 100 per cent correspondingly.

In turn, the growing participation of foreign firms as both investors and buyers of property in these cities was a key factor in the consolidation of an international property market which, while formed in 1980s, took off particularly in the 1990s. In the case of São Paulo, for instance, these firms have usually been American ones – but closely followed by German and French firms – which have entered the local market by making joint ventures with local developers (World Architecture, 1997). In the case of Beijing, these firms have usually been Japanese ones, which have entered and still operate in the market in joint ventures with publicly owned local construction institutions. The entry of institutional investors into the financial market has also contributed to the expansion of the property industry throughout the world (Sassen, 2001). The financial industry, in this regard, has now become a key industry in this field, not only occupying but also owning a large share of urban property.[11]

In this context, prices of urban land in major cities have risen out of proportion to the overall national economic profile, also showing a huge disparity of land price between core and peripheral urban areas. As a consequence, the consolidation of transnational urban spaces has sharpened within cities, also contributing to attract more and more international biddings to specific locations (for example, high profile business districts). Castells (1996) goes further in this observation and shows how, besides accentuating the emergence of transnational spaces within urban areas, the sharp increase in inner city property prices has also contributed to further agglomerating the economic activity within the urban space. According to his explanation, investments in property imply fixed costs to a firm, therefore a move to suburban areas, where the cost of land is less costly, would imply a devaluation not only of its fixed assets but also of the corporate image of the firm. Several major property undertakings started thereby to emerge in core areas – either restoring old structures or producing new developments – and these areas, in their turn, have become part of an international, high profile property market, including the participation of foreign investors, architects, designers, auditors, suppliers, and so forth. In Asia, for instance, some 1800 skyscrapers were constructed in the 1990s; in Shanghai alone 138 towers were added to the skyline during this decade.

As a consequence, the urban space has been largely undergoing a homogenization process, becoming more and more alike from city to city, particularly in such transnational spaces as the business districts. This similarity can be noticed in buildings individually, as they start applying similar designs, construction techniques, equipment, and so forth, a fact that is largely related to the intense participation of foreign contractors, designers, auditors, suppliers and clients. And it can also be observed at the district level, as the density of the tissue of such major cities is extremely increased – densified and verticalized – insofar as these cities enter the network of 'transnational urbanization' and increasingly absorb investments brought about by globalization. Major cities and their transnational spaces have indeed become large agglomerations of people, high-rise buildings, cars, pollution and everything that follows. As Castells puts it, these cities concentrate both the best and the worst (1996).

Although the internationalization of the property market plays a great role in homogenizing urban spaces, to further understand the logics ruling the spatial transformation of major cities and thereby contributing to the growing similarity of particularly such transnational spaces it is necessary to also understand processes that are somehow triggered *at the locality*. For this purpose, and parallel to the internationalization of the property industry, it is also important to look at the local managerial élites – which have a great influence on the local property market – to understand why certain aspects of the urban space are growing more and more alike, while others are diversifying with globalization. These élites, unlike 'common' people, are typically cosmopolitan. Moreover, it is their dominant interests that govern society and, to a large extent, its spatial logic. Their cosmopolitanism, however, plays a dual role: on the one hand it supersedes any specificity of the local, lifting them to ahistorical, placeless spaces of the globalized order; on the other, it embeds them in new forms of social cohesion so as to escape such global cultural codes (Castells, 1996). In other words, while the urban élite seeks to be connected to the global world, it also seeks to maintain its specificity so as not to become an anonymous, somewhat obvious facet of globalization.

Thus, their influences in terms of spatial manifestation are also dual, so to speak. On the one hand, élites build their own world, distinct from the global, impersonal world. In terms of architecture, this includes differentiated residential and to some extent leisure places, such as spaces of culture and art, which largely vary from city to city. On the other, they also need to create a lifestyle that unifies or connects them *symbolically* with the élite around the globe, particularly where their work habits are concerned. And here the spatial manifestation supersedes the historical specificity of each place and develops this anonymous and obvious facet of globalization. Illustrative can be the diverse business districts around the world and its support facilities – such as international hotels, airport lounges, sports installations, global chain restaurants and shops – in sum, 'transnational buildings' which have all developed a similar shape, a similar culture and a similar meaning.

Global Architectures

What is interesting, and not coincidental, is the fact that the consolidation of such transnational buildings has taken place at the same time that postmodernism started to dominate as an architectural style, since the early 1980s onwards. As explained by Hardt and Negri (2001), the passage from modernity to postmodernity took place insofar as European customs and values were supplanted by American ones; a culture that is all-inclusive, which is no longer dominated by an aristocratic élite, but by a business class in which everyone has, in principle, the same chances. In architecture, postmodernism materialized as a movement in which buildings, particularly office buildings, started to divert from the pure, austere industrialist forms of modernism and the International Style, which had emerged in Europe with the Bauhaus, whose orthodox forms could only be understood or interpreted by aristocrats or intellectuals. The proposal of postmodernism was instead to generate forms to be understood and interpreted by everybody, and this would be achieved by incorporating ornaments such as allusions to historical motives and other local specificities (such as those deriving from vernacular traditions, for instance). Starting in 1978 with the headquarters of AT&T in New York, designed by Phillip Johnson, postmodernism proposed a discrete ornament (a Chippendale top in the construction façade). But what happened was that it developed fantastic proportions in the following years, particularly under the practices of American architects as Michael Graves, Robert Venturi and Charles Moore, and became a colourful, exaggerated, even dyslexic style. What is paradoxical is that, instead of accomplishing a worldwide heterogenization of architecture, as architects of this movement had primarily sought, the fallacy of postmodern architecture is that it became an end in itself. It became another style, where historical motives had to be reproduced in contexts deprived of any historicity, such as business districts, resulting in a confused ensemble, the reproduction of hybrids at the crossroads of 'spaces of flows'. It thereby led to the homogenization, from city to city, of a huge architectural cacophony in the era of globalization, which, according to some authors, seals the end of history, where everything is mixed, where things have gone out of control (Castells, 1996).

This said, the influences and dynamics of globalization that have been funnelled to the urban space throughout the 1980s and 1990s with the internationalization of the property industry, together with the influences of the urban élite and of the post-modern movement, particularly in terms of corporate buildings, have been manifested in an architecture that symbolizes the popularization or democratization of the urban space in view of the rise of a global business culture, the architecture of the globalized world. A global architecture that is furthermore characterized by transparency, where the massive use of glass seeks to allude to the integrity and reliability of the company that inhabits the building. But what in fact happened was that, by replicating itself, the homogenization of the urban architecture has also turned the global city into a large experimental laboratory, where new construction sites are incessantly opening up, where every building strives to be bigger, more colourful, more spectacular than the other. And this homogenization, as we will see below, has also entailed enormous environmental costs, which only recently started to be taken into account, not only associated with the sheer magnitude and agglomeration of these developments, but also regarding the (too often) inadequacy of their technologies.

Transnational Buildings in between Global Capitalism and Local Infrastructures

This discussion on the homogenization of transnational spaces brings us back to the debate on the homogenization/differentiation of culture in the age of globalization, and to the (contradictory) theories put forward by Cohen and Robertson mentioned in the beginning of this chapter. Upon closer examination, and in line with Robertson's argument, perhaps the similarity noticed above is more visual than real. Without doubt, to a certain degree differentiation still exists in such transnational spaces. Real estate researcher Juriaan van Meel (2000), for instance, carried out a detailed study of the relationship between office design and national context and identified that, although from the outside office buildings may look very similar, in each country their layout will vary enormously in view of the different laws, market characteristics, cultural issues, labour relations, urban settings, and so forth. What is interesting to analyse, in this respect, as urbanist Nezar Alsayyad observes, is that 'in the era of globalization, when culture is becoming increasingly placeless, urbanism will maintain some relevance because of its ability to explain the specificity of local cultures' (Alsayyad, 1996, p. 108).

In contrast, it is undeniable that to a large extent such transnational spaces are indeed undergoing a growing homogenization, standardization or even

McDonaldization process. Transnational buildings such as office buildings, shopping outlets, chain hotels, and so forth, are still 'global products' too often designed by the same global architects, and occupied by the same global economic agents. In this sense, returning to Cohen's analysis in the beginning of the text, there is to an extent an urban convergence process indeed taking place, which is besetting large metropolises in the age of the global economy in several ways. Looking at the major cities from this standpoint opens up a universe of critical urban problems that are emerging with globalization, thus showing 'the other side' of the global city research: the realm of rising urban environmental and infrastructural challenges.

To begin with, it is clear that in terms of infrastructure major cities in both North and South underwent a slow economic growth in the late 1970s and early 1980s, attributable not to the advent of globalization itself but to the worldwide economic recession following the oil crisis. This was immediately reflected in a slow growth of public investment in infrastructure – such as roads, water supply, wastewater treatment, solid waste collection, electricity supply and telecommunications – sealing in turn a growing gap in urban infrastructure provision. As a result, even in rich countries such as the USA, a debate has been raised about a possible infrastructure crisis following electricity blackouts on the eastern coast, failed water and wastewater services provision in Chicago and Washington, and problems with road maintenance in other large cities. In the South, conversely, this has contributed to widening the gap in urban environmental management, leading to an estimated 170 million urban inhabitants presently without clean water supply or a proper urban sanitation infrastructure. In Latin America, for instance, a survey conducted in 1994 by the World Bank revealed that only two per cent of all urban waste was treated before disposal, a figure that has probably remained more or less stable. In addition, the problems related to urban transport in major capitals of the South are clear indicators of the deficient infrastructure performance of these cities. This leaves us little doubt that both types of cities have been increasingly facing a lack of financial resources – as well as a weak management capacity – to be invested in urban infrastructure ever since.

It was in this context that the concept 'urban environment' – and subsequently 'environmental management' – arose some 20 years ago, also coinciding with the advent of globalization as a key notion of modernity. This took place first in the North, and has now achieved a more or less worldwide scope. Since then, there have been many attempts to mitigate environmental damage, particularly in the North, several of which have been considered fairly successful. Yet, in most cases, according to numerous studies, the overall urban environmental quality tends to deteriorate rapidly in cities both in the developed and the developing countries, demanding urgent attention. In the North this is taking place particularly due to the depletion of natural resources, urban pollution and weakness of environmental governance. In the South, the difficulties encountered by the already precarious environmental infrastructure and governance have been exacerbated by the rapid speed at which cities are growing, where two main environmental priorities are dominating. One of them is the pollution of water resources deriving from untreated wastewater. Needless to say, the growing urban population, overconstruction, infrastructure overload and poor housing provision for those with the lowest incomes are the main driving forces for this. The urban deficit in terms of adequate sanitation has reached a very high level in the South, for instance, 80–90 per cent in cities such as Karachi in Pakistan. The result is disastrous to both the environment and human health. The second main urban environmental challenge in these cities is vehicular atmospheric pollution that is taking over after polluting industries migrate to other areas. Mexico DF, for instance, has a population of around 20 million inhabitants and is also home to four million cars which produce toxic atmospheric gases six times beyond the acceptable standards set by the World Health Organization. When vehicular pollution is too intense, industrial production is halted and the public is urged to stay indoors. In Bangkok, another example, over 100,000 masks have been handed out to traffic policemen in response to the hospitalization of one of their members, who had severe lung complications from breathing stifling air. Other critical problems include deficit in green areas, inefficiency in energy and water consumption and the heat island effect, among other things.

But parallel to such declining investments in urban infrastructure that have taken place since the early 1980s, the spatial transformation and growing homogenization of major cities *due to* globalization has also been playing a key role in adding to such rising environmental challenges. First of all the density of the urban fabric in such cities has been increased considerably due to the agglomeration of economic activities in core regions, where three main morphological trends are developing in parallel and leading to converging environmental problems. The first is a process of *verticalization* and densification of core regions, resulting from the transformation of these cities into international business centres and national economic engines. The presence of foreign firms and high-income workers has contributed to sharp increases in urban commercial and residential property prices, particularly during the past decade. This has led to the proliferation of high-rise buildings and high-density land usage resulting in the formation of 'urban canyons', which threatens the natural ventilation and lighting inside buildings. Therefore, more indoor artificial lighting, refrigeration/heating and ventilation are frequently required to operate buildings in such cities, with higher energy consumption implications. High-rise buildings also imply increased wind speed at pedestrian level due to the formation of such urban canyons, leading to reduced outdoor activity and increased use of indoor space. And the less friendly the outdoor environment, the more people rely on indoor comfort, resulting in more energy consumption (Santamouris, 2001; Schiller, 2000).

Secondly, as urban land prices have risen significantly, these cities have also been undergoing a rapid process of *expansion* and suburbanization – as peripheral areas are more affordable, hence attractive, particularly for residential developments – entailing more energy use and pollution from transport for commuting. In this context, economic and real estate pressures too often prompt alterations in the local building and urban planning codes so as to facilitate construction permits. And in this process, environmental considerations usually fall short, leading to a type of 'spontaneous' urban growth trend. Many metropolises nowadays suffer from heat island effect as the expansion of urban areas implies a decrease in green areas, more vehicular pollution, as well as paving and other heat absorbing/reflecting materials – which in combination increase urban heat sharply. Temperatures may reach up to ten degrees Celsius higher than those of adjacent non-urban areas, severely increasing the need for air conditioning in buildings and aggregating energy consumption of these cities. In addition, more complex and environmentally intensive systems of water supply and treatment are required to pump water over longer distances in expanding cities. Finally, complex drainage solutions are required to cope with urban flooding problems, making their environmental and energy load tremendous (European Academy of the Urban Environment, 1997).

The third trend is towards a general of *decontextualization* of buildings. As discussed above, the presence of foreign firms – active investors, buyers and users of property – has contributed to the internationalization and homogenization of the property sector. This, in addition to the worldwide, converging architectural preferences of the local managerial élites, has led too often to the reproduction of similar buildings within the global network of cities. As a result, the building stock of major cities is now seeing a process of homogenization, hence of decontextualization in many cases, as more and more it responds to international standards of design, construction techniques and building services, usually employing glass and hermetically isolated façades. Though often seen as an appropriate solution to avoid the external polluted environment of major cities, such 'environment rejecting' techniques are nevertheless being employed indiscriminately, which often does not correspond with the local climatic context. As a result such techniques end up provoking further environmental problems as buildings require more and more energy to be cooled and lit, and their glass façades contribute to increase urban heat.

Numerous studies have pointed at the environmental footprint of such transnational buildings, as they converge in themselves elevated indexes of worldwide energy and water consumption, raw material employment and usage of land, making their impacts on both the local and global environment massive.[12] In chapter 3 we will discuss these indexes separately, and in more detail. Statistics also suggest that poorly designed buildings consume significant amounts of the world's energy supply, potable water and raw materials being thus accountable for a significant share of the world's climate change, also for gas emissions, stratospheric ozone, potable water and other non-renewable resource depletion, in addition to deforestation problems.

In this sense, however glamorous they may appear, transnational buildings should also be seen as sources of environmental hazards. This requires an urgent revision of urban environmental management approaches, which still largely focus on and try to deal with traditional problems of urban pollution, sanitation and deficits in energy and water supply, but too often overlook the roots where many such problems rest. Indeed, although conveying a glossy image of global capitalism and local wealth, these buildings are in fact at the crossroads between the highly dynamic world of global exchanges (on the one hand) and local, deteriorating urban environmental infrastructures, governed by the dynamics of place (on the other).

Conclusions

The essence of this chapter was to provide an overview of the main implications of globalization to the urban space, and the related environmental transformation that cities are undergoing. We started by defining main concepts and debates on the relationship between globalization and modernity – such as the implications for the domains of culture, economy, politics, also referring to the environmental question. We subsequently described the new urban dynamics that emerged with global-ization, and finalized by discussing the implications that globalization has for urban space and for the urban environment.

In major cities, the urban space has undergone marked transformations with glob-alization, leading to the rise of 'transnational buildings' within urban areas. These are, for instance, office buildings, global restaurant chains, shops, international hotels, and so on, buildings that in addition now also belong to an international property market. In this context, they have become global products often produced by same international designers, investors, construction companies, and so on, and often occupied by the same global economic agents, such as multinational companies and financial institutions. By providing a direct link between local and global social practices, these buildings have eventually also contributed to the consolidation of a context of 'transnational urbanization' among cities, in view of the growing linkages, interdependencies, diffusion of diverse flows of information, and so forth, that now occur from city to city, across the countries.

As a result, while still maintaining certain local characteristics, major cities have also been increasingly undergoing a homogenization process. This is reflected not only in the new economic, societal and institutional dynamics that take place in particularly their transnational spaces, but is also manifested in their spatial forms, environment and infrastructure. For this reason, their transnational spaces are also being plagued with a set of critical (similar) problems, which somehow intensify to the extent that cities absorb investments and increasingly participate in the global economy. Among these problems there are environmental setbacks, resulting from the massive spatial and environmental transformation once investments are funnelled to the urban space, and materialized in the form of high-rise, high-density developments.

As we attempted to demonstrate in this chapter, we can assume that the building stock of the world's major cities portrays a typical example of 'diffusion of sources' of environmental pollution, standing at the crossroads between the wealth of global capitalism and local environmental and infrastructure problems. In addition, it also implies the 'diffusion of impacts', which not only affect the local environment, but the global sustainability of the planet, concomitant to the loads of energy and other resources that they require to operate. Nevertheless, and being a transnational space within the urban area, we can also assume that transnational buildings do also represent a great channel through which environmental management and reform practices may be distributed along a transnational urbanism system, in view of the city-to-city, transterritorial interactions, carried not only by international property investors and related professionals, but also by its global occupants such as corporate clients. Hence, to the extent that globalization contributes to the environ-mental deterioration of major cities, as we explored in this chapter, it may, as we will see in the following ones, also contribute to their environmental reform. Standing between global flows and local infrastructures, transnational buildings can and in many cases are already triggering the ecological restructuring of the urban environment.

Notes

1   Theories of globalization are not restricted to this continuity/discontinuity dichotomy,
     however. Authors such as Scholte (1996) and Held *et al.* (1999) tried to distinguish other
     schools of thought in the globalization debates. Beyond those that decry a globalization
     hypothesis (what they call conservatives or sceptics), these authors also identify what can
     be called the hyperglobalist thesis, advanced by critics mostly concerned with issues
     regarding power and politics, claiming that the nation-state is weakening *vis-à-vis* the
     growth of global business practices, particularly of transnational networks of trade,
     finance and production. This group thus sees globalization as the current imperialistic
     trend of rich countries exploiting poorer ones, in other words, the Americanization or
     westernization of the world. Unsurprisingly, at the other end of the spectrum, Scholte also
     notices the emergence of a liberal group, made up of neo-liberals and reformists, who are
     now celebrating globalization and its fruits. In fact, Scholte identifies three main schools
     of thought – namely the critics, the liberals and the conservatives – while Held *et al.*
     identify the sceptics, the hyperglobalists and the transformationalists, the latter
     comprising of those that analyse globalization as a social phenomenon that has brought
     qualitative changes in cross-border transactions, such as Giddens and Castells with the
     notions of 'time-space compression' and 'space of flows', respectively.
2   The social system theory was elaborated by Talcott Parsons, defining that any social
     system comprises of four subsystems, whose related functions serve to uphold the whole,
     which are: the cultural, the economic, the political and the social.
3   Social/urban 'transformation' can be understood as a change in the social system's objec-
     tives and values, turning it into a different system. In turn, when the system changes the
     institutionalized ways to achieve its systemic goals, there is a process of social/urban
     restructuring or reform (see Castells, 1989).
4   An example here could be the growing awareness that environmental problems that take place
     in the Amazon, for instance, will affect the environmental quality of other parts of the planet,
     or, another example, that deforestation in Malaysia will bring air pollution to Singapore.
5   Although both Giddens and Robertson focus on the local/global relations, Robertson
     emphasizes the cultural dimension, while Giddens focuses on social relations. Robertson
     has therefore criticized Giddens for overlooking cultural issues, and also for seeing glob-
     alization as a consequence of modernity, while the other author sees it as a condition that
     has facilitated modernity.
6   Although much discussion has arisen over the effectiveness of such standards as well as
     on the question whether they are affecting industries at all.
7   The main possibilities of global environmental agreements with a homogenizing intent
     are at the moment the Multilateral Agreement on Investment (MAI) and the Article XX
     and the Multilateral Environmental Agreements (MEAs). The MAI was introduced in
     1995 by the OECD as a decision to homogenize general agreements on investment (not
     only regarding the environment) in view of the growth of foreign direct investments by
     OECD members. Due to the intense criticism it attracted, negotiations have been
     suspended since April 1998, and the idea of creating a 'level playing field' for foreign
     direct investments remains unachieved. The Article XX was introduced by the General
     Agreement on Tariffs and Trade (GATT, which came into force in 1948), listing certain
     provisions for environmental regulations. The MEAs are trade provisions designed to
     exert control over world trade (under the auspices of the WTO, in turn founded in 1993,
     at the end of the Uruguay round of GATT, to serve as un umbrella organization supporting
     the GATT and the international trade system).
8   Although Friedmann credits Harvey as well as Castells for the research they had been
     carrying out since at least the early 1970s, linking larger developments of industrial capi-
     talism to processes influencing and transforming the urban space. According to

Friedmann, it was precisely these authors that revolutionized the sociological concept of the city as a contiguous ecological ensemble subjected to the dynamics of local population and space to the one in which the city started to be interpreted as a product of social forces also triggered by world capitalism and the relations of production. But it would be only by the late 1970s that the city would start to be associated with the globalizing economy as such.

9 A previous article by Friedmann, *World City Formation: An Agenda for Research and Action*, co-authored with Goetz Wolff, had been published in 1982, introducing the first ideas, which would be further elaborated in the 1986 publication.

10 In distinguishing between the semantics of the terms transnationalism and globalization, anthropologist Michael Kearney (1995, quoted in Smith, 2001, p. 3) argues that the latter is mostly concerned with social processes that are 'decentred from specific national territories', while transnationalism indicates transnational social relations as being 'anchored' in a place while also transcending to other places.

11 To corroborate this, Sassen points at a study published in the journal *Real Estate Finance*, in which the authors demonstrate that the ownership of such transnational spaces lies in the hands of private, usually foreign firms, particularly those of the financial sector. In 1997, for instance, the financial sector owned 27 per cent of the property of London City (see Sassen, 2001, and Baum and Lizieri, 1999, 'Who owns the City? Office Ownership and Overseas Investment in the City of London', *Real Estate Finance*, 16(1), pp. 67–100).

12 See, for instance, Baker *et al.* (2000); Hawkes (1996); Jones (1998); Littlefair *et al.* (2000); Roodman *et al.* (1995); Watson (1993); Edwards (1996); Anink *et al.* (1996).

Chapter 3

The Environmental Restructuring of Urban Office Buildings

Ecological buildings and neighbourhoods started to be constructed in the 1970s as a response to the energy crisis following the oil embargo and a growing sense of environmental awareness. While most of the achievements at that time took place in housing design, notable works were also done in the field of office buildings. Since then the attention of architects, clients and policy makers has been increasingly drawn to the energy and environmental dimension of office spaces, eventually prompting a whole new research agenda and literature on the subject.

A leading argument in this chapter is that a major shift has been taking place in the transition from the approaches developed in the 1970s to those of today. While in the 1970s green designs were conceived in terms of local, contextual, low-technological solutions, usually applying the 'eco-community' discourse, now at the turn of the century the issue is no longer whether the building is low or high technology, but whether it achieves a better environmental performance in general. Thus, while in the 1970s solutions tended to explore options of *self-sufficiency* – or disconnectivity from the mains grid – sustainable office buildings are now primarily exploring *environmental efficiency* approaches and being carried out in contexts of relatively strong connections to networks of existing infrastructure. Their greening turns into assets for the companies that inhabit them, for whom environmental concerns are high on the agenda but are still intermingled within other logics, such as the survival in the marketplace.

In the pages that follow I will provide an overview of the environmental restructuring of urban office buildings, with respect to technological aspects as well as actors (local, global) and policies carrying environmental innovations. The chapter starts with an historical description of the transition of the logic of ecological design, that is, from sufficiency to efficiency approaches, showing how the deployment of environmental control[1] in office buildings is evolving from *mechanical* to *passive* solutions, while at the same time discarding approaches of full disconnectivity to systems of infrastructure for achieving environmental efficiency. Following that I will explain current innovations in design techniques of both individual office buildings as well as office districts, describing issues of energy, water, materials and indoor environment, also paying attention to the social context and degree of connectivity to infrastructure systems. Thirdly, I change the focus from analysing techniques in their social contexts, and look at two other – related – dynamics in bringing about environmental change: that of politics (government policies) and that of management (policies prompted by companies, the main occupiers of office spaces). The chapter concludes with some observations about the changing character of the environmental restructuring of urban office buildings within the overall context of late modernity.

Historical Overview

Although the history of office buildings and the issue of environmental control obviously dates further back, it was in the early twentieth century that a kind of 'administrative revolution' took place, resulting in the creation of large companies and large buildings. With the subsequent growth in the demand for office space in central districts, office buildings started to verticalize and dominate the landscape of major cities like London, Chicago and New York. What is interesting to see in these buildings is that in certain aspects they had much in common with what is understood as ecological building design today. That is, due to the technological limitations of the time, such as lack of air conditioning, for instance, environmental control would be achieved via passive means (for example, through passive cooling). In this sense, their interiors tended to explore the use of daylight through large windows, resulting in narrow floor plates to achieve lighting control. And, like today, natural ventilation was also somehow hindered due to urban air pollution and noise, as cities of the industrialization period were not only filled with polluting factories but were also joined by railway transport systems with noisy and polluting coal-burning engines (Cook, 2000). It was therefore in this context that environmental control was developed in these buildings: within a conflict as to the usefulness of windows to address daylight but to avoid the entry of pollution.

Dealing with this environmental conflict in cities of the early twentieth century led to two types of solutions. On a macro level, urban designs encouraged the separation of city functions – such as the residential, industrial and commercial functions, so as to control the spreading of pollution and provide a certain degree of urban hygiene – and the creation of traffic corridors to link them. On the level of individual buildings, massive investments were carried out to improve the technologies that had emerged during the previous century – such as the combination of steel and glass in the building envelope, and the introduction of mechanical appliances such as heating, sanitation and subsequently artificial lighting. With the expansion of these technologies, the construction of office buildings became increasingly rationalized, standardized and eventually industrialized. An early type of air conditioning for buildings emerged,[2] making use of a system of grilles, which deterred the influx of polluted urban air (Cook, 2000). As a result, office buildings grew increasingly 'sealed' from the outside, as environmental control would be achieved more and more through artificial means. A typical example of such period is the Larkin Administration Building, in the state of New York, designed by Frank Lloyd Wright and completed in 1904, later to be demolished in the 1950s (Banham, 1969; Cook, 2000).

While monofunctional urban development was confirmed in the ensuing decades, so was this tendency of sealing the building from the outside insofar as refrigeration and fluorescent lighting systems were consolidated, allowing larger and deeper floor plans. These systems were also coupled to further innovations in the envelope design, especially with the introduction of the curtain wall, marking altogether a worldwide turning point in architecture and construction techniques. While coming as an aesthetical response to the eclectic, bourgeois style of buildings that dominated the cityscape at the turn of the century (including neo-classic, neo-gothic, and so on), these new technologies established new parameters within the modern movement in terms of a worldwide *homogenization* – or even proletarization[3] – of construction techniques. In addition to that, they also marked the worldwide *internationalization* of architecture, by which one single building design could be applied in any city, be it in a cold, arid, tropical or moderate climate. On the other hand, these new technologies also carried within themselves enormous hidden costs – in terms of energy efficiency, environmental damage and human health – that would only much later on become evident (Banham, 1969; Baker *et al.*, 2000; Hawkes, 1996; Jones, 1998; Littlefair *et al.*, 2000; Roodman *et al.*, 1995; Watson, 1993; Wilson *et al.*, 1998).

Yet, it would be incorrect to say that with the increasing worldwide rationalization of office buildings no further passive environmental solutions were explored during the modern movement of architecture. Although several authors contend that modernism might have been somehow antithetical to local environmental considerations – particularly under the practices of large corporate architectural firms, such as those established by Walter Gropius, Mies van der Rohe, Marcel Breuer, Philip Johnson, Skidmore Owings and Merrill – some of these same architects also made their contributions in terms of reducing the energy and environmental load of mechanical systems in buildings. Walter Gropius and Marcel Breuer, for instance, analysed the local climate and sun angles as determinants in the design process, and the Lever House – designed by Skidmore Owings and Merril and built in Chicago in 1952 (one of the iconic buildings at the time) – used in its glass envelope a heat-absorbing tint to reduce undesired solar gains (Watson, 1993). Of course, more 'organic approaches' such as those proposed by Alvar Aalto, Frank Lloyd Wright and Eric Mendelsohn have always, one way or another, expressed more concerns for the environment, although perhaps embedded in more complex architectural languages (Jones, 1998).

From the late 1950s onwards some important publications emphasizing passive environmental control in buildings started to emerge. A series of articles published in magazines such as the *Bulletin of the American Institute of Architects*, for instance, presented the use of climate-responsive architecture, such as white reflective roofs for warm climates and earth-sheltering and solar orientation for cold ones (Watson, 1993). The first contemporary ideas regarding 'bioclimatic architecture' also emanate from this period, mainly developed by Victor and Aladar Olgyay as an integration between design, climate and human comfort, where 'environmental control would be achieved through *working with, rather than against, climate*' (Hawkes, 1996, p. 13, italics added; Olgyay, 1963). Eventually, in 1969, the publication by Reyner Banham *The Architecture of the Well-tempered Environment* added an important contribution connecting the environmental crisis with the growing energy consumption of buildings while, on the other hand, also exploring the role of environmental technologies in the context of the modern movement or the International Style of architecture (Banham, 1969). Although the work of these authors paved the way for the development of more sustainable buildings, of course the energy crisis following the 1973 oil embargo played a major role particularly in questioning the use *and cost* of air conditioning in offices, as well as the efficiency of large, open floor plates.

The energy crisis of the 1970s affected Europe above all. Whereas the city-zoning concept had predominated until then, urban planners started to encourage urban compactness and mixed-use developments to save on car fuels. In offices, employers were suddenly concerned with the sharp rise in prices to heat and cool the work-places and on top of that employees started to also express their complaints about such large and open office floors, in view of noise and lack of privacy. In this context, while optimism regarding technology declined in Europe in the 1970s, employees became more and more influential within organizations – particularly in continental Europe – resulting in the tightening up of laws to guarantee their right to sit at the supervisory board of a company, which in turn secured, among other things, their right to daylight, natural ventilation and an outside view[4] (Meel, 2000).

This, of course, had a direct effect on the way office buildings were designed and maintained, and environmental control would be achieved. In contrast to open floors, preference was now given to cellular layouts or a combination of both (the 'combi-office'), and here architects started to experiment with new solutions, such as the building of Centraal Beheer in Apeldoorn, the Netherlands, a large insurance company, designed by Herman Hertzberger and completed in 1972, where the 'human scale' and the feeling of a 'working community' were the key ideas. By contesting the deep floor to a large extent and by seeking human comfort, this building became an influential example during the 1970s in terms of improving the indoor environmental quality and reducing energy consumption. Other similar examples would also influence the way of addressing the environmental (and human) dimension of buildings by then. Among these, the NMB (now ING) building in Amsterdam, designed by Alberts and van Huut, and completed in the mid-1980s, proposed somewhat radical ecological measures trying to make an autonomous, 'self-standing' building. Although we will return to this case with more detail in chapter 5, what should be stressed now is that solutions such as those applied in the NMB remained relatively small in number. In line with alternative, eco-community ideals, the NMB project attempted to fully disconnect the building from the systems of infrastructure, particularly those regarding energy supply. Its aim was to propose an alternative lifestyle, even in the context of working places, and a break from unsustainable modernity. Nowadays, these approaches – once known as 'organic design solutions' – which in themselves present remarkable technological solutions, are nevertheless largely seen as naïve, since they failed to be applied on a large scale in view of the overall framework of the business world – capitalism, commercial property development, globalization – and remain as scattered, sporadic, even as exotic cases; in short: models of a kind of utopia.

In Great Britain the context was both similar and different. On the one hand, the social, operational and environmental grounds of large and open office spaces and monofunctional zoning systems also started to be questioned from the mid-1970s onwards (Meel, 2000). But on the other, solutions did not necessarily try to radically break with local infrastructures, and were more pragmatic in some ways. The engi-neering firm Arup Associates, for instance, completed in 1981 the Gateway Two building in Basingstoke, the first large office building to incorporate a central atrium, acting as a buffer for air temperature control between internal and external conditions. Although this was one of the first office buildings to be referred to as 'low-energy' in the world, it was still designed to be connected to the mains grid.

And it proved to be a prime example in fact: the central atrium, some contend, has developed into an essential condition of contemporary bioclimatic office buildings, particularly in temperate climates. This design paradigm, which may be referred to as 'sustainable building', has actually become the most popular approach of ecological design.[5] These are buildings that try to minimize their environmental impacts by evoking topics such as ethics, environmental sustainability and reduction of the ecological footprint. Another example is the headquarters for the National Farmers Union Mutual and Avon Insurance at Stratford-upon-Avon, designed by Robert Matthew, Johnson-Marshall and Partners and completed in 1984. In addition to the atrium, this building also employed several other bioclimatic features, such as cross-ventilation, external fixed solar control, generous floor to ceiling heights, good daylighting, high insulation, night-time ventilation, sensitive controls, and so forth (Jones, 1998).

Again, also unlike continental Europe, on a more social level, proposals to empower employees and their union representatives in Great Britain were practically unanimously opposed (Meel, 2000). Therefore, in a way, the more hierarchical British working tradition has hindered the development of egalitarian or more human physical spaces, such as those offering access to daylight, natural ventilation and outside views to the majority of employees. This helps explain why environmental design in British offices developed different approaches as compared to continental Europe ever since. Cellular office layouts have been combined with – still – large, open and deep floor plates. Therefore, the logics of addressing sustainability topics in the 1980s were, in the 1990s, also joined by concepts of flexibility and physical performance, with environmental efficiency to be achieved primarily in contexts of strong grid connection and combining passive with active technologies. Most British architects now use climatic buffer zones (such as atria), high-performance materials and smart appliances to achieve environmental control. And this has also enabled them to start *exporting* their environmental design logic to the world, including continental Europe, particularly in terms of 'low-energy' office building solutions, with a number of British architectural firms making the bridge between global solutions and the specifics of the local.

So here we are speaking of a paradigm that may be termed 'building as a smart asset' (cf. Guy and Osborn, 2001), in which deep ecological buildings are developed in strong grid connections; sharply in contrast to the solutions of the 1970s. Nowadays this has grown to be the most often evoked logic of green design above all in corporate architecture, and, it goes without saying, in major cities.[6] Renowned examples of this logic are the Commerzbank (Frankfurt, 1997), the RWE Tower (Essen, 1996), the Menara Meseniaga (IBM Tower, Kuala Lumpur, Malaysia, 1992), the Four Times Square (New York, 1999) and a rapidly growing number of others. These buildings are not only icons of the post air-conditioning generation of architecture, combining low and high technologies, but also icons of globalization and, respectively, reflexive modernity.[7] Paradoxically, there are a number of energy companies that actually occupy such buildings, for instance, EdF in France, ENI in Italy, Tokyo Gas Co. in Japan, in addition to RWE in Germany, among others. And interesting, too, is the fact that solutions have now started to address issues regarding water efficiency as well as environmental management at the district level, with projects such as the Shanghai Master Plan of Richard Rogers (unbuilt), the

Gannet/USA Today Corporate Headquarters in the United States, the Berlin
Potsdamer Platz and the Business and Advanced Technology Center in Malaysia, the
latter currently in construction, revolutionizing urbanism.

In the coming section we will briefly explore the main techniques that are being
deployed in such buildings – how they are conceived and embedded in systems of
infrastructure – as well as give an account of the indoor environmental quality and
issues related to the urban environment and infrastructure.

Ecological Building Techniques

Since the late 1960s and early 1970s major transformations started to challenge the
environmental dimension of buildings, particularly – but not only – concerning
systems of acclimatization and lighting. These transformations resulted in a number
of new solutions for achieving indoor environmental control and comfort, which are
in certain countries more or less becoming commonplace nowadays. These are, for
instance, the opening of façades to natural ventilation, the creation of atria and halls
as climate buffer zones, the improvement in insulation and sun protection and the
introduction of renewable energy systems (Daniels, 1997). Furthermore, a major
shift occurred in the way such solutions have been conceptualized and implemented,
as nowadays the environmental performance of urban office buildings is achieved in
contexts of strong grid connection – somehow contradicting the initial attempts of
the 1970s.

In this section we will provide a closer understanding of how solutions are being
conceptualized for the development of ecological office buildings and districts, in
terms of technology, and related degrees of connectivity to infrastructure and
embeddedness in local/global social dynamics. For this purpose we subdivide environmental themes into three main groups: 'real' environmental technologies
(addressing issues of energy, water and materials), indoor environment and urban
environment. For each group a short account is given of the impacts that such
themes pose individually on the environment, followed by a description of the state
of the art of the main techniques which are being deployed to curb them: how these
are put in use in view of main social – local and global – carriers, and how these are
finally connected to networks of infrastructure.

Environmental Technologies

Energy. As analysed by Jones (1998), modern buildings consume energy in five
phases. The first is related to the manufacturing of materials, components and
systems, which is termed *embodied energy*. The second, which is associated with the
energy consumed for the transportation of materials to the site, is known as *grey
energy*. Third, *induced energy* applies to the energy expended in the construction
itself. Fourth, the *operating energy*, the form of energy that has prompted most
consideration, is the energy actually spent in the running of the building, as long as
the building is occupied. Finally, a building also consumes energy in its final
disposal or, eventually, in its recycling, which is the *disposal and recycling energy*
phase. All things considered, the most energy-intensive phase is the operational one

which corresponds to the running of the building throughout its life cycle – usually estimated at 60 years or as long as the building stands and is occupied – and is therefore related primarily to the energy dispensed in the systems of acclimatization and lighting. Nevertheless, energy consumed at the manufacturing of building products is also very high; in England, for instance, embodied energy of construction materials accounts for ten per cent of the nation's total industrial energy use (BRE, quoted in Smith *et al.*, 1998).

Ideally, reducing the energy consumption of an office building should address these five stages. However, attention is currently focused on the operational phase and strategies are thereby deployed in view of different, though interrelated, considerations, mostly in the design phase, combining both active and passive resources. First and foremost, a building should pay attention to *passive solar issues*, such as orientation and siting, glazing size and location, natural ventilation, as well as shading strategies, so as to work *with* – not isolated – from the surrounding environment. This implies, for instance, the placement of windows in strategic locations so as to capture sunrays, but avoid glaring, and also to capture air but ensure the building's structural stability. Once these issues are determined, the building may then turn to *energy-efficient materials*, including high-efficiency windows, insulation, bricks, concrete, masonry, as well as interior finishing products, which are basically higher quality, superior building materials. Thirdly, the building may adopt additional *high-performance technologies*, advanced in terms of (helping in) energy saving, such as energy-saving appliances, advanced lighting controls and thermostats, activated blinds, strategic fans, efficient heating and cooling systems, solar water heating systems, as well as heat-recovery systems, wind turbines and photovoltaics, among other alternative energy solutions (Passive Solar Industries Council, 2003).

The combination of such strategies has resulted in interesting innovations, of which two cases deserve to be mentioned. The first one is the *wind tower*, which is a re-adaptation of a vernacular solution commonly applied in arid places (see, for instance, Jones, 1998; Baker *et al.*, 2000). In combination with modern technologies, these towers are powerful ventilation systems, which induce air circulation through the building, drawing warm air upwards and capturing fresh air in. An example is the Ionica Headquarters in Great Britain, where the architects also introduced, in addition to the towers, an interactive façade, a central atrium, as well as ventilated hollow-core slabs, which altogether allow the building to be air conditioning-free.

A second example combining these innovations is the *double skin* façade, which is claimed to reduce energy consumption and running costs by 65 per cent, and carbon emissions by about 50 per cent (Battle, 2003). The double skin, for instance used in the Commerzbank in Frankfurt and the RWE in Essen, consists of a double envelope system with a cavity between (of around 50 centimetres, see Davies *et al.*, 1997). It can act as a thermal buffer zone in winter, reducing space-heating requirements, as a source of natural ventilation in mid-season, even in high-rises, as well as a solar control system in summer, as the skin may be sealed and blinds activated, reducing cooling loads. It is therefore most appropriate for temperate climatic regions.

As can be noted, the optimization of energy use in buildings is a product of both local and global embedded solutions. To begin with, all passive measures are to be taken according to the local environmental conditions, thus following the logics of the place. Here the client and the design team do indeed play a crucial role in determining how these measures will look like, involving, for instance, the way how local, traditional design solutions may be used in modern buildings. Conversely, energy efficient materials as well as high-performance technologies are in fact global by nature. They are usually designed by multinational manufacturers (for example, Lucent, Siemens and American Standard), and applied transnationally, following specifications by architects and contractors according to the requirements of the place. Therefore the two hybrid solutions described above – the wind tower and the double skin – are in fact already to a certain extent 'glocal' combinations, synthesizing the logics of the local, in their passive character, but above all developed according to trends determined by the global state of the art of technological development.

Finally, in terms of connectivity, we see two main trends taking place. These solutions may either be applied in weak grid connections or in contexts of strong grid links. The latter is of course usually the case, and this is explained due to two reasons. First, office buildings are generally located in contexts of strong grid infrastructure (urban areas), therefore they do not particularly need to 'turn their back' to existing systems, although they may, indeed, use them less or more efficiently. Secondly, office buildings are still energy-intensive structures, arguably requiring a backup system in case, for instance, the solar panels cannot cope with the energy demand, the winds are not sufficient to run wind turbines, and so forth. Here a context emerges in which the roles regarding flow management between the building and the energy infrastructure are redefined, meaning that loops are partially closed at the same time that the existing infrastructure is partially used. Here perhaps utilities may play a role in providing services in energy-saving strategies, as is already the case in most developed countries.

As for weak connections, conversely, one could say that these would take place more sporadically, when the client proposes, jointly with the architect, a kind of demonstration project, by considering the building and the system of infrastructure as two independent systems. As yet, and to a certain degree, such demonstration projects are still somewhat unusual, even naïve solutions, so to speak, particularly in contexts of strong grid infrastructures, as they propose a conflictual breakaway with logics – such as those of the government, local utilities and global capitalists – that are still rather imperative (see Guy and Osborn, 2001; Jensen, 2001).

Water. The current system of decentralized water supply and wastewater disposal is one of the legacies of the nineteenth century, introduced in European cities and quickly adopted by the rest of the world. Although this system helped reduce cholera and the typhus epidemics of that period, at the same time it laid the groundwork for many of the environmental problems confronting us today. The destruction of natural landscapes, for instance, such as water ecosystems, wetlands and streams that serve as water reservoirs, in addition to the so-called city sinking effect (the lowering of the urban soil due to the decrease of the volume of underground aquifers) happens on a large scale due to the excessive level of water consumption in buildings (a significant amount of the world's potable water is estimated to be consumed in buildings). The respective consequences are: rapid groundwater depletion, microclimatic change, species extinction, the killing of forests when the tree roots can no longer reach the groundwater and the deterioration of the built environment. Moreover, long-distance water pipelines are needed for water provision in large cities, accounting for high maintenance costs and high-energy consumption to pump large volumes of water in and out of vast urban areas. A survey carried out in Germany, for instance, pointed out that Frankfurt gets its water from Vogelsberg (100km away), Hanover from the Harz region (more than 100km away) and Stuttgart from Lake Constance (approximately 200km away, see European Academy of the Urban Environment, 1997). The treatment of wastewater, in turn, also entails high costs and energy-intensive systems to transport the emissions from their sources to treatment plants. Several problems regarding urban sanitation, particularly in third world cities, derive from the incapacity for coping with such a complex – and costly – system of infrastructure, which nevertheless has become the most commonly used model worldwide.

However, innovations are currently emerging, apparently worldwide, involving the reuse of water in buildings and, to some extent, the disconnection of water-related infrastructure systems. In terms of water consumption, an appropriate planning may include a wide range of water-efficient fixtures – such as low-flow taps and low-flush toilets – to reduce the volumes of water used in an office building. In addition, rain or 'grey' water[8] may be used as second-quality water to reduce the volumes of water expended in flushing toilets, in watering gardens, and so forth (Ibid). These are fairly promising water-saving options, although current regulations, particularly in OECD countries, commonly put rainwater on a level with wastewater, overburdening the sewage treatment systems. Sewage can also be treated more rationally, usually involving a disconnection from mains grid, using nature-based systems for wastewater purification. Besides decreasing the overburden on conventional sewerage systems, these kinds of systems also minimize the energy use for operating large, centralized sewage treatment plants.

A number of office buildings have started to incorporate water conservation and reuse strategies, whose appliances are often provided by global manufacturers, such as American Standard. Examples that may be given are: Commerzbank in Frankfurt, Swiss Re in London, Menara Meseniaga in Kuala Lumpur, Malaysia and Lloyd's of London, London (Gissen, 2003). In many cases, utilities are playing a major role in providing services in water-saving strategies to help such buildings achieve desired reductions in consumption and emission, particularly due to the urgency of the problem of water scarcity.

Yet, like the energy infrastructure, the optimization of water-related services in urban office buildings is also taking place in contexts of strong connection to existing infrastructure, although urban buildings may harvest water from underground aquifers and try to treat sewage in decentralized plans. Examples of disconnectivity to systems of water infrastructure, however, would perhaps be most common in cases of office parks located in peri-urban large sites supplied with large quantities of fresh water, which could be used to secure the building's demand of water, as well be able to serve as nature-based water treatment plants, for instance through ponds, or other in-site solutions.

Materials. To discuss the use of materials and the related environmental implications, we have to bear in mind that a distinction should be first made between environmental pollution from the use of materials, such as depletion of resources and indoor pollution, related to the use of toxic materials inside buildings. In this section we describe issues related to environmental pollution.

Each year an estimated three billion tonnes of raw materials (40–50 per cent of the total flow in the global economy) are used in the manufacturing of building products and components worldwide (Roodman *et al.*, 1995; Anink *et al.*, 1996; UNEP, 1996). Raw materials for the building industry must be extracted, processed, transported, added in the construction phase and finally disposed of, and there are certainly many environmental impacts related to all these stages.

The pursuit of technological development since the industrial revolution and the gradual emphasis on generating a common international language in architecture, as we explained in chapter 2, particularly soon after the Second World War, developed a building culture where the use of steel, glass, aluminium and concrete dominated, starting in developed countries and then in the rest of the world. It is realized now that these materials present high embodied energy – as they are too energy-intensive to process, which frequently leads to pollution – and are increasingly depleted as finite resources, which puts a burden on architects worldwide to reclaim a more sensible approach towards their use. Furthermore, because they belong to an international style rationale they are also international in origin, which immediately increases their grey energy potentials, that is, the energy expended for their transportation. Paradoxically, many buildings nowadays referred to as ecological or low-energy hide high levels of grey and embodied energy.

Several buildings, however, are now attempting to minimize the use of materials with high embodied energy, such as aluminium, plastic and cement, as much as possible, and particularly to avoid those with high grey energy. These buildings try to use materials closer to their natural states, such as timber and bricks and other renewable ones, also making sure they are extracted in such a way as to ensure regeneration and avoid depletion. In addition, many attempts are being made to minimize waste and encourage the recycling of scraps resulting from construction debris, for instance, as well as of the whole building once it is decided to be disposed of. An example here is the Alterra office complex in Wageningen, the Netherlands, which has not only used renewable materials but has also been designed to be totally recycled once disposed of. All its components are therefore cut in such a way that they may be reassembled in another building in the future (Koster, 1998). Other buildings that have adopted a similar approach are the National Audubon Society in New York, the Greenpeace USA Headquarters in Washington DC and the HEW Customer Center in Hamburg (Gissen, 2003). These are buildings that are developing an intelligent economy of cycles, based on sustainable principles, trying to optimize the usefulness and durability of the materials applied by avoiding waste. Therefore, the flow of materials is being analysed in the sense that waste is prevented in different phases: from the extraction and processing of construction materials, to the construction or renovation of the buildings and eventually to their final demolition. On the question of selection of materials, a remark should be made regarding the way these materials are embedded in local and global infrastructures, which is now leading to a paradoxical discussion. As described above, at least since the modern movement of architecture the possibility of using construction materials of 'global' origins – such as aluminium, glass and steel – was enabled, also revolutionizing and somehow homogenizing the conception of façades. Nowadays, however, to the extent that this possibility has been intensified with other 'global' materials, such as prefabricated ones, it has also been challenged by the issue of grey energy expended in transportation, calling into question the international procurement of construction materials. And here office buildings designed for global cities, though seeking to achieve an image of globality also through the materials used in their façades and interiors, are increasingly challenged to adopt materials of local sources if they want to comply with ecological conditions, eventually requiring a formulation or conception of 'glocal' architectural identities in the envelope/interior design. In this case, the selection of construction materials will be more and more embedded in the local infrastructure, though decisions regarding this selection will still remain among actors which may often be 'global', such as clients, contractors, architects, at least insofar as regulations on this matter are not yet well defined. Here the participation of certain environmental NGOs has been significant, particularly concerning the use of non-renewable materials, such as timber from non-managed sources in the Amazon and Malaysia.

Indoor Environment

A perspective on the indoor environment is relevant here as it complements the above discussion on environmental technologies and pressing environmental concerns. Modern buildings are pathogenic in various ways. Generally speaking, as most people spend at least 80 per cent of their lives indoors, predominantly in their homes and offices, it is of great importance that the indoor environment is favourable to the buildings' occupiers (European Academy of the Urban Environment, 1997). This pathogenicity of the indoor environment was first detected after the 1973 oil crisis, when people started to suddenly fully insulate their houses so as to save energy. As cases of sicknesses resulting from indoor contamination sharply rose, several studies were in turn carried out, eventually detecting that there are many materials inside buildings which may be harmful to human health, many of which are even carcinogenic.

These studies on sick building syndrome and indoor air pollution have revealed that the modern building industry, pressed to generate its products *en masse*, has developed a wide range of synthetic materials to be commercially accepted on a large scale, most of which are harmful to human health. Wood, for instance, has been replaced by uPVC for windows, wool in carpets by synthetic fabrics, wooden furniture and fittings by plastic, and so on, and a series of electrical appliances have been introduced (Smith *et al.*, 1998). Of particular concern are exposure to electromagnetic fields, volatile organic compounds and nowadays legionnaires' disease. The sick building syndrome has become so alarming that the United States Environmental Protection Agency (EPA) already considers it among the five greatest threats to human health. Accordingly, the American Medical Association and the United States Army performed a survey to investigate the consequences of poor indoor environments and estimated that inadequate indoor air quality costs about 15 billion dollars in lost productivity each year in the United States (Ibid.). Therefore, improving the indoor environmental quality implies more productivity and lower absenteeism levels, in addition to sparing companies litigation risks, as a number of studies on the subject have demonstrated (see Roodman *et al.*, 1995; Wilson *et al.*, 1998; Heerwagen, 2000).

As a result, optimizing the use of materials in buildings as we discussed above should also pay attention to the other side of the environmental equation, that is, the people who inhabit the building. Therefore, while preference should be given to endogenous and renewable materials to avoid environmental pollution, these very materials are those that should be most appropriate to human health, for example, mud, natural rocks, ceramics, certain minerals and natural floor coverings (European Academy of the Urban Environment, 1997). Illustrative is the Greenpeace USA Headquarters in Washington DC, which paid particular attention to indoor sustainable design in its renovation, selecting low volatile organic compound materials, in addition to other environmental and human health considerations (Gissen, 2003).

In terms of embeddedness within local/global infrastructure, and unlike the issue of grey energy of construction materials as described above, major worldwide efforts are apparently being made to control indoor pollution. The prohibition of asbestos cements and the control of legionnaires' disease, for instance, is now more and more commonplace. But in any case, although the global diffusion of ecological building technologies does also concern the indoor environment, regulations on this are still strictly made on a local basis, differences between which may sometimes be an obstacle toward the import or local development of technologies regarding the improvement of the indoor environment. In this case, architects and clients play a decisive role in defining the quality of the indoor, while local policy-makers play a decisive role in promoting active policies to control indoor pollution.

Urban Environment

Finally, we can explore the greening of office buildings from the perspective of the urban environment, which involves three main dimensions: the spatial structure of the place, the local transport infrastructures and the city's overall political/utility planning setting.

Starting with the first, the greening of urban office buildings involves the implementation of design and construction techniques to be integrated within the spatial structure or the place. To begin with, this means paying attention to issues such as local climate, prevailing winds and urban fabric, in the sense that individual buildings will be able to fit well – individually as well as collectively – within the space and be less resource intensive by exploring natural daylight, passive cooling/heating, and so forth, according to the local requirements (cf. Girardet, 1997, 2001). Individual buildings may also contribute to enhancing urban green areas, not only on the surface, for instance, on the roofs and ground, but also vertically on the envelope. There are now interesting examples of buildings that have developed *vertical gardens*, which not only contribute to balancing energy use in their interiors, by minimizing cooling loads for instance, but which do also help to reduce pollution and urban warming. A radical case in point here is the renovation proposal for the ENI headquarters in Rome which, though never built, suggested the recovery of an obsolete façade by adding a second layer to it, a dense vertical garden, which would at the same time solve the problem of rain infiltration and avoid overheating in summer. As is implicit here, there are basically two dynamics that would influence the greening of office buildings from this perspective. One of them concerns local building codes and master plans, which should elaborate policies to allow such optimization of the land use so that buildings require fewer resources to operate, although still maintaining such buildings connected to systems of infrastructure. The other regards the role of (motivated) architects and clients – regardless of their origins (local, global) – which play a decisive role for proposing innovations, by carefully studying the local spatial organization and which designs and construction techniques would be most appropriate.

The second perspective of the greening of urban office buildings has to do with the local transport infrastructures. As discussed in chapter 2, inner city industrial pollution is largely giving way to vehicular pollution with its consequences for human health and the environment. In this regard, what is currently being proposed in order to mitigate the environmental problems related to transportation is a combination of land use and transportation policies, usually applying the systems of *compact mixed-use urban nodes*, which concentrate mixed-use developments (commercial and residential at the same time), minimizing the transport needed to commute from one zone to another. This system, although contested for concentrating pollution, avoids the single-function development and the dominance of the car, favouring thus multi-functional buildings and clean transport systems like bicycles (see, for instance, Rogers, 1997). Empirical evidence demonstrates that the compact model is successful, not only in terms of relieving some of the urban environmental problems, but also in terms of enhancing the quality of life the city offers. An example that can be given is the master plan for the Potsdamer Platz in Berlin, designed by the Italian Architect Renzo Piano, proposing the rehabilitation of a large area of urban wasteland into a mixed use development, including offices, retail, housing, entertainment facilities and public amenities, also addressing public transport issues. In this case, broader (local) urban planning strategies would be decisive for implementing compact, mixed-use developments. However, clients and architects may also play a role in this regard in the sense of proposing mixed land use and accessibility to public transport as part of their environmental planning strategies. Examples that may be given along this line are: Condé Nast and Reuters in New York, HEW in Hamburg, Deutsche Messe in Hanover, ABN AMRO in Amsterdam, Gap Inc. in San Francisco, Helicon and Swiss Re in London, Commerzbank in Frankfurt and the Greenpeace USA Headquarters in Washington DC, among many others.

Thirdly, the overall political setting of the city would be crucial in promoting active policies and programmes to improve the environmental performance of office buildings. These could involve not only the design of better master plans – such as the above-mentioned Potsdamer Platz – but also the promotion of other solutions such as urban cooling where applicable, through urban agriculture and expanding green areas to alleviate the heat island effect by improving natural shading, heat absorbing and humidifying capacities. A study performed by the Lawrence Berkeley National Laboratory in Los Angeles, for instance, where trees and high-albedo surfaces (that is, with high reflectivity of solar energy) were theoretically added to about 15 per cent of the city, indicates that peak summer temperatures have dropped by ten degrees Celsius, and smog production decreased by ten per cent – equalling the removal of three to five million cars from the roads (see also Rosenfeld, 1999). Studies using high-albedo roof-coating materials in California and Florida found that cooling energy use was reduced by as much as 67 per cent. These are solutions that will certainly be applied following the degree of environmental ambition of the government in power. And here, finally, utilities may also play a role in trying to optimize the use of resources in urban areas. Although their objective is of course of maximizing profits by selling more and more basic services, they are also now facing the contradiction that the resources they sell (for example, energy and water) are also becoming scarcer. In this sense, many utilities are now also favouring a more rational environmental performance of urban settlements, promoting programmes of energy/water saving also concerning office buildings.

Innovations in Governmental Policies

To this point I have mainly discussed the general technical solutions that are being deployed to increase the environmental performance of office building stocks and the social context in which they are being adopted, with respect to connectivity to infrastructure and embeddedness to local/global societal dynamics. Now I will shift the focus from the techniques and discuss the general policy scenario influencing the way such buildings and districts are designed and operated. This discussion starts with an overview of the governmental actors and institutions (with a special focus on the transnational, national and local urban policies promulgated in the European Union, also mentioning examples elsewhere when relevant), and on the section that follows, of market actors, focusing on corporations that occupy the office space.

Two main historical contexts have influenced the development of governmental policies with regard to the building industry: the energy/environmental crisis of the 1970s and the problem of global warming together with the rise of a 'risk society' in the 1990s. In both scenarios, national development patterns based on resource-intensive and fossil fuel energy have been put into question; and, equally, and in both cases cities and their buildings have been identified as among prime targets to reduce the country's aggregate energy consumption and environmental impact. In terms of policy development, both contexts have gradually prompted a number of innovations in different countries. Among these, Europe has become one of the most advanced regions, turning into a case worthy of special attention:

In retrospect, the development of such policies in the European Union started in the 1970s, when concern over the effects of technological development, growth in energy demand and environmental disruption started to attract the attention of the middle classes (Edwards, 1996). These, in turn, pushed authorities to take a stand and ensure above all their energy security. Among the consequences, the building industry was challenged to quantify and qualify its level of environmental impact and energy consumption, and identify the extraction and use of resources. A new energy and environmental policy was developed leading to the grant of subsidies for the development of the first solar houses, as well as incentives for experiments with the first passive office buildings, such as the NMB described above. In the urban policy field, attention was given to small-scale development and compactness, to encourage sociability and discourage the use of cars. Albeit being viewed as too idealistic on that occasion, these new policy approaches have in fact boosted a new generation of buildings and urban designs that have given an important step toward improving the energy and environmental performance of the built environment.

In this regard, to the extent that the energy and environmental crisis of the 1970s was gradually solved, energy and environmental efficiency continued to be an issue within the building industry in Europe. A number of programmes were developed in housing, office buildings and urban design, among others, from the late 1970s to the early 1990s. Their problem, however, was that they were scattered and uncoordinated, thus unable to boost results. It would only be in the early 1990s that governments would start to take a serious stance regarding the building sector – particularly in face of the uncertain policy implications regarding global warming[9] – and try to synchronize policies. Although these policies to curb carbon emissions have now come to a standstill, the 1990s have indeed prompted many innovations in the energy and environmental policy field. Europe has again taken the lead in this respect,[10] where some of the policies are transnational (applied across European countries), while others are more national in character and others still developed at the urban planning scale. In the following paragraphs a description of such policies is provided, also exemplifying to a certain extent cases outside the European Union.

In relation to transnational policies, various directives and research funding programmes have emerged related to the building sector in the European Union since the early 1990s. In the year of 1990, for instance, the European Commission's *Green Paper on the Urban Environment* was a turning point in environmental issues *vis-à-vis* the building industry, regarding primarily the establishment of a broad framework for effective action on a diverse range of environmental problems from energy to noise, global warming and water pollution (Edwards, 1996). The Green Paper listed seven important areas of action or policy change to facilitate the transition necessary in European cities.[11] The next significant development was the publication by the European Commission in 1992 of the *Task Force Report on the Environment*, acknowledging the importance of the urban quality of life and its important links involving health, environment and amenity. Finally, the Maastricht Treaty, signed in February 1992, introduced the concept 'sustainable growth respecting the environment', proposing a wide range of implications for the future practice of the building industry, among which were: (i) preserving, protecting and improving the quality of the environment; (ii) protecting human health; (iii) prudent and rational utilization of natural resources; and (iv) promoting measures at international level to deal with global environmental problems. It is evident that many of these are related to the building industry. The Treaty also recognized that environmental action must be taken across national boundaries to avoid one Member State from gaining competitive advantage over another in the case of policy discrepancies. Thus the harmonization of European environmental policies has been an imperative objective of the European Union and the practical effects of the Treaty, also concerning the building industry, are gradually emerging.

In this respect, two important policy principles have emerged in the European Union Treaty changing the relationship between clients and their professional advisers on the question of environmental pollution: the principles of 'polluter pays' and 'pollution should be dealt with at the source'. The former shifts the emphasis away from governments to the environmental contaminator exposing thereby clients and architects to the risk of litigation from third parties. The latter implies taking preventive measures to avoid remedial action later. In this sense, it is implicit in the principles of the European Community policy that it is now necessary to implement projects with minimal environmental and health impacts.[12]

Although these measures were launched in a transnational perspective, in the light of these principles individual governments within the Community have introduced a number of policies to curb the energy consumption and environmental impacts of buildings and districts, including offices. Of these, some are voluntary measures while others are more command-and-control. Among voluntary based approaches, a successful example is the one of *eco-labels*, which assess the environmental performance of buildings so as to grant them points. Their aim is to encourage the voluntary self-monitoring of the market, in the sense of enhancing the 'image' of the building (and the companies that inhabit them), promoting better marketability, such as commercial advantages through lower energy and water bills, in addition to achieving higher environmental sustainability to influence clients (Daniels, 1997). The most renowned of such schemes currently deployed is the Building Research Establishment Environmental Assessment Method (BREEAM), applied in Great Britain since 1991, first for office buildings, and subsequently for industrial facilities, supermarkets and private houses. Concerning office buildings, the BREEAM uses a system of evaluation according to criteria grouped in three levels of environmental impact.[13]

The BREEAM has been the first approach of its kind in the world, and comparable methods are nowadays being developed and applied in other countries, such as France, Norway, Spain, United States and Canada. In the United States a similar system has been launched – the Leadership in Energy and Environmental Design (LEED) – which is also a consensus-based national standard for encouraging high performance and increasing the sustainability of buildings in a voluntary way. Developed by the United States Green Building Council, it provides a common 'green building' standard across the country to encourage integrated design practices, and promote environmental leadership and competition in the market through raising consumer awareness (LEED, 2003). Similarly to the BREEAM, LEED also provides a comprehensive framework for assessing the environmental impacts of buildings in different levels. In addition to the LEED, the United States government introduced in 1992 the Energy Star programme (through the Environmental Protection Agency under the Clinton administration), which is also a voluntary labelling scheme designed to promote energy-efficient products, so as to reduce carbon emissions. In office buildings, for instance, the Energy Star applies to office equipment, such as computers, monitors and printers, which in fact has been the sector in which it achieved the greatest market entry. In 1998 the Energy Star merged with the Green Lights programme, which had been promoting energy-efficient lighting in commercial buildings. By 1999, more than 100 buildings were awarded the Energy Star label in the United States (Brown *et al.*, 2000).

In contrast, more command-and-control approaches are also being experienced by governments with the introduction of minimum energy performance requirements in the building code, in other words, the use of energy standards. Here the Netherlands has taken the lead, followed by Canada, where these requirements are usually complemented by a series of regulations, such as the minimum performance and labelling of energy-consuming products, collection of statistics on monitoring, in addition to subsidy schemes (Larsson, 1996; MINEZ, 1999). The energy performance of a building has therefore to be demonstrated in the documents for the application of a building permit.

In Europe, and elsewhere too, governments are also experimenting with the deployment of economic instruments such as tax abatements, improved mortgage conditions, creation of investment funds and other benefits to encourage developers or owners of ecological buildings as well as incentives to utility companies, whose market has now been deregulated at large. As for improvement in mortgage conditions, for instance, two illustrative examples can be given: one of them is the Bank of Montreal, which reduces its interest rates by one fourth for green constructions; the other is the largest Swedish housing bank, the Hypoteksbanken, which announced that it would only lend money to ecological-oriented projects (although also to the housing sector, see Roodman *et al.*, 1995). Although promising, these instruments are nevertheless still incipient. Taxes can for instance be levied at different stages of the production and operation of buildings, ranging from materials to energy and water consumption. Concerning energy use, product charges – which can be laid upon the price of products which cause pollution, either through their manufacture or consumption – and tax differentiation can be applied on electricity generated by fossil fuels so as to create incentives for the introduction of more sustainable technologies. In this context, investment and research and development (R&D) subsidies on new, more sustainable technologies in different areas of the construction industry are currently been experienced (particularly in north-western European countries) in order to encourage innovation and development of environmentally friendly technologies (Edwards, 1996).

Finally, at the urban level, local governments in various countries are now making use of covenants, concerning both buildings and urban designs, which are among the most reasonable solutions to encourage actors to take environmentally friendly actions. Covenants are usually developed according to a pre-established framework (which may be introduced at national level), developed by the government in collaboration with the market, specifying numerous measures to be taken voluntarily so as to decrease the environmental impact and energy consumption of buildings or districts. This framework is thus a way of homogenizing the adoption of sustainable measures in a country, in other words, of providing a common understanding on the issue of sustainability among different stakeholders. In the Netherlands, for instance, a series of National Packages for both ecological building and urban design was signed by stakeholders in the mid-1990s serving to clarify, both to the building industry and to public authorities, what exactly an ecological building practice implies (VROM, 1996, 2001, cf. chapter 5). Although not mandatory, local governments may influence the decisions of developers, for instance, by facilitating projects that comply with certain criteria put forward in the Package. Denmark is another country that has also adopted a similar covenant applicable to the building industry.

As a last word, several governments are also influencing the environmental performance of buildings and districts by requiring the application of an Environmental Assessment during the planning and design phase of projects. These are usually prescriptions also within the urban planning sphere. The Environmental Assessment is usually applicable for projects above a predetermined area, including mostly biophysical criteria,[14] for which a large amount of information is needed, ranging from the visual aspects of the design, to effects on health and safety, pollution and land take and its agricultural capacity (Edwards, 1996).

Innovations in Corporate Policies

Corporate innovations in environmental policy are of course manifesting in different segments of companies within the building industry nowadays – ranging from product manufacturers, development, to construction and facility management companies, among others. Above, for instance, we incidentally mentioned a few companies such as Siemens, American Standard and Lucent, which are now globalizing environmental technologies for buildings. In this section we will however provide a general discussion on environmental innovations promulgated by companies that *occupy* office spaces and how.

In the past decade, environmental management in companies has become more and more commonplace, with corporate environmental management practices developing according to at least three main stages or situations. The first one is called the *crisis-oriented stage*, where firms are compelled to control their environmental impact dimensions to comply with existing laws and regulations. At this stage, the firm usually finds solutions among end-of-pipe technologies and their internal motivation is strictly restricted to the compliance with the law. Secondly, the *process-oriented stage* is characterized as an attempt to achieve eco-efficiency, in which firms, knowing in advance about the legal implications of their activities, try to control their environmental performance in a cost-effective way, usually making use of preventive programmes. The third stage regards the *chain-oriented process* in which environmental management systems, including the whole chain of production, takes place: from materials extraction, to manufacturing, use and, finally, to the end disposal. Firms that undergo such a stage try to fulfil a kind of green identity, by means of such concepts as 'win-win' and PPP (people planet profit), and often make use of this to achieve a marketing differentiation. To date, most of the firms fall into the process-oriented stage, although the number of firms trying to go beyond efficiency issues is growing.

Regarding the companies under the second and third stages, four main innovations have been introduced in recent years influencing environmental management issues, also affecting the way these firms deal with the environmental dimension of their offices. The first of these is signing up to *international voluntary business programmes*. These business programmes – such as International Chamber of Commerce Business Charter for Sustainable Development, Agenda 21, OECD Guidelines, Coalition for Environmentally Responsive Economies (CERES) Principle, UNEP codes of conduct, and the like – are a framework of corporate environmental policies with a particular interest in regulating the international dimension of the environmental performance of companies such as in the case of foreign direct investments. By endorsing these principles, companies claim to benefit by improving their image, public relations and reputation, gaining more credibility with the market (see Adams, 1999).

The second of these innovations are the ISOs (issued by the International Standardization Organization) and the Environmental Management Systems (EMS).

The ISO 14000 series is a way of homogenizing environmental standards across borders, but has rather been considered as a kind of missed opportunity, as it did not achieve the expected market penetration among different industrial sectors (Mol, 2001). However, in the European Union case, for instance, the European Committee of Standardization has adopted the 'ISO 14001 Environmental Management Systems' as the main European standard (Edwards, 1996). The Committee thus requires organizations to publish an independently validated statement of their environmental policy so as to bring their environmental factors to the notice of the general public.[15]

Thirdly, and parallel to the ISOs, the EMS are another environmental management tool. The differences between both are in fact small: the ISO 14000 series provides the *certification* of environmental performance, which is universally applicable, while the EMS provide an *analysis of production processes* so as to detect environmental implications and increase the environmental performance of production or operation. Thus, the identification of environmental aspects of an organization's activities, products or services is the basis upon which the EMS will be built. In turn, environmental objectives and targets are required to form the basis upon which progress towards improving environmental performance will be measured. These must be consistent with the broad environmental policy of the company, including commitment to the prevention of pollution.

Finally, and in order to ensure that the EMS or ISO certifications are consistent over time, companies are increasingly undertaking Environmental Audits of their own environmental performance. These are periodical assessments usually done by external experts so as to determine the performance of the EMS undertaken by a company, by providing a feedback loop for the managerial board as well as suggestions for corrections.[16] Companies are gradually using Environmental Audits as a management tool in order to gain a competitive advantage due to a number of reasons, including in particular the ever-stricter environmental legislations and the liability implications, the rising energy, materials and waste disposal costs, the competitive pressure (as other companies start pursuing environmental objectives) and a growing public awareness. The result of the audits may be incorporated in the company's annual report.

In line with these instruments, companies do increasingly recognize that besides 'branding' their products with an environmental certificate, endorsing international sustainable business programmes, and the like, it is equally important to provide an appropriate 'branding' of their workplaces. Raymond (2001) analysed in this regard, how companies are using a sensitive approach in the architectural style to reinforce the principles of the corporate culture and strengthen their image, which can for instance be of a progressive, trustworthy, conservative or caring enterprise. The corporate architecture, in addition, also demonstrates whether the company fosters communication, teamwork or individualization, or hierarchies, among other important issues, also influencing the profile of employees it will attract. In this sense, while most companies start applying such new instruments of environmental management for their products, some of them do also start moving to a more chain-oriented approach (the third corporate stage above described), and include their premises in their environmental programmes.

Illustrative here can be the case of several energy companies that have started to explore a new approach to the (re-)design, construction and operation of their premises in the sense of furthering environmental considerations. Electricité de France (EdF), for instance, which since the 1970s has generated and distributed energy based on nuclear sources, specified in the brief for the commission of its new headquarters in Bordeaux that the complex should be energy-efficient. Together with the six main electricity utility companies of the world (Edison, Enel, Hydro Quebec, Kansai, Ontario Power, RWE and Tepco) EdF is part of the E7 Group, which plays an active role in global electricity issues and is also committed to promoting sustainable development, considering environmental management as a high corporate priority. For this purpose, the group has developed a joint policy framework for implementing initiatives in both domestic and international markets, as well as for providing information and expertise on the efficient generation and use of electricity. Also, as part of their environmental policy commitment, these companies have individually engaged in innovating their corporate offices, in the sense of providing benchmarks to be followed by the market. Besides EdF, another renowned example of ecological building promoted by an energy company within the E7 Group is the RWE AG Headquarters in Essen, completed in 1996, which became a landmark for the entire Ruhr Valley region with its 30-storey cylindrical tower, 32 metres in diameter, the fifth-tallest German building, and one of the first on such a scale to provide natural ventilation.

Energy companies, and utilities in general, are a particular case in point. In the era of deregulation of the public services market, such companies are now at a cross-roads between stricter environmental regulations and campaigns targeting the reduction of consumption of, for instance, energy and water, and their business objectives of increasingly selling the services they provide. It is in this context that some of the business rules of utilities have changed in recent years, as these companies start also selling 'efficiency' besides electricity and water. In the United States, the National Association of Regulatory Utility Commissioners worked on a task force to change the electricity utility profit rules to reward investments in Demand Side Management (DMS[17]) and, beyond premium rate of return on efficiency investments, utilities would start to engage in 'shared savings' systems. That is, for every dollar saved from the customer, the utility was allowed a small rate of participation in the saving, allowing its stockholders to earn an extra $0.15, while the customer remained with the saving of $0.85 (Rosenfeld, 1999). In this case, 'teaching' the market – including companies – how to be more efficient in energy consumption has become a sound economic solution. In the United States, since 1990 the Shared Savings idea, together with DMS programmes, grew at about three billion dollars every year, with some slumps since 1996 (Ibid.). Hence why environmental innovations in office building start to be an appealing trend also for those who sell 'environmentally intensive' products.

In addition to the utilities, if we also look at the briefings of the most significant examples of ecological buildings in the world owned/maintained by regular companies, we see that in most cases it is the companies themselves that indeed trigger the greening process of their buildings. In the late 1970s the NMB (or ING) headquarters in Amsterdam commissioned an 'innovative architecture', with environmental considerations. IBM in Kuala Lumpur, Malaysia, required an architecture to reflect the 'progressive character of the company', remaining sensitive to the environment, while EdF in Bordeaux built a cellular office space to achieve energy efficiency, and RWE in Essen included natural ventilation to reduce energy consumption and increase indoor comfort. The ENI in Rome requested a renovation project to demonstrate the 'ecological equilibrium' of the company. This indeed points at a trend in which companies head towards a more chain-oriented environmental policy, as mentioned above, so as to attain a green identity, also with the architecture of their offices.

Similarly, and considering the way that companies deal with the operations of their offices, we see that examples are numerous of companies that are extending the environmental management routines (including audit schemes and public reporting) of their activities to also encompass issues such as water and energy use in their offices, environmentally efficient systems of waste disposal, and so forth. Examples that may be given here, besides the companies just mentioned above, include The Gap Inc., Duracell, Herman Miller SQA, Nike, Schlumberger and Ford. These are companies that are certainly not only seeking to improve their environmental image with more sensitive architectures, as one may perhaps claim, but which are also revolutionizing ways of carrying out corporate environmental programmes, at least as far as their home-country contexts are concerned.

Conclusions

This chapter sketched the circumstances in which environmental concerns are being internalized within the construction and operation of urban office buildings and districts. It first provided a chronological overview of the changing approach to dealing with the environmental aspects of office buildings and districts. A particular concern in this overview was given to systems of acclimatization and lighting, which historically have been dealt with as the most environmentally intensive components of office buildings. After the historical description, it outlined the main techniques and related societal dynamics that are currently being applied to mitigate the environmental impacts of office buildings and districts, which were analysed in terms of systems of environmental technology, indoor environment and urban environment, respectively. Finally, it also explored the main policy innovations that governments and corporate actors have begun developing to deal with the ecological footprint of office buildings and districts.

From the information gathered in this chapter it seems that a major transformation has been occurring since the early 1970s, when the first important considerations for the energy and environmental dimension of buildings and urban areas took hold. In the 1970s, by the time the first energy crisis hit the West, environmental themes were to a large extent rather marginal within the construction and operation of (office) buildings and districts. While to a certain extent research on this theme had already been carried out for decades by then, practical examples were still scarce and likewise not institutionalized within either governmental or corporate policies. In addition, solutions tended to approach 'de-modernization' designs, or a disconnection from systems of infrastructure, which was largely viewed as too idealistic by then.

However, and somewhat surprisingly, to the extent that the energy and environmental crisis was gradually solved, environmental innovations that were introduced during the 1970s increasingly grew in importance since then, leading to the development and maturation of many programmes targeting different sectors within the building industry. These programmes gained a particular momentum since the early 1990s, when the second energy crisis hit the West, drawing attention to the issue of global warming and leading to a more mature public concern over ecological issues. Since then, examples of sustainable office buildings and districts have increased rapidly, at the same time that governments started to increasingly institutionalize environmental issues within their urban policies, and companies, similarly, started increasingly to apply environmental programmes to their activities, eventually also encompassing the dimension of their offices. Thus, while in the 1970s environmental issues were to a large extent only marginal within the construction and operation of office buildings and districts, these issues started to gain a core importance in the 1990s. Likewise, de-modernization solutions of the 1970s questioning the overall technological optimism of the modern movement of architecture have now given way to a new 'enchantment' of technologies, in a way forward in modernity. Finally, during the last decade the environmental reform of office buildings and districts has been further strengthened by other policy and managerial innovations that have been deployed with an increasing intensity, such as rating systems, 'shared profits', improved mortgage conditions, corporate environmental management programmes, and so forth.

In the light of these developments, it no longer seems possible to surmise that the environmental reform of office buildings and districts is mere wishful thinking today, as it was in the 1970s. It is now recognized at large, among governmental, technical, corporate, as well as societal circles, that improving the environmental performance of buildings and districts is an achievable, pragmatic and necessary move towards ensuring the sustenance base of the planet in terms of natural resources – a move in which solutions for greening are embedded in contexts of strong grid connectivity as well as enmeshed in a dynamic local-global societal interaction.

Notes

1   Environmental control should be understood as solutions developed to achieve *indoor comfort*, such as desirable levels of temperature and lighting, which can be attained via mechanical or passive methods. As I will explain later on in this chapter, mechanical systems of acclimatization and lighting have become the most energy-intensive components of a building.

2   Air conditioning was first introduced in the United States into the textile industry, in the nineteenth century, where the incoming water vapour reduced thread breakage and the effect of static electricity (Cook, 2000).

3   Although the modern movement and the International Style were seen as a proletarization of construction techniques, aiming at the provision of housing for everyone with industrialization, it would become clear later on that the austerity of forms did not really communicate with the proletariat, being appreciated only by intellectual élites. It would be in this context that postmodernism would supplant modernism, as we explained in chapter 2.

4   This took place in Italy (1975), Germany (1976), Sweden (1977) and in the Netherlands (1979).

5   Nowadays, however, the term sustainable building has become a kind of catchword to refer to all buildings that are designed in a more environmentally friendly way.

6   According to Guy and Osborn (2001), five main 'competing logics of green design' may be identified, ranging from lower to higher technological approaches: The first and lowest-

technology of these preaches the creation of buildings to reinforce the notion of *self-sustained eco-community*, totally disconnected from the main infrastructure networks, and mostly expressed in terms of organic housing design for alternative lifestyles, seeking to break away from unsustainable modernity (for example, the Eco-Village Network, Findhorn in Scotland, and so on). This approach is followed by the *healthy building* paradigm, which evokes issues as sick building syndrome and psychological aspects of the indoor environment. Subsequently, the sustainable architecture or *sustainable building* story line as such (or as Guy and Osborn call it: 'the building as ecological polluter') should be understood as the one in which buildings try to minimize their environmental impact or footprint by evoking ethics and sustainability topics, such as renewable materials, soft and appropriate technologies, use of local knowledge and resources, and so forth. (This is in fact the story line most popularly associated with the image of green building, although to date mostly advanced through demonstration projects, cf. National Dubo Centrum, 2000, for instance). The fourth approach in turn refers to *neo-vernacular architecture*, seeking to recreate symbolic social values by shaping and contextualizing modern looking buildings according to local traditional design criteria. Finally, the last of such logics is the one closest to ecological modernization theory (cf. chapter 4). Guy and Osborn call it as the 'smart asset' logic, which evokes topics such as flexibility (particularly of the workspace), efficiency, cost-savings, intelligent technologies, and so forth.

7 Reflexive modernity stands for the confrontation that modernity is facing with its own problems, cf. chapter 2.

8 Water discharged particularly from sinks, which may be used as second-quality water.

9 Such as the United Nations Framework Convention on Climate Change and the proposals of the Kyoto Protocol. In 1992 a text for the United Nations Framework Convention on Climate Change (UNFCCC) was first adopted at the United Nations Headquarters in New York regarding the reduction of greenhouse gas emissions. By 1997, the Kyoto Protocol determined that developed countries should decrease the emissions of greenhouse gases (primarily CO_2) by seven per cent, based on 1990 figures, during the period 2008 to 2012; up to 1999, 84 countries had signed up to it.

10 In the United States, conversely, energy and environmental policies have been somewhat offset by powerful economic forces, reducing to a certain extent the value of environmental solutions, also affecting the ecological reform of the building sector.

11 These included: (i) the abandonment of zoned land-use principles and adoption of policies encouraging mixed-use and denser development; (ii) a switch from investment in roads to support the public transport; (iii) the protection of urban cultural heritage; (iv) the protection and improvement of open spaces in towns to enhance visual pleasure, improve microclimate and reduce air pollution in urban areas; (v) the improvement of wastewater treatment; (vi) the reduction of air pollution and more efficient use of energy; and (vii) the avoidance of waste generation at the source (Ibid.).

12 In the European Union context, the general debate regarding environmental issues, particularly global warming, prevails under the 'precautionary principle' according to the European Community law, where Member States are increasingly required to take preventive actions concerning environmental damage, which should be rectified *at source* (see, for instance, Edwards, 1996).

13 The first of these is the 'global evaluation and resource utilization' including potentials of CO_2 emissions, acid rain, ozone depletion, in addition to the use of natural resources, recycled materials, renewable materials and longevity. Secondly, the 'local evaluation' assesses issues regarding transportation, water management, noise, shading and other local ecological features. Thirdly, the 'interior evaluation' corresponds to an assessment of the use of dangerous materials and systems of indoor comfort (Ibid.).

14 The Directive 85/337 of the European Community, for instance, defines two project categories: Annex 1 projects (mostly including industrial facilities, for which a formal

Environmental Assessment is required) and Annex 2 projects (which may include office buildings or districts, for which the assessment is required as long as Member States so consider). Since the definition of works under Annex 2 is quite vaguely expressed, different European countries have adopted varying standards (Edwards, 1996). In 1997, however, after discussions on a possible harmonization of screening procedures, Directive 97/11 extended the categories of developments subject to formal Environmental Assessments. These include: major out-of-town developments (like shopping complexes, theme parks, office parks and leisure centres), golf courses, multiple cinemas, stadia, major holiday villages or hotel projects and certain infrastructure projects (such as yacht marinas and industrial estates), ski developments and smaller categories of power station.

15   Such a statement has to include commitments to the prevention of pollution, continual improvement in environmental performance and a record of compliance with relevant environmental legislation (Edwards, 1996). The latter is of course the minimum standard any organization needs to achieve.

16   An environmental audit involves the evaluation of the operational practices so as to determine whether these can be made more efficient in terms of resources use and waste production, or altered to minimize risk of pollution. It examines the way in which the company deals with the waste it produces and seeks more efficient waste management options that may be employed. It analyses the material and energy resources the company uses to see whether more environmentally sound alternatives can be applied. Moreover, it develops contingency plans for environmental accidents.

17   According to Chappells *et al.* (2000, p. 30), DMS studies have the objective of 'reducing the need for products or services by better managing their storage and supply'.

Chapter 4

The Ecological Modernization of Transnational Buildings

While in the preceding chapter I described the main trends in the environmental restructuring of urban office buildings, the focus of this one is to put these trends into a theoretical perspective which will help us to analyse and evaluate the greening of transnational buildings in major cities. The theory of ecological modernization suits this purpose as it combines a focus on the rise of environmental technologies and related policies within a broader sociological perspective on the relationship between globalizing modernity and environment.

Ecological modernization theory emerged as a distinct school of thought in environmental sociology in the early 1980s, primarily in north-west Europe, and has now grown into a leading worldwide model of environmental reform. The concept 'ecological modernization' denotes a paradigm bringing together economic growth with environmental protection. At its core lies the idea that 'all ways out of the ecological crisis seem only possible by going further into modernity', in that environmental problems of modernity are to be solved in a further, ecologically radical modernization process, by refining polluting industrial processes into cleaner ones. The theory presents thereby a series of propositions – ranging from technological, to political, societal and economic issues – to put an end to the 'industrialism versus environmentalism' conflict of modernity. It suggests that it is indeed *viable* to combine further industrial growth with environmental objectives, without changing the institutions and societal dynamics of modernity in their fundamental traits.

Several studies on different industrial clusters have taken ecological modernization theory to ground their analyses and propose policy directions, for example, the chemical industry (Mol, 1995), domestic consumption (Spaargaren, 1997), utility services (Chappells *et al.*, 2000, van Vliet 2002), to mention a few. While some of these have emphasized the role of science and technology (cf. Huber, 1985, 1991, 2000), others have focused on the importance of economic and market dynamics in bringing about ecological reform (cf. Mol, 1995), and still others on the changing relations between state and market (cf. Jänicke, 1993). Furthermore, another body of research has centred on the changing discursive practices within environmental politics (cf. Hajer, 1995). Finally, since the mid-1990s onwards, research into ecological modernization theory has also started to pay attention to geographical areas beyond north-west Europe, most notably to other industrialized and newly industrialized countries, such as the United States, Japan, Lithuania, China and Vietnam (cf. Rinkevicius, 2000; Frijns *et al.*, 2000). Central to all these studies is the notion that environmental and economic objectives *can* be met within the existing political and economic spheres of the societal system of the contemporary world.

In order to better grasp the framework of ecological modernization theory and its usefulness in analysing sustainable building practices, the chapter starts with a general introduction to the historical development of environmental sociology so as to review how the ecological modernization discourse emerged and evolved. We will then go on to discuss some of the dominant characteristics of ecological modernization theory and analyse how these may be linked to our discussion on globalization and urban environmental change. The chapter finalizes by putting forward a set of hypotheses about the greening of office buildings in global cities following the ecological modernization logic.

From Limits to Growth to Ecological Modernization

The first debates on the relationship between society and environment took place in the early twentieth century, focusing primarily on the issues of the degradation of natural resources and built environments (Dunlap, 2000). These debates, however, though resulting in the institutionalization of the first nature reserves, national parks, and the like, did not significantly contribute towards building a theoretical perspective in sociology, as they failed to question the underlying causes – economic, social or political processes – leading to environmental conflicts. As certain environmentalists suggest, a more concrete upsurge of environmental concerns would only take place in the 1960s and 1970s, when notions of radical change or limits to growth revolutionized discussions on the transformations of the social order required for our survival on earth. This period is frequently designated as the first wave of environmental concern, a period which also coincided with the first attempts to promote industrial pollution control.

Environmental sociology was introduced as a sub-discipline in social sciences during this first wave of environmental concern,[1] as discussions about the relationship between social dynamics and environmental deterioration/reform started to gain increasing ground. Rachel Carson's volume *Silent Spring* published in 1962 was in this regard unarguably one of the first and most influential of the period. These early discussions about the environmental question were also largely influenced by a series of events, culminating in 1972. First, the Apollo 8 expedition to the Moon in 1968, for instance, strengthened the notion of a 'spaceship earth', or the awareness of a common 'shelter' that needs to be safeguarded. Second, the first (United Nations) conference on the environment, held in Stockholm in 1972, initiated a process of institutionalization of environmental concerns. Finally, two other important publications – the report to the Club of Rome *Limits to Growth* and a special edition of the journal *The Ecologist*, *A Blueprint for Survival* – both issued in 1972, consolidated the notion that a fundamental change was imperative: While *Limits to Growth* drew attention to the existence of an 'environmental problèmatique' and a future environmental predicament, *A Blueprint for Survival* not only alerted people that 'radical change is both necessary and inevitable...,'[2] but also proposed a model for an alternative, ecocentric society. A society that would consist of numerous small-scale units of settlements, where people would live close to and subsist on nature, where technology would be adapted to a proper scale, and where the political system would be autonomous (*A Blueprint for Survival*, 1972; cf. Spaargaren, 2000).

As expected, the notion of ecocentrism and radical change sparked a major controversy during this first wave of environmental concern. On the one hand, traditional capitalists and the right wing of the time believed that the rising ecological questions were largely overestimated, and that environmental problems ought to be solved according to Adam Smith's invisible hand or market equilibrium theory. Conversely, a more leftist approach argued that a radical anti-growth political culture was necessary to curb environmental problems, somewhat reviving the zero-growth theory of John Stuart Mill (cf. Huber, 1991). This leftist line in time bifurcated into two streams of thought, which, albeit related, gave rise to two distinct schools in environmental sociology: the neo-Marxists (on the one side) and the counter-productivity scholars (on the other). While the former blamed capitalism per se, counter-productivity theorists – also known as de-modernization, de-industrialization or eco-anarchists – blamed both the capitalistic and industrial clusters of modernity for causing environmental problems (Mol, 1995). Hence, an early body of literature on environmental sociology was originally formed on the grounds of a dialectical debate on the institutional traits of modernity – capitalism and industrialism – in the identification of prime agents bringing about environmental disruption. Before analysing the major outcomes of the first wave of environmental concern, let us have a pause and explore these slightly differing approaches.

According to neo-Marxists like Allan Schnaiberg, James O'Connor, David Goldblatt, Peter Dicken, Ted Benton and David Pepper, it was the *treadmill of production* – that is, the capitalistic character of the organization of production – that was responsible for bringing about the continuous disruption of the sustenance base. For them, such disruption is primarily initiated by a small number of powerful companies, which, by propelling the process of capital accumulation, make use of nature as a production force, causing environmental harm and trapping capitalistic societies into a kind of treadmill of economic production and environmental disruption. In this sense, the key to understanding – and reverting – the environmental crisis of modernity lies in departing from the capitalistic mode of production, which is essentially detained by such companies.

This school, though still subsisting as one of the dominant academic traditions in environmental sociology (particularly in the USA), was widely criticized for its unilateral perspective about capitalism causing environmental problems. A more radical school of thought thereby emerged, advocating that both capitalism and industrialism should be considered on the question of environmental threats. Advanced particularly by the group of counter-productivity theorists – including Barry Commoner (USA), Ivan Illich (France), André Gorz (France), Rudolf Bahro (Germany), Otto Ulrich (Germany), Wolfgang Sachs (Germany) and Hans Achterhuis (the Netherlands) – this group developed a line of reasoning based on the concept of 'net-balancing' or *Total-bilanzierung*. Still writing in the light of Marxist thought, these theorists were nevertheless somehow critical to Marxism in its disregard to the *character* of the forces of production (such as technological options), as Marx's accounts were exclusively focusing the *social relations* of production (Spaargaren, 2000). Therefore they postulated that in order to have a correct measurement of the productivity of a technology or a certain sector of industry, all *real* costs involved with production processes, including environmental harm, should be taken into account.

This net-balancing approach tackled in particular technological systems known as 'slum-technologies' or 'dead-end technologies' – such as nuclear energy and the chemical industry – meaning, in practical terms, that the welfare brought about by such industrial segments in the short term reaches a socio-critical point in the long term, at which gains start to run counter to the emerging (environmental) consequences. As a solution this line proposed not only changing the realm of the *relations of production* (that is, capitalism) but also the realm of the *forces of production*, in other words, dismantling of (such) industrial systems, mostly encouraged by grassroots initiatives belonging to the 'new social movements' including NGOs. In turn, the counter-productivity school was also criticized, but mostly for leading to conflictual relationships between state and industry. And in this context another group of environmentalists would eventually come to the fore with a more positive appraisal of the logics of industrialism, the ecological modernization theorists.

As some scholars contend, the limits to growth debate – as this first wave of environmental concern became known – despite its importance as having introduced a definite discussion on the relationship between nature and society, and for inaugurating disciplines such as environmental sociology and environmental economics as sub-disciplines within sociological and economic studies, cannot be considered to have led to successful results, at least not in economic or political terms. Mol (1995), for instance, describes that during this period the first government departments for the environment and environmental legislation and planning were instituted in most industrial societies, followed by an increase in the number and membership of non-governmental environmental organizations. But as an ecological reform carrier, he argues, this first important debate on environmentalism was not effective in 'affect[ing] the basic institutions that were held responsible for environmental disruption' (Mol, 1995, p. 2), that is, capitalism and/or industrialism, in their fundamental traits. Options of environmental reform created mostly divergences in opinions rather than solutions to tackle the problems – the envisaged environmentally sound society proposed during this period was often viewed as too idealistic or even inconceivable within the logics of modernity.

A new wave of environmental concern occurred when the environmental movement lost this trait of impracticality in the mid-1980s, when attention was drawn to the *structural design fault* of industrialism, whereby the concept 'sustainable development' started to gain increasing ground, giving the environmental question an overall more positive appraisal[3] (Mol, 1995; Spaargaren, 2000). According to Adams (1990), two main publications laid the ground for most environmentalist thinking on the sustainable development field:[4] *World Conservation Strategy* (IUCN, 1980) and *Our Common Future* (Brundtland, 1987). Although with a strong focus on the dual crisis of third world countries – namely the crises of development along with environmental constraints (such as desertification, deforestation, and so forth) – the sustainable development debate basically brought to the fore two notions: first, as an overriding priority, the call for the upgrading of the living conditions of particularly the fourth world. Second, the 'belief…that equity, growth and environmental maintenance are simultaneously possible with each nation achieving its full economic potential and at the same time enhancing its resource base' (Kirkby *et al.*, 1995, p. 7).

In this regard, and no longer so much questioning the economic fault of modernity (namely, of capitalism) *vis-à-vis* the environmental crisis, there was now a new environmental politics discourse, whereby a sustainable level of production was encouraged: supporting growth but at the same time reorienting technology, managing risks and merging environment and economics in decision-making processes (Brundtland, 1987). As a result, and again in contrast to the 1970s' debate on limits, the 1980s celebrated an expansion of capitalist development, as 'the concepts of economy and ecology were no longer regarded as antithetical' (Spaargaren, 2000, p. 45). This not only meant that the third world could develop within the planet's carrying capacity, but also that industrialized countries should adjust the structural design faults of their industrial systems according to sustainability parameters.

It was within this new policy outlook that a third group of environmental sociology theorists emerged, originally in Germany, recognizing this '*structural* character of the environmental problèmatique' leading to the burdening of the sustenance base, yet assuming that exiting political, economic and social institutions can internalize environmental care (Hajer, 1995, p. 25, italics added; Mol, 1995; Spaargaren, 2000). These theorists started out by observing that environmental protection could be achieved in frameworks of economic growth, leading to the assumption that material flows could be 'decoupled' – that is, dissociated – from economic flows[5] (Mol, 2000a). As a result, and challenging the notion of de-industrialization and limits to growth, these scientists started to explore new directions or options for understanding the dynamics of environmental deterioration and reform in view of the main social practices and institutions of modernity in a scenario of further growth – of modernization. Their central object of reflection has since then been the changing social practices and institutional transformations bringing about the environmental reform of modern societies. According to ecological modernization theorists, the institutionalization of environmental care into all spheres of society is a viable condition for the further development and subsistence of mankind, even under conditions of capitalism.

The theory of ecological modernization originally matured against the backdrop of two dominant, though slightly different, debates, put forward by two of the major German social scientists in the mid-1980s. Although, by now, several authors have contributed to the theory's development, eventually leading to a refining of its original propositions, a few topics still remain imperative for understanding both the core of this school of thought and how it diverges from or converges with other theories. In the section that follows I briefly review the most distinct characteristics of ecological modernization, starting with the issue of emancipation of ecology and then moving on to the question of the changing relationship between state and market, and the concept of social change (the two main debates originally put forth by the theory), the theory's descriptive and normative connotations, as well as the issue of substance/environmental flows and the role of science and technology. Following this review I will finally explore the theory under the present conditions of globalization and its applicability in the building field.

Premises of Ecological Modernization Theory

A central theme of ecological modernization theory is the notion that ecology has been growing as an *independent rationale* or criterion within modern industrial societies.

Unlike other important movements that have emerged since at least the 1960s onwards (such as feminism, peace and nuclear disarmament), it is unarguably the environmental movement that has been most quickly ascending and growing in importance within the modern societal system. This trend can be confirmed to the extent that departments and ministries for the environment have been established (1970s), green parties instituted (1980s) and several market-based mechanisms have started to incorporate 'ecology' as a distinct product criterion (1990s), through eco-labels, environmental auditing, green financing and through concepts like environmental performance, for instance. According to ecological modernization theory, the institutionalization of environmental care is a process that cannot be only reduced to an economic or political reasoning, insofar as ecology is becoming a distinct rationality of modernity.

Against this backdrop, ecological modernization theory developed two complementary debates. One of these was presented by Martin Jänicke (1985, 1986, 1993), bringing into focus a discussion on the *failures of the modern state.* According to this, the classical environmental policy-making paradigm – centralized, inflexible, developing 'curative' policies of command-and-control – has to a large extent been incapable of dealing with or controlling the environmental crisis of modernity, in view of monitoring massive loads of natural resources and related emissions that are used in and produced by the world economy. Likewise, the bureaucratic state has also failed in promoting substantial advances in technological innovations and incentives for companies to adopt more environmentally sound strategies. Jänicke elaborated thereby on a *political modernization* discourse, in which environmental policy making is set about by horizontal cooperation and consensus among actors, on the basis of dialogical decision making and covenants, and in which the state somehow 'retreats' in the implementation of environmental care and transfers certain responsibilities in this matter to non-central level actors, such as the market. Without of course losing grasp of certain tasks that remain indispensable for the state in bringing about environmental reform, this proposal is not a simple 'laissez faire' policy, but rather a changing paradigm in which the state becomes an 'enabling state', in the sense that it creates appropriate conditions for the market to carry out environmental management and reform.[6] In addition, he also notes that in this process the environmental policy discourse shifts not only from command-and-control to more negotiated approaches, but also from 'curative' and 'demodernization' solutions to 'preventive' and 'technologically progressive' ones.

The other debate was initiated by Joseph Huber (1985, 1991, 2000), identifying that this new environmental reform discourse was not only restricted to the government-industry relationship but that it also concerned the societal sphere, in view of the role of civil society in pushing for ecological reform, such as consumer pressure and environmental NGOs. He thereby elaborated a *theory of social change* – or a radical programme of ecological reform – in which 'economy' and 'ecology' became intertwined concepts. The essence of Huber's thinking is that ecological modernization is a way to overcome environmental problems by making use of the same institutions of modernity – such as political and economic ones – in a project of 'modernizing modernity', by re-institutionalizing environmental concerns (or by 'economizing ecology' and 'ecologizing economy', above all in the sense that ecology starts making an impact on the business world rationale).

These two streams within the theory have resulted in two (or three)[7] main bodies of literature. The first one deals with ecological modernization as a *descriptive* or *substantive theory*, which analyses the (historical) changing political concepts and societal developments to deal with environmental problems by applying theoretical premises as a vehicle for describing society. The main observation made here is that environmental issues have been moving from the periphery to the core of societal concern, affecting the policy-making practice of politicians, managers, financiers, consumers, and so forth, also converging at the idea that the state is becoming less and less bureaucratic and hierarchical at dealing with environmental problems, delegating environmental care responsibilities to the market. The second highlights ecological modernization as a *normative* or *formal theory*, which prescribes alternatives to deal with environmental problems. Here again the main observation is that ecology is moving from peripheral to core debates of modernity, eventually developing its own rationality. To explain this, adherents of ecological modernization present a set of some five interlinked hypotheses, which have been tested since at least the mid-1990s:

- The first hypothesis corresponds to the criticism that traditional judicial-administrative structures based on the 'react-and-cure' formula dominant in the 1970s have received, whereas a second-generation 'anticipate-and-prevent' regulatory framework or corporate policy has started to gain increasing credibility.
- Related to this, the second hypothesis stresses that science and technology have started to play a new role *vis-à-vis* ecologically-informed transformations of modernity, not only discarding the 'react-and-cure' (end-of-pipe) formula, but also manifesting such important new concepts as 'multiple stress' or 'critical load' – emphasizing integrative ecological responses to industrial processes and the levels of pollution that nature can endure.
- Thirdly, and while the state retreats in view of environmental care issues (cf. above political modernization),[8] market actors – such as producers, R&D institutions, business associations, recyclers, as well as end users – start to play a pivotal role as ecological reform carriers, moving away from the concept that environmental protection implies increased production costs towards the concept 'pollution prevention pays'.
- Fourthly, decision-making processes regarding the management of public assets (such as nature) have also been joined by external actors, such as environmental NGOs, which do not only further push for environmental protection but have also started to develop environmental reform proposals.
- Finally, the fifth hypothesis can be defined as the changing environmental discourse paradigm, moving away from the 'ecology versus economy' discourse introduced in the 1970s towards a more consensual approach, in reference to and intrinsically interlinked with the above-mentioned four other hypotheses, whereby concepts such as win-win, people-planet-profit and pollution prevention pays, among others, have emerged.[9]

As can be noted, a common denominator to these hypotheses is the issue of managing environmental flows – such as the use of energy, water, materials and the related emissions at the end of the production line. The theory's essence is therefore to provide an understanding of how environmental flows may be managed in a more ecologically rational way, in view of developments that take place interdependently within socio-economic and political-cultural transformations resulting in technological change. According to the theory, the contemporary environmental crisis is above all a *social crisis* of the structural design fault of modernity, leading to the burdening of the sustenance base, which needs therefore to be reconstructed in the sense that production as well as consumption processes start to minimize the extraction of resources, particularly non-renewable ones, being more efficient in the industrialization process and minimal in terms of emissions.

And in order to achieve this, three main projects have been advanced by the theory. First, the shift or substitution from curative (*Entsorgung*) to preventive (*Vorsorgung*) technologies, in a paradigm of further industrialization with clean production processes, as opposed to end-of-pipe strategies and de-industrialization solutions. Second, the partial de-industrialization or dematerialization of certain technical systems or economic sectors that are fundamentally maladjusted still remains imperative in this new context, such as certain segments of the chemical industry, nuclear energy, and so on. Third, the close monitoring and subsequent monetarization of nature; in other words the better control of resource streams and the attachment of an economic value to them, through, for instance, the introduction of economic concepts, mechanisms and principles aiming at environmental protection.[10]

In its essence, ecological modernization theory suggests that these projects are leading to an ecologically radical kind of industrial revolution in which environmental externalities are being internalized in a way forward into modernity, in an ecological *modernization* process. According to the theory, de-industrialization solutions certainly do exist, but are developed on a smaller scale as compared to further modernization approaches.

To finalize, the theory also highlights that to the same extent that ecology is growing as a new criterion of processes of production and consumption, it is also growing into an independent criterion of *modernity* itself, as the environmental question is now also being raised in the general literature on sociology. Illustrative of this achievement are the works by such key scholars as Anthony Giddens and David Harvey, who are now formulating concepts in which the ecological crisis becomes pivotal for understanding the current, 'reflexive' phase of modernity in which we stand.

The Globalization of Ecological Modernization Theory

From the early 1990s, new environmental issues like global warming, ozone depletion, desertification and the destruction of rain forests have strengthened the idea that environmental problems are not only interlinked among themselves but also resound on a more global level. It is within this context that a 'second environmental crisis' emerged in contrast to the 'first environmental crisis' of the 1970s and 1980s, usually defined by environmental sociologists as the phase of 'global environmental change'. While the first environmental crisis tried to tackle environmental problems at the local level, the second crisis introduced 'new' debates on the urgency of environmental problems and the need for international or even global coalitions to deal with them (cf. Spaargaren, 2000). These new challenges have eventually also affected the framework of ecological modernization theory, particularly for putting into question the role of science and technology as environmental reform carriers, and also for stressing the need for transnational environmental policy agreements – an element that the mainstream elaborations of the theory do not address.

One of the leading theorists of the second environmental crisis is Ulrich Beck with the concept of *Risikogesellschaft* (risk society, cf. Beck, 1992, 1999), through which he points to the emergence of a society where fear and anxiety dominate, where environmental problems have gone out of control. Also tackling modernity and its industrialist dimension, he suggests that the production of 'wealth' is accompanied by the production of 'risks', with incalculable side effects. Such risks are in turn bringing modernity to a new phase, one in which it becomes reflexive, where society is confronted by hazards and insecurities 'induced and introduced by modernization itself' (Beck, 1992, p. 21). Terming this new phase 'reflexive modernity', Beck explains that unlike in 'simple' modernity, the global consequences of such new risks – such as radioactivity, toxins, genetic engineering – belong to a different age, as they induce irreversible and generally invisible harms, thus in principle only existing as long as they are scientifically proven. Additionally, and paradoxically, risks of reflexive modernity, according to Beck, act in a kind of boomerang effect, sooner or later affecting the same agents who produced them, thereby breaking up or democratizing,[11] or at least to a certain extent, patterns of social class or developmental status.

It is within this framework that, besides the role of science and technology and the urgent need for transnational policy agreements, the role of multinational companies in the diffusion of environmental 'bads' or 'goods' has also been increasingly called into question. In general, environmental sociologists argue that it is precisely the economic dynamics of global capitalism that holds the greatest share of responsibility for triggering and worsening environmental problems. Yet, while there is evidence that multinationals are making efforts to deal with their environmental externalities – or at least as far as their home countries are concerned – environmental sociologists *do not* yet share a consensus regarding their environmental conduct on a worldwide level.

In this regard, such scholars as Bradford Gentry (1999), Lyuba Zarsky (1999), Jan Adams (1999) and Arthur Mol (2001) have in general a positive appraisal of the environmental performance of economic agents in the era of globalization. Defending the thesis that globalization mechanisms may encourage the distribution of 'goods' (such as better technologies and improvement in living standards) to different localities, they suggest that it may thereby trigger a 'race to the top' in terms of environmental management particularly where developing countries are concerned. Other scholars including Ulrich Beck (following Vandana Shiva, 1993, and particularly dependency theorists) are more sceptical, claiming that the foreign direct investment-environment linkages are far from evident. In the face of this dichotomy, a question to be raised, also defying the principles of ecological modernization theory, is: in the era of global environmental change, to what extent do global market actors indeed play a role in diffusing global environmental reforms?

*   *   *

The ecological modernization theory has been (and still largely is) worked out in the context of north-western European countries, tackling the local dimension of environmental problems, such as through the improvement of environmental flows within industrial sectors. Many of the elements put forward by global change theorists – such as the environmental dimensions of globalization processes or the global dimensions of environmental problems – do not appear in the classic elaborations of ecological modernization theory. Also, the theory does not have a strong focus on the risks in everyday life but rather on institutional adaptations to cope with ecological problems. In a way, ecological modernization theory is much more concerned with issues regarding *institutional reflexivity*, than with the reflexivity of risks and threats to everyday lives (Hogenboom *et al.*, 1999).

In some respects, however, the arguments put forth by Ulrich Beck do not necessarily contradict those of ecological modernization scholars, in the sense that both schools combine the idea of continuing with modernization processes while trying to encompass their side effects. But when it comes to issues regarding the institutionalization of doubt or the globalization of uncertainties, risk society theory seems to be much closer to the principles of the counter-productivity school, as it implies the disenchantment of science or the inability of technology to solve environmental problems, unlike ecological modernization theory.[12]

All in all, and in line with the discourse on global environmental change, discussions have already started to emerge as to the suitability of ecological modernization for explaining or predicting ecological reform in non-EU areas, most notably in developing countries or in the so-called double-risk societies[13] (for example, Rinkevicius, 2000; Frijns *et al.*, 2000). Although the theory has received rather critical remarks in this regard, also stemming from ecological modernization scholars themselves, its applicability to other countries is still intriguing adherents as well as sceptics of ecological modernization theory.

In its current conceptualization, the theory presupposes some socio-political, economic and cultural conditions, as well as institutional characteristics that become decisive to its application. Frijns *et al.* for instance mention (i) a democratic and open political system; (ii) widespread environmental consciousness; (iii) well-organized environmental NGOs and business organizations to defend public interests in negotiations; (iv) a tradition in negotiated policy making; (v) advanced technological development in a highly industrialized society; (vi) a detailed and reliable system of environmental monitoring; and, finally (vii) 'a state-regulated market economy that dominates production and consumption processes, covering all the edges of society and strongly integrated in the global market' (Frijns *et al.*, 2000).[14]

A major argument here is that an ecological restructuring of developing countries according to western models is already in progress due to globalization mechanisms themselves. These include for instance the numerous international development programmes promoted by multilateral organizations such as the World Bank, IMF and UNEP, as well as activities and programmes diffused by diverse international NGOs and multinational companies – which are in a way encouraging developing countries to 'leapfrog' the first technological generation of polluting industries and directly adopt better, ecologically sound approaches. For adherents of ecological modernization theory, it is therefore not incorrect to say that the rising economic interdependence, political interaction and collaboration, global diffusion of 'western' technologies and the emergence of global consumers may well push for somewhat *converging* tendencies, which also apply to environmental reform issues.

In this case, the globalization of the ecological modernization theory seems to be pertinent, although researchers still suggest that its applicability to areas outside northwest Europe will probably require some adaptations.

Ecological Modernization Theory and Transnational Office Buildings

As mentioned in the beginning of this chapter, ecological modernization theory has been used in studies of different industrial sectors and policy contexts. Two main questions are thus in order at this point: how and to what extent may ecological modernization theory contribute to a study of the greening of transnational office buildings in different cities; and, conversely, how can a study of the greening of transnational office buildings in different cities contribute to substantiate the theory of ecological modernization.

Starting with the former, ecological modernization is in the first place a theory that helps us to analyse the ways in which substance-flows can be organized and managed in modern societies in a more appropriate way. This implies at least three main kinds of environmental innovations to solve the structural fault of modernity – (i) dematerialization, (ii) monitoring and monetarization of resource use and (iii) substitution of unsustainable resources with renewables (cf. above). The relevance of each type of innovation varies according to the context that is being studied.

In analysing the greening of building practices all three forms of environmental innovations seem to be relevant, insofar as buildings incorporate technological options in their production, and yet become a kind of *industrial agent* in their operation, metabolizing environmental flows such as water, energy, materials, exhausts and wastes in their running. Dematerialization in the context of buildings implies for instance the shift from the provision/consumption of products to the provision/consumption of services, with lower environmental impacts. Thus, instead of introducing 'air conditioning', introducing simply 'cool air' means that the air conditioning machine may be replaced by other means to achieve cool air, through, for instance, natural ventilation. Monitoring, in turn, means a continuous and detailed assessment of the environmental flows, including resource use (energy, water) and waste streams (wastewater), which may take place in the operation cycle of offices. This corresponds to turning the invisible aspects of the operation of offices into visible or quantifiable ones. Monitoring is usually accompanied by the monetarization of resource use and wastes, giving thus a price to environmental externalities (through eco-taxations, for instance). Finally, substitution has to do with the replacement of technologies that are unsustainable by sustainable, clean ones, or, similarly, of non-renewable resources by renewable ones. This is for instance the case of renewable energy sources (such as wind turbines or solar panels) to replace fossil fuels, although here a gradual substitution is more likely to occur in view of the arguments discussed above.

Secondly, and to analyse how such innovations are coming to the fore, ecological modernization theory provides a framework for assessing and understanding the *social context of technological change* – that is, the interdependency between technological change and socio-economic and political-cultural transformations. It predicts that environmental reforms are most likely to occur in frameworks of 'modernizing modernity' – refining production and consumption processes towards clean technologies, ecologizing economy and economizing ecology – hence without altering fundamentally the main institutions that make up modern, capitalist societies (cf. above).

Along this line, we may use the ecological modernization theory to assess and compare the role/interaction of different actors involved in the organization of production and operation of office buildings and related districts for bringing about environmental innovations and reforms. When reflecting on the ecological restructuring of transnational office buildings we are dealing with a dynamic of actors belonging to a public-private continuum, and of both local and global origins: such as multinational companies, local policy makers and urban planning authorities, energy and water utility managers, as well as architects, contractors, suppliers, investors and representatives of credit institutions, among others, that may be either local or international. Questions one should thus ask to analyse the theory's adequacy for explaining environmental change in the building field include the following. How are environmental criteria emerging in the design and operation of office buildings in different cities? Are technologies of office buildings in different cities moving towards cleaner ones? If so, are local governments of different cities introducing 'enabling' policies to instigate a dynamic of radical environmental change, thereby moving away from purely command-and-control and curative instruments and with what results? And in turn are global market actors such as multinational companies – which occupy a significant share of the urban office-stock – playing a key role in implementing, worldwide, urban environmental change?

To analyse how environmental innovations emerge amid the dynamics of the actors of a specific industrial sector, the theory proposes a system to distinguish among three main analytical spheres or networks[15] in which such transformation processes take place: the policy, economic and societal spheres. This system – defined as the triad-network – offers 'the advantage of combining both the structural properties of institutions and the interactions between actors constructing a network' (Mol, 1995, p. 63). The policy network concentrates on the government-industry interactions based on the political-administrative perspective, in which transformations can be detected regarding the way laws, regulations, standards and other instruments are formulated, passed and enforced. Secondly, through the economic network,[16] which concentrates on economic interactions via market mechanisms throughout the production-consumption processes, it is possible to see whether innovations stem from the market (including supply and demand forces) towards ecological reform and eventually towards its self-regulation in terms of environmental control. Finally, within the social network – concentrating in its turn on social-cultural relations between economic sector and civil society – one can observe whether social movements exist calling for an ecological reformation process.

The relevance of these networks also depends of course on the context in which they are applied. In the case of production and operation of transnational office buildings, where connections to local grids and global/local social interaction are rather strong,[17] the policy and economic networks seem to be most relevant. The societal network, which mainly relates to civil society movements such as environmental NGOs, is somehow of less importance, at least up to the present date, as apparently there is limited societal pressure demanding an ecological reform of office buildings.[18]

Thus, with respect to policy networks, office buildings are traditionally produced at the crossroads of policies and regulatory instruments (such as those determined by master plans and building codes), and by their enforcement and monitoring methods. The way they operate will also depend on the way they are served by systems of infrastructure provision such as utilities (energy, water, wastewater, and so on). These connections take place basically within government-industry/local-global linkages, determined *a priori* by local planning agencies (although the efficiency of these becomes rather ambiguous in a context of transnational spaces). How, if anything, are environmental innovations emanating from within this network? How do interactions between global actors and local ones in this public-private continuum take place; what is the role of the local government in bringing about the environmental reform of transnational spaces? By answering these questions we will also revert to the debate of Sassen and Smith as for the role of the local government in managing transnational spaces (cf. chapter 2).

As for economic networks, transnational office buildings can be seen as commodities that will be produced and operated in an international market, determined thus by both local and global stakeholders. Here a strong interaction exists between suppliers (including suppliers of energy and water, of construction materials such as product manufacturers, of design, such as architects, of money such as financiers, and so forth) and consumers (such as companies and building owners, in other words, those that will use the office space) – both with varying origins (local, global) and diverging interests – regarding the way offices will be conceived and operated and environmental innovations will emanate. In this book, our second concern is thus to assess the role of global and local economic actors in bringing about environmental reform: how decisions are guided in each context, and how they may be channelled, if anything, from place to place. Here the role of multinational companies remains of crucial importance for determining the ways through which environmental innovations are being promoted by global occupiers of transnational spaces and whether such companies are encouraging a global virtuous circle of environmental change.

Hypotheses about the Ecological Modernization of Transnational Buildings

Ecological modernization theory has been developed in the context of north-west Europe and in relation to industrial production and consumption processes primarily. So in order for it to be useful for assessing ecological reforms in different economic and policy contexts we should be aware of the problems which can arise when dealing with a transnational perspective and the office building sector mainly. Some of the elements of the theory are useful without much adaptation/reformulation, while others need to be complemented with additional theoretical notions.

Assuming that ecological modernization may indeed be of relevance for areas outside the context of north-west Europe, this book uses the theory in its *descriptive dimension* and will assess how its core assumptions vary, if anything, from place to place. With the objective of better understanding both how the environmental reform of office buildings develops in different places as well as how the theory applies in different economic and policy contexts, this investigation will be carried out on two levels. First, the triad-network is partly applied[19] to help in the assessment of how ecological reforms may be under way in different cities in view of the interaction between local/global and public/private actors. Second, and based on this information, the main tenets of ecological modernization are assessed and compared among different urban contexts. For this purpose, a series of hypotheses on the greening of transnational spaces in the light of ecological modernization theory is herewith suggested, which will help us to evaluate the ecological restructuring of transnational buildings in major cities:

1. Besides economic criteria, ecological criteria are now also applied in the design and operation of office buildings, favouring in general a more efficient – rather than self-sufficient – use of resources. Buildings are therefore still connected to existing systems of infrastructure while better monitoring and partially dematerializing the use of environmental flows, as well as substituting inadequate technologies.
2. Governmental policies in major cities are moving towards consensus-based policy-making approaches for the environmental management of transnational spaces, launching conditions (enabling policies) for the market to carry out environmental reforms. These approaches are in addition also favouring a shift from curative strategies to preventive ones. The role of the state in governing both environmental reforms as well as transnational spaces in general is therefore proactive.
3. Economic actors and market mechanisms are thereby playing a key role in diffusing ecological criteria in office buildings. While in the earlier periods of environmental reform, policy makers had a crucial role to play in the agendizing and formulation of the (hierarchical) policies, nowadays market actors are becoming key vehicles for implementing environmental reforms.
4. Global market actors such as multinational companies may thereby turn into vehicles for triggering worldwide environmental reforms, homogenizing a rationale of environmental management applicable to (transnational) office buildings.

In a way, while the theory of ecological modernization lays a foundation for understanding empirical transformations leading to the environmental restructuring of transnational stocks of offices, by approaching these hypotheses, on the other hand, we may also contribute to the theory's development. This investigation may thus be constructive for two possible reasons. First of all, there are few relevant studies that have analysed the greening of buildings or offices according to the ecological modernization theory. However, as the environmental impact of office buildings is a subject of particular importance, environmental innovations are increasingly taking shape. This is therefore a fruitful field of research for assessing the validity of the principles of ecological modernization. A second reason is related to the fact that, in the context of globalization and global environmental change, the role of ecological modernization theory in analysing and prescribing environmental reform in different state-economy contexts still remains to be further explored. Therefore, widening the understanding of how ecological modernization occurs/applies in different economic and policy contexts is crucial for substantiating arguments favouring the theory's global reach.

In order to analyse the adequacy of these hypotheses an overview of contemporary events taking place in three major cities at the interface local-global, public-private is provided (chapters 5, 6 and 7). These three cities, Amsterdam, São Paulo and Beijing, provide a sample of fundamentally different 'state-economy' combinations, that is, of cities with different political and economic backgrounds, which presumably affect the way environmental innovations emerge in transnational buildings amid public-private/local-global social actors. As will become clear in the coming three chapters and particularly in the conclusion, these differences serve as a backdrop to allow us to analyse and compare how the ecological modernization of transnational buildings is developing in various urban settings. The selection of Amsterdam is also notable due to the fact that this city is located in a place with a well-developed environmental management capacity, where environmental innovations are taking place. Moreover, while Amsterdam is found in a partially state-regulated market economy, Beijing is notable for being located in a so-called socialist market economy and São Paulo in a relatively free market. The three cities also diverge in terms of political decision making and priority assigned to environmental issues, yet levels of technological development in the building field, including possibilities for the ecological modernization of building technologies, are relatively high in the three of them.[20]

Finally, a number of multinational companies are also selected to allow us to analyse and compare the interface of local and global environmental management strategies in the three cities: these are ING, Andersen, ABN AMRO and IBM. What these companies have in common is the fact that their offices in Amsterdam are globally renowned in the literature as examples of sustainable building. The dynamics of environmental change in their buildings at the local-global interface will be analysed in the three cities, where environmental innovations deployed in Amsterdam will serve as a kind of benchmark to be sought after in the buildings/offices these firms maintain in São Paulo and Beijing. While investigating the dynamics of environmental change in these cities at the local-global interface, we will determine how far globalization is bringing about urban environmental reforms from the perspective of multinational firms.[21] The conclusions on the greening of transnational buildings from this local-global social dynamics and in a cross-city perspective, also in relation to ecological modernization theory, will be elaborated in chapter 8.

Notes

1   In one of the inaugural articles demonstrating an intertwinement of social theory and environmental issues, Catton and Dunlap proposed in 1978 the 'new theoretical perspectives in sociology', defining a new field of study focusing on the 'interaction between the environment and society' (cf. Dunlap, 2000).

2. '...because the present increases in human numbers and per capita consumption, by disrupting ecosystems and depleting resources, are undermining the very foundation of survival' (*A Blueprint for Survival*, 1972, p. 15).

3   Paradoxically, however, as Dunlap (2000) observes, this new wave of environmental concern was triggered by three major environmental catastrophes – Three-Mile Island (1979), Bophal (1984) and Chernobyl (1986). These catastrophes, while provoking a shift in the focus of environmental concerns from issues regarding scarcity to the impacts of certain technological options on humans, finally called into question the *structural design fault* of industrialism, that is, the inadequacy of certain technologies (cf. also Giddens,

1990, pp. 151–2). In time, as debates eventually reconnected the relationship between human health and the issue of environmental scarcity, leaving the question of the relationship between capitalism and environmental problems somehow untouched, the notion of a 'burdening of the sustenance base' (Mol, 1995, p. 2) started to advance in environmental sociology debates. Societal attention was now focused on the mismatch between the 'capacities of the natural systems of the earth and humanity's ability to fit its activities into this framework' (Kirkby *et al.*, 1995, p. 7). These questions finally paved the way in the 1980s for the emergence of the concept of 'sustainable development', which came as a proposal to deviate from the conflictual environmental sociology and policy models of the 1970s. The environmental question was to be solved insofar as this three-sided mismatch of industrialism, scarcity and human health was adjusted.

4   However, he claims, the concept of sustainable development had already been brought into focus at the Stockholm Conference on Human Environment of 1972 – where the clash of interests between environmental conservation and development was pointed out – and subsequently employed by a number of authors, receiving various interpretations, such as Riddell, Sachs, Eckholm and Glaeser.

5   In other words, that economic flows and environmental resource flows develop *independently*.

6   For instance, by introducing eco-labelling schemes and other mechanisms to instigate a market dynamics towards environmental reform.

7   In reality, Mol (1995) identifies three main bodies of literature, the third one referring to programmes of political parties.

8   More recent definitions on the role of the state divert to some extent from this idea of retreating and are also somehow more sceptical regarding the role of the market as an ecological reform carrier (cf. below).

9   For these hypotheses see Mol (1995) and Hajer (1995).

10 In view of these claims, ecological modernization has been often connected to the idea of being a mere technocratic or technological fix approach. In addition, the assumption that large-scale technologies, which cause environmental harm, may be reverted into instruments of environmental reform has likewise incited much critique, particularly by neo-Marxist schools. For these schools, by tackling environmental problems via 'new and more intelligent technologies', ecological modernization may also result in negative social effects due to the increased costs these technologies may imply in the short-term, and benefit economies of scale, such as large corporations. And these corporations, in turn, cannot be reverted into instruments of ecological reform, as they are in fact the main agents causing environmental disruption. In short, according to these scholars 'ecologizing economy' and 'economizing ecology' by delegating certain environmental reform tasks to the market is on the whole incapable of resulting in more than window dressing environmental reforms or technological fixes.

Ecological modernization theorists have argued back against these criticisms and explained that at the heart of the theory is an attempt to bridge the gap between technological change and environmental social sciences, by looking at how such environmental flows are being *managed* by society on a large scale. In general, technological developments are already being designed according to ecological criteria, and environmental problems of modernity cannot be tackled without considering that technologies – and large corporations – are indeed intrinsic aspects of modernity or, ultimately, that modernity and industrialism are an *inseparable and probably irreversible project*. Therefore the phrase: 'all possible ways out of the environmental crisis cannot but be ways further in modernity'; as modernity is far from being in its end and industries, which will continue to subsist, will need to be refined in an ecologically rational direction. In any case, ecological modernization theorists posit that political modernization may *perhaps* not suit conditions of 'pure free' markets. Although this is an issue that in its turn calls into question how far the theory can be generalized, it should be also clear that pure free markets do not in fact exist, and that, to varying extents, all market economies are state-and-society regulated, similarly to the context of north-west Europe.

11 The idea of democratization of the distribution of risks has been contested by particularly dependency and neo-Marxist theorists, who claim the poor always suffer most (Mol, 2001). Beck later on explained that 'globality of risk does not, of course, mean a global equality of risk' as the first law of environmental risk is that 'pollution follows the poor', the sanitation deficit in the third world being a major indicator in this regard (cf. Beck, 2001, p. 5).

12 As expected, the criticisms it has thereby attributed to ecological modernization are fairly in line with those made by counter-productivists, see Mol, 1995, p. 44. Conversely, ecological modernization has claimed that risk society, in spite of being a prominent and influential political appeal, somehow fails to provide a concrete framework for the development of environmental policy proposals.

13 Societies not only facing risks of late modernity but also development constraints (such as poverty, monetary deficits, institutional shortcomings, and so forth).

14 It is evident that institutional conditions of north western Europe diverge in many aspects from those in developing countries. The third world itself is also quite plural, consisting of newly industrialized countries, 'underdeveloped' countries and transitional economies. In this regard, the theory does certainly not correspond to the conditions of underdeveloped economies (for example, sub-Saharan Africa), where there is no welfare state with articulated and institutionalized environmental tasks, hardly any advanced technological development or state-regulated market economy connected to the globalized world market and, above all, very weak institutionalized environmental consciousness (Mol, 1995). But with respect to transitional economies and newly industrializing countries, however, the theory seems to be more adequate as a number of them have a relatively strong welfare state, an (emerging) market economy, relatively high level of (environmental) technology, a transitional process of democracy and public participation, although quite a poor level of environmental awareness and relatively powerless (relevant) environmental organizations (Ibid.).

Here again the theory has been contested by particularly dependency theorists and neo-Marxists for being viable, in the first place, only due to the 'net withdrawal of natural resources from and a net addition of pollution to developing countries by the industrialized nations' (Mol, 1999). For such theorists, in addition, the general 'imposition' of a western model of environmental reform is unsuitable to non-OECD countries, due to their different local socio-economic and cultural conditions. Although part of these arguments may be true, other arguments, in contrast, would suggest that ecological modernization, as a western ecological reform model, may be indeed suitable for non-OECD countries, as modernity is mainly a western or triad project (which has already been globalized), in which the dominant models of development – and consequent ecological restructuring concepts – do emerge, though not exclusively, in the west.

15 Networks, in this respect, can be understood as social systems in which actors operate in more or less permanent institutional interactions.

16 The economic network is in some works also referred to as industrial network.

17 Reverting to what was said in chapter 3, according to Guy and Osborn (2001), the logic of green design closest to ecological modernization theory is that which can be referred to as a 'smart asset', in which topics such as flexibility, efficiency, cost savings and intelligent technologies are evoked. This is the main logic of green design of the world of commercial property development, thus of the development of ecological office buildings in large cities, such as the Commerzbank in Frankfurt, Four Times Square in New York and Swiss Re in London. The ecological reform of buildings is therefore carried out in contexts of (i) strong grid connectivity, (ii) where environmental concerns are high on the agenda but still enmeshed within the logics of business survival, and (iii) of strong

local/global interaction. Therefore, and in view of all the actors that are related in the production and operation of office buildings in such contexts (and beyond the decisions made alone by architects/clients), environmental reforms in such contexts will tend to develop environmental solutions that (i) do not disconnect from mains grids, (ii) are both a means to reduce expenses and an asset to brand the overall economic and societal performance of the companies that inhabit them with an environmental image, and (iii) make use of both locally embedded techniques (such as passive solar design) and of global technologies, such as those related to saving equipment (energy, water devices) and efficient materials (cladding, windows and so forth).

18   Although society may exert pressure on companies to improve their environmental performance, eventually affecting the environmental dimension of office buildings.

19   I emphasize 'partly applied' as in general I will neither analyse the societal sphere nor all the organizations pertaining to the economic and policy spheres.

20   But besides the institutional differences, the cities also have physical and environmental variations. Although these variations may prompt different solutions in terms of techniques (particularly as far as passive solutions are concerned, cf. chapter 3), this book is mainly interested in exploring the *societal processes* that foster or hinder the adoption of environmental techniques. In this sense, the technologies that are applied in view of the different environmental priorities are considered to be subsequent to the rationale of politics, policies and management that are required to achieve environmental change, with whom we are mostly concerned.

21   Another remark to be made at this point regards the issue of freehold or leasehold, whether it has an influence on the incorporation of environmental concerns in the company's office. As will be demonstrated, not all the offices analysed in this book are the property of the companies selected, particularly those in Beijing. However, even tenant companies may very well 'push' for the ecological upgrading of the building they occupy as this condition does not rule out the possibility of the company choosing among different buildings in view of their environmental status, regarding, for instance, several indoor technologies, appliances and equipment, including lighting and sanitation systems, equipment (computers, machines), layout (of desks, for instance), indoor shading devices, and so on (Bouman, 2000). In addition this does not rule out companies being obliged to apply environmental management systems, monitoring procedures, and the like, in the running of their (rented) premises.

Chapter 5

Amsterdam

Figure 5.1   Amsterdam South

Throughout the 1980s and 1990s Amsterdam consolidated its position as an international business capital, attracting an increasing number of corporate headquarters. During these decades, environmental topics grew into a key theme of both corporate and governmental agendas in the Netherlands owing to a number of factors: conventions regarding global warming, stricter regulations and higher fees for the consumption of energy and water, pressure from civil society, and so on. As a result, and as the city's stock of office buildings started to grow, environmental management practices stemming from global and local actors began to intermingle in Amsterdam: first, local environmental policy agencies, which had traditionally played a prime role in the city's development, started to prompt a number of new strategies to manage its environmental and infrastructure challenges, made more pressing by the increasing internationalization of its business activities. And second, several multinational companies, which migrated to the city, also started to advance environmental strategies for their offices, all in all boosting the ecological reshuffle of Amsterdam's office buildings.

The environmental restructuring of Amsterdam's office buildings is the core subject of this chapter. In the first section we outline the characteristics of the place, describing the composition and operation of the city's stock of office buildings, the local infrastructure and environmental challenges, as well as the general regulatory framework governing them. Subsequently we move to the heart of our debate and provide an analysis of the environmental management practices of both local and global actors, describing the approaches adopted and the interplay of social action in furthering technological change in four corporate buildings (ING, Andersen, ABN AMRO and IBM). In the conclusions we achieve a synthesis as to how the environmental reform of Amsterdam's office buildings is developing in view of the influences and interactions of such two spaces, the local and the global, of social agency.

The Urban Setting

Amsterdam grew from about 1000 AD on the banks of the Ij River, although it was the river Amstel – dammed and canalized around 1270 – that gave the town its name. Most of the topographical contours and natural boundaries of the Amsterdam of today were delineated during this period, when two harbours were created, an outer and an inner one, and a series of dikes was raised to contain the banks on which buildings and circulation routes for land traffic were constructed.

Historically, further adaptations to the natural geography were advanced as the city expanded, including the construction of new dikes to improve safety and the drainage of lakes towards the north of the Ij and towards the south adjoining the city. And as the population grew, various urban planning concepts were deployed to control and accommodate Amsterdam's spatial needs. Although now criticized for inconsistency – as these concepts ranged from urban expansion and functional separation approaches to city compactness and mixture of uses – environmental preservation has always remained a constant, probably in view of Amsterdam's susceptible topographical constitution (Fainstein, 2000).

Amsterdam has undergone three distinctive economic periods. First it developed as a trading town at the crossroads of local and regional networks of traders; an economic activity that largely benefited from its favourable geographical location and from the exemption granted to it from paying tolls on Dutch waterways. Subsequently, Amsterdam grew into an industrial centre, towards the mid-1800s, a period during which Bremen and London had surpassed its trading importance. Nowadays, it has grown to be an internationally oriented business city, enjoying rapid economic growth, often being referred to as the 'gateway' to Europe. With Schiphol airport (the fourth-largest European airport) and Westpoort (currently the fifth-largest harbour in Europe), Amsterdam has during the past decade attracted an increasing number of headquarters, of both multinational companies and national firms.

Nowadays Amsterdam's stock of office buildings is distributed along two main business centres. One of them is situated in the waterfront and dockside development along the banks of the Ij River, mostly around the Central Station, in an area known as the Ij-oevers. The other is located in the city's southern suburbs – known as Amsterdam South – an area that has been developing over the last 15 years predominantly along the A10 highway, connecting Schiphol Airport to the city centre (see Figure 5.2). Amsterdam South is the fastest growing business centre in the Netherlands as well as the largest office-building site of Europe (Kemme, 1996), in which the financial and service sectors predominate. Its growth is largely related to the proximity to Schiphol Airport, the country's main international airport, in which one of the first landmark buildings or 'image signifiers' of the global economy – the World Trade Centre (WTC) building – was constructed. This

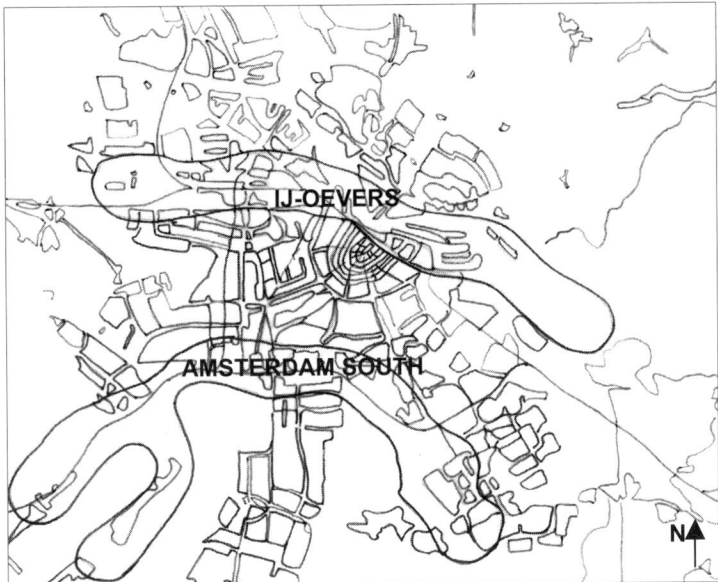

Figure 5.2   Distribution of Amsterdam's office-stock

building, completed in 1985 and located in front of the airport's main entrance/exit, is a strong symbol for those arriving to Amsterdam by plane; a fact that certainly helps the city secure its importance as an international business centre – yet, unlike other Dutch large cities, preserving its historic cityscape.

Nevertheless, Amsterdam is not the only headquarters location in the Netherlands. In spite of accommodating a large number of corporate headquarters of both Dutch and foreign firms, Amsterdam's total office-stock area is too small to make any impression in the international property market (Koster *et al.*, 1997). In terms of area, in 1990 Amsterdam totalled one fifth of London's office space, and one seventh of that of Paris (Rienstra *et al.*, 1999). This is partly explained as Amsterdam is not a dominant national market for office space, like London is in England or Paris in France, nor does it accommodate large state-owned companies.[1] This fact sometimes calls into question Amsterdam's status as a global city, although the city is many times referred to as the 'gateway' to the unified Europe. Instead of Amsterdam, it is usually the Dutch Randstad[2] that is designated in academic literature as the 'Dutch global city', which, despite not being a jurisdiction, ranks as the third most important metropolis in Europe after London and Paris, and ahead of Frankfurt and other German cities. Amsterdam's economic role within the Randstad is nevertheless crucial, and the city is commonly regarded as the country's cultural, finance and service capital, being thereby formally addressed as a 'secondary global city'[3] (Ibid.; Nijman, 2000; Koster *et al.*, 1997). Yet, according to a new master plan for the South Axis region, Amsterdam's total office area is bound to see some expansion as objectives have been established to finalize a total 650,000 square metres of office space in the coming years, where transport infrastructure will be eventually redirected underground (Amsterdam Physical Planning Department, 2002; World Architecture, 1998).

The greater Amsterdam area currently includes offices of approximately 1800 foreign companies – counting the European headquarters of around 250 foreign companies as well as major Dutch corporate headquarters. A particularity of Amsterdam is the fact that the city is currently turning into one of the main European financial centres, employing almost 45,000 people in the financial market (Amsterdam Economic Development Department, 2002). The southern axis along the A10 highway is becoming the country's 'financial mile', as many say, with head-quarters such as those of ABN AMRO Holding and ING Group.[4] Amsterdam also has more than 70 foreign banks with offices in the city, the oldest stock exchange in the world (currently ranking fifth in Europe and eighth in the world), in addition to highly specialized training institutions (such as Amsterdam Institute of Finance and two universities), which altogether strengthen the city's importance *vis-à-vis* the global economy. Other major sectors present in Amsterdam are publishing and accounting.

Most such transnational spaces are owner-occupied; in fact, at the moment around 50 per cent of the whole Dutch office-stock is owner-occupied. This implies that office buildings tend to adopt a corporate identity through the architecture rather than pursuing pure marketability from the investors' point of view (such as construction efficiency, capitalization over land values and gross-to-net ratios). As a consequence, organizations are also more eager to experiment with new building types and innovations in office concepts, including environmental innovations (Meel, 2000). This is also favoured by the fact that the cost of property in Amsterdam is rather low as compared to the other economic capitals, owing to the inability to concentrate a large office-stock area and subsequently a high number of corporate offices, which automatically increases the budget of firms to invest in architectural features. Still, trends indicate that this high rate of ownership – as well as property prices – is probably going to change in the coming years as organizations start to prefer renting their office spaces instead of owning them, leading developers to boost a commercial office development market.[5]

In terms of architecture, the office design pursued in Amsterdam seems at first sight to have a strong international orientation. This is due to the fact that a large number of foreign architects, particularly British and American ones, practice in the Netherlands either for international clients or for Dutch commissioners. Nevertheless, it can also be argued that despite the apparent international orientation, the office architecture pursued in Amsterdam in still very Dutch (Meel, 2000). In the first place, greater Amsterdam is not particularly dominated by high-rise office buildings as compared to other business cities. A survey conducted by the property company Jones Lang Wootton revealed that Amsterdam has in fact one of the smallest concentrations of high-rise buildings of any economic capital, less than a third of the square metres of Singapore or Kuala Lumpur (Koster *et al.*, 1997). This is partly due to its status as a historical city, in which a specific urban setting (char-acterized by narrow streets, the absence of a straight street pattern and a sensitive soil) has rather hindered the development of tall structures.[6] Secondly, although building façades give the impression of being fairly similar to American or English ones, their floor plans are in general quite different. While deep floor layouts dominate the latter, Dutch buildings usually present shallow ones.[7] The Rembrandt

Tower, for instance, one of the tallest buildings of Amsterdam (135m) has a floor depth of only nine metres. This of course affects several internal components, such as lighting, ventilation, isolation, and so forth. In addition, open-plan offices are also rather rare whereas cellular office spaces predominate in the office layout. This is probably also related to the egalitarian society that is so fostered in the Netherlands. An office module of 1.8m × 5.4m is the standard; the number of modules an employee occupies is directly proportional to his hierarchy in the firm (Meel, 2000). This is also facilitated by the highly developed industrialized construction techniques in the Netherlands, in which products' dimensions (such as slabs, ceilings and units of heating, ventilation and air conditioning) are highly standardized. However, current trends indicate that this situation may change as cellular office spaces hinder communication among employees to a certain extent, where the need for working in teams may lead to more flexible layouts. Finally, desk sharing and teleworking systems are also fostered in the city, which have tremendous implications for the office space layout. Among European countries, the Netherlands has the highest rates of teleworking, around nine per cent of the working population (European Commission, 1999). This has implications for the occupancy rate and subsequently on operational issues, among which are the offices' energy and water consumption levels.

Amsterdam is not considered a polluted city. Most public complaints usually concern noise and odour nuisances, the former particularly around Schiphol airport and the latter usually related to traffic emissions. Apparently there are no major air quality problems, or infrastructure weaknesses (such as those related to energy and water supply and waste/wastewater collection and treatment), except for the emissions of carbon dioxide for which the city is accountable. However, as Amsterdam is growing to become a major information technology-oriented city, where information and communication technology companies are extremely heavy energy consumers, energy supply is starting to suffer some constraints.[8]

There are around 338,000 people working in 49,000 business establishments in Amsterdam, consuming water, energy[9] and other natural resources, as well as generating waste and wastewater. Statistics demonstrate that Amsterdam's office-stock consumes around 550 million cubic metres of natural gas and 2000 million kWh of electricity per year, also revealing a gradual increase in the consumption. This implies a total of some six million tons of carbon dioxide emissions per year. Amsterdam's office-stock also generates about 160 tons/year of freon gases (that is, CFC, HCFC, HFC and halon gases), with consequences for stratospheric ozone depletion. With respect to water infrastructure, surveys conducted by Amsterdam's department for the environment demonstrate that the city's office-stock consumes about 16 million cubic metres of water per year, and has around 16,000 water meters installed. Estimates also indicate that Amsterdam's office buildings generate around 300,000 tons of waste per year, excluding construction and demolition waste, approximately one third of which is waste paper (Milieudienst Amsterdam, 1998).

In turn, regarding the overall regulatory framework affecting the urban setting, the Dutch building industry – thus Amsterdam's office buildings – operates under the Dutch building code, which is specified by the Ministry of Housing, Spatial Planning and Environment (VROM). Although local municipalities cannot add extra clauses to the code, as these might lead to unfair competition among the building industry's professionals, they can influence it slightly so as to suit local specificities.

Building permits, in this regard, are issued and checked locally, particularly by the local housing and environmental departments. In addition to the building code, the VROM also puts forward a set of standard rules (AMvBs) applicable for different building types (such as restaurants, shops, offices, and so forth), which, albeit nationally issued, leave a great margin to be locally interpreted.

Apart from these prescriptions, the Ministry of Social Affairs and Employment (SZW) has established national rules concerning health and safety issues for the interior of the workplace. These rules, known as Arbeidsomstandigheden (or simply Arbo) regulations, determine a range of aspects concerning the indoor environment, particularly the dimensions of workplaces and the access of workers to daylight. With regard to dimensions it specifies that a workstation should comprise of at least seven square metres (gross) – a fact that goes some way towards describing the reasons behind the large office areas so common in the country as compared to England or North America where these dimensions are set at half this size by law. As for daylighting, they stipulate that workstations that are being used for more than two hours per day need to have access to natural lighting. Although there are no standard rules specifying the distance from the workstation to the window, the regulations state that the window surface has to total at least $1/20^{th}$ of the total floor area of the office space.

As for the municipality itself, there are basically two main sets of regulations, which render the city's office-stock particularly distinctive. One of them governs Amsterdam's land use system, by which land is let on the basis of long-term leases, and through which market speculation can be controlled. Property developers, whether profit-oriented or not, have to participate in government biddings, and as a result cannot press for speculative building production despite the fact that demand for constructed space is far higher than the supply (Kahn *et al.*, 1999; Fainstein, 2000). This municipal land tenure system is rather rarely applied, not only in the Netherlands but also throughout the world.

The other set of regulations concerns the office buildings' height, where the municipality of Amsterdam allows a maximum constructed height of about 90 metres in sub-centres provided it is in the vicinity of a public transport intersection[10] (Kloos, 1995). In Amsterdam South particular attention has to be also assigned to air traffic due to its proximity to Schiphol airport. The restrictions concerning height have one drawback, as the region's limited vertical space imposes a constant search for vacant space on the city's outskirts (Kahn *et al.*, 1999). Yet, plans for high-rise buildings in Amsterdam are treated separately by the city council, enabling participatory decision-making processes during development negotiations.

Local Environmental Management

Up to this point we have discussed the particularities of Amsterdam's transnational buildings in view of their historical development, market, architectural typology, local infrastructure and environment, as well as their main regulatory framework. In order to understand how environmental management is being thereby introduced, this section reviews how environmental principles, policies, strategies and instruments are being advanced within the city's main policy networks, including different levels of governmental bodies, utility companies and relevant agencies. In so doing it also outlines how these networks interact in implementing environmental policies, focusing in particular on energy- and water-related issues.

Amsterdam is governed by three major departments – housing, urban planning and land-lease – in addition to others of lesser importance: environment, infra-structure and traffic, welfare and economic affairs. Environmental themes, including those related to the office-stock, are basically dealt with by the Department for the Environment, the Milieudienst Amsterdam.

Within the municipality the division of tasks is fairly decentralized as Amsterdam is divided into 14 sub-districts each with its own administration, operating with quite a high degree of autonomy. Each of the sub-districts has to perform certain tasks such as local spatial planning, maintenance of public areas and environmental upgrading and preservation. The Zuidas region (a district located in Amsterdam South), however, due to its economic importance and rapid development with not only local but also regional implications, is still largely controlled by the central municipal government.[11] The municipal government is in turn responsible for the provision of drinking water and the operation of rail, road and public transport infra-structure for the whole city.

Where environmental management is concerned, Amsterdam's stock of office buildings is primarily influenced by the Dutch building code, which contains several specifications or requirements – such as safety rules, structural issues and other tech-nical requirements – but says little about environmental topics. In fact, such topics are identified in certain regulations restricting the use of materials that radiate toxic gases – for instance radon and asbestos – and others related to construction and demolition waste, which are required to be separated into three fractions for ease of handling and recycling. As for water use or water performance in offices, the building act apparently does not contain any specific regulation.[12] The same applies to wastewater in office buildings, or the use of rainwater/grey water.[13] It does, however, include an important component, which is the energy performance standard (EPN), a standard that determines the quantity of energy that a building is allowed to use based on the calculated energy consumed by the building by a reference consumption figure (Dutch National Team, 1998).

The EPN was introduced in 1995, under an energy policy framework established by the Ministry of Economic Affairs (MINEZ) in conjunction with Novem, the Dutch energy and environmental agency (MINEZ, 1999). It was originally outlined in the Energy Report, a document issued by the MINEZ containing long-term energy strategies. The EPN is in this sense a standard regarding *new* industrial and office buildings (not housing), compelling them to comply with a required performance. This performance decreases over the years; in 1995, for instance, it was set at 1000 $MJ/m^2/year$, whereas it is now 850 $MJ/m^2/year$ and in the future it is aimed to be 600 $MJ/m^2/year$ – a reduction that the government believes to be easily achievable. For *existing* buildings, the MINEZ launched a programme known as 'long-term agreement' (LTA) – requiring such buildings to reduce their energy consumption by 25 per cent, based on the 1995 levels within a period of ten years. Both the EPN and LTA have been launched in conjunction with an Energy Performance Advisory system (EPA), an advisory scheme provided by the government that determines the energy consumption of existing buildings by means of a scan, to which recommendations for improvements can be added. Nowadays the EPN is instituted in the building code, which is under the VROM,[14] and controlled locally in the proceedings of building permits issuing.

Apart from the building code (and the above-mentioned standard rules or the AMvBs), the Arbeidsomstandigheden (Arbo) regulations also play a decisive role, particularly in terms of dictating certain aspects of the indoor environment, such as interior dimensions and daylighting issues. As for the latter, although the Arbo regulations do not impose standard rules specifying the distance from the workstation to the window, the guidelines suggest that lack of daylighting or outside view can result in dissatisfied employees. This may explain the reason why Dutch floor layouts are rather shallow, a fact that is embedded in the Dutch 'consensus' culture in which the issue of egalitarianism is highly praised (that is, an outside view not only as a privilege of directors but a right of everyone). In this respect, about 80 per cent of Dutch office buildings have openable windows and possibilities for individual climate control, aspects that are crucial in the overall office's energy balance.

The environmental performance of Amsterdam's stock of office buildings is also influenced by the city's department for the environment, which makes use of two main sets of instruments – covenants and environmental permits – in addition to the application of standard rules and enforcement procedures, although the deployment of such instruments in daily environmental management routines is apparently limited. Covenants, which allow the addition of extra requirements, are a traditional Dutch way of environmental policy making, by which negotiations play an important role. This is particularly clear in the city of Amsterdam, where the land use system is based on municipal land tenure, by which companies that seek to build in the city have to create long-term partnerships with the government; the government, in turn, may decide on which partners to work with. This encourages both companies and authorities to reach agreements, which may touch upon environmental issues. The covenants, in this context, are usually based on the ALARA principle, by which environmental impacts may be reduced to 'as low as reasonably achievable'. It thereby introduces the idea that as zero impact is practically unachievable efforts should be made to reduce the impact only where it is either intolerable, or where the cost of its reduction is reasonable. For the construction of office buildings, this means applying all available means to mitigate the environmental impacts and to improve the building's performance (not only regarding energy) as long as they do not entail exorbitant additional costs, which would hamper the economic feasibility of the investment.[15]

In general, the environmental component of covenants is to be worked out within the department for the environment, although through consultation with other governmental bodies, including the VROM and the MINEZ. Although most such covenants are elaborated according to the ALARA principle, they may also be based on the National Packages for Sustainable Building, an initiative of the MINEZ and the VROM, gradually institutionalized since 1996. The packages are themselves kinds of covenants, which have been signed by different stakeholders from different branches of the building industry, including authorities. They contain vast specifications promoting environmentally friendly solutions, from the building to the urban design scale, at the same time demonstrating actions expected to be taken voluntarily by the market (see VROM, various years). Parallel to the packages,

VROM has started an environmental policy including a climate programme (for carbon dioxide reductions) and a new sustainable building programme, by which it tries to shift the emphasis from 'environmental efficiency of buildings' to renovation and maintenance of the existing building stock, including demolition and recycling, issues that can also be raised in the covenant and decision-making processes in Amsterdam.

The department for the environment may also influence the environmental performance of office buildings by compelling certain projects to undergo environmental audits, by which environmental permits may be granted. These audits are usually requested for large-scale projects, such as buildings using heavy machinery; office buildings usually do not fall into this category. The department may in addition add some extra clauses (the so-called 'expanded scope of the environmental permit' – Verruimde Reikwijdte van de wet Milieubeheer), by which extra environmental demands can be made also based on the ALARA principle. However, if the requirements are regarded as too strict, contractors may contest them in court. The department may also make use of the standard rules (AMvBs) to influence the environmental performance of office buildings, as they can be locally interpreted (VROM, 1998a). Requirements may also be based on the ALARA principle. Finally, the department has a team of inspectors, which attempts to check buildings periodically, particularly concerning their machinery. However, when it comes to the environmental performance of office buildings, these inspections are said to fail since priority has to be given to companies that usually cause public annoyance, such as bars and nightclubs.

Moving now to the energy sphere, the energy performance of office buildings in Amsterdam is also influenced by different actors and their related policies belonging to the energy network. In the Netherlands, the main governmental body responsible for the elaboration of energy policies at the national level is the MINEZ. At the local level, the main actors responsible for energy issues, including energy preservation, are the utilities. In between them, the Dutch National Agency for Energy and the Environment (Novem) plays a quite important role in supervising and managing the realization of energy and environmental programmes in view of the tensions that usually arise among conflicting interested parties, such as the government, the market and society. Novem brings together government policy and market developments so as to bridge the gap between theoretical knowledge and its practical application and provides support for the upgrading the energy performance of buildings nation-wide, with several examples in Amsterdam (Novem, 1991, 1999; European Commission Thermie Project, 1998a, 1998b).

In addition to assisting the government in implementing energy and environmental programmes, Novem also executes subsidy schemes for energy audits for buildings, provides for an adequate exchange of knowledge bringing in foreign expertise and supports the government in designing policies by providing consultancy services. In this respect, it facilitated the development of the energy performance standard (EPN) and its implementation, in conjunction with the MINEZ (Dutch National Team, 1998; Novem, 2000a, MINEZ, 1999). Several buildings in Amsterdam have undergone energy audits so as to achieve energy reductions below those set by the EPN and consequent improvements under subsidies granted by Novem (see Novem, various years).

Yet, major policies regarding energy efficiency are determined by the MINEZ, the organization responsible for deploying instruments tackling the different stakeholders involved in the energy sector. But since January 2002 the Dutch electricity market has been privatized allowing a number of energy companies to serve the city of Amsterdam and compete for the kilowatt-hour cost; the most prominent of which are Nuon and Essent. As part of the privatization agreement, such private electricity companies are required to implement schemes of 'energy premium', as stated in the MINEZ' Energy Report. These schemes are grants allowed by the government (a budget of approximately 180 million euros/year) to be invested in energy-efficient appliances and in facilities that conserve energy. The energy companies, in turn, have stated their principles regarding energy conservation in a so-called 'green paper', published in 1999. Due to the fact that it is difficult to reach agreements between users and commercial energy providers, or even to manage costs, energy companies can provide consumers with energy saving services, something that is in fact consistent with their profile as market actors, ranging from energy efficiency advisory schemes, which screen the energy performance of the building, for instance, and propose tools that can be used so as to lower energy bill costs, to related subsidies schemes. Usually they are approached by the clients (for instance, companies) as for the delivery of such services, although they run marketing campaigns for such services on the web and through leaflets that are given to potential clients. In addition, they are now also offering green electricity – that is, electricity deriving from renewable sources – which is slightly more costly than conventional electricity, the additional money to be ploughed into projects for the generation of alternative energy sources. There are also some incentives for long-term contracts to be made, by which energy supplying companies install PV (photovoltaic) cells on site, each panel currently generating 80 kwh/m^2/year. All these issues are discussed in the Energy Report, defining the position of the energy distribution companies and the implementation of statutory duties by the various parties in the liberalized energy market.

Regarding the water network, the publicly owned water company serving Amsterdam is the Gemeentewaterleidingen Amsterdam (GWL), which is in fact the oldest water company in the Netherlands. Its total water production capacity is 101 million m^3 of drinking water, from two plants – Production West at Vogelenzang (near Haarlem) and Production East at Weesperkarspel (in Amsterdam East) – both undergoing environmental management schemes. Since the building code does not impose strict rules regarding water consumption and wastewater emissions in office buildings, the company takes some environmental initiatives due to the fact that water is gradually becoming a scarce resource, the price of which is increasing, so that water reserves have to be preserved. These initiatives consist of continuous publicity to encourage the population to save water in buildings, R&D programmes (including some concerning nature conservation) in addition to water-saving services conducted upon request (usually made by hotels), by which the company sells monitoring systems, water-saving devices and performs risk assessments concerning legionnaires' disease,[16] the latter according to a temporary law passed by the VROM. Interactions, in this regard, between the water distribution company and other governmental bodies responsible for environmental management issues – such as the department for the environment, the VROM, or the water board – mostly concern water quality, at least so far, rather than water efficiency.

The same applies to the water treatment company. Wastewater emissions in Amsterdam are dealt with by Dienst Waterbeheer en Riolering (DWR). Water treatment in the city of Amsterdam applies a pipe system which separates rainwater from grey/brown water, the former not undergoing any treatment and being disposed on surface water resources, such as the canals. As for the decentralization of wastewater treatment services in order to reduce the volumes of piped water to the main treatment plants, the city does not yet make use of such solutions, as far as office buildings are concerned, the exception being industrial facilities. However, a new policy is currently being studied for the development of a decentralized treatment facility to serve the Ijburg area, where a number of office buildings will be completed in the coming years.

Global Environmental Management

Ecological modernization theory postulates that market actors play a crucial role as environmental change drivers. One of its central themes is that ecology is becoming an independent rationale of modernity, a claim that is evidenced by a number of new ecological criteria that have recently started to emerge: such as eco-labels, environmental auditing, green financing, concepts like environmental performance, and so forth (cf. chapters 3 and 4). For the theory, while the state still remains imperative for launching adequate environmental management tools for the market to adopt, the main argument is that the dynamics of environmental change mostly takes place within the market itself, which eventually shifts to a self-regulatory paradigm. Based on this claim, one of the hypotheses put forward in this book is that global economic agents, as multinational companies, may be thereby playing a crucial role in the implementation of urban environmental reforms worldwide.

In the light of this hypothesis, and while the preceding section described the main policies and instruments applicable to office buildings deployed by local utilities and environmental agencies in Amsterdam, this section will investigate how programmes and strategies of energy and water conservation in office buildings are happening – being initiated or processed – within a market of global economic actors such as multinational companies and financial firms. More specifically, we will see how environmental flows are being managed in the office buildings of four multinational companies in the city of Amsterdam, namely ING, Andersen, ABN AMRO and IBM, by describing how environmental management solutions and practices are decided upon and operated, as well as fit within the local management of environmental flows described above.

ING Group

ING-Groep N.B. is a multinational financial institution of Dutch origin, operating in 65 countries in the fields of banking, insurance and asset management. Instituted under this name in 1992, ING Group is a result of a succession of mergers and acquisitions with a long historical background. It currently holds several branches, known as ING brands, such as ING Real Estate, ING Barings, ING Bank and Nationale-Nederlanden, all part of the Group's equities, and therefore under the Group's liability. ING Group is currently the second largest financial institution in the Netherlands.

ING maintains several landmark buildings both in the country and abroad – including the headquarters of ING Bank and the headquarters of ING Group, both located in Amsterdam – in addition to important buildings located in other Dutch cities, such as the Nationale-Nederlanden headquarters in Rotterdam, the tallest skyscraper in the Netherlands (150 metres high). ING's buildings tell much of the Group's history and evolution in management styles in view of a changing society that the bank has been working for. Despite more recent accomplishments – among which the new ING Group headquarters recently constructed along the A10 road in Amsterdam – it is probably the ING Bank headquarters (completed in 1987, formerly known as NMB Bank) in Amsterdam Southeast that can be considered to be the Group's most remarkable building, a building complex that has indeed marked a period of environmental policy making, trying to achieve passive architectural solutions and an environmentally self-sufficient structure, still being frequently cited today in literature particularly due to its outstanding energy-saving features and related cost savings (see, for instance, Vale *et al.*, 1991; Wilson *et al.*, 1998). As environmental management in this building was mostly defined at the design phase, we will provide a description of how decisions prior to the construction were made and environmental management issues incorporated below.

The complex was built in 1984–87 to headquarter the NMB Postbank (Nederlandse Middenstands Bank), a bank which had resulted from the merger between the Post Bank, a government-owned banking institution, and the Nationale-Nederlanden, an insurance company.[17] As its name indicates,[18] the NMB was a bank created for the Dutch middle class, which, unlike the ING Bank of today, was a Dutch-oriented institution. Its board of directors constituted in part of members keen on the anthroposophical philosophy of Rudolf Steiner, who commissioned a building to be above all very human, aiming not only to improve the staff's well-being but also to provide the image of a 'people friendly', non-intimidating bank.

To begin with, the site acquisition took place after an offer made by the municipality of Amsterdam by which a large area would be sold rather inexpensively, provided the bank would construct a shopping mall in addition to the office complex. This area was located near the Bijlmermeer housing complex, in the city's southeastern suburbs, a place that was becoming derelict and facing numerous social problems, but which provided for good public transport access. As for the bank, the returns on its investment in the mall would help finance the construction of the headquarters, which would require a large office area to accommodate 1200 people, totalling 50,000 square metres. The idea was to construct ten mid-rise towers (approximately eight storeys each) interconnected by a large internal street – instead of a high-rise one in case the bank decided to sell or lease one or some of the buildings in the future if the total number of employees should be downsized, something that in fact never happened.

The commission was given to the Amsterdam architects Alberts & van Huut, specialists of the so-called 'organic architecture' style inspired by anthroposophical concepts by which the building provides a 'third skin' for people (after skin and clothing), so that the architecture attempts to represent as much as possible the natural environment. The design was carried out in participatory way, in which several round tables took place, including the architects, members of the bank, the engineers, the landscape architects and some technicians, where all stakeholders had equal decision-making powers as well as the right to give their opinions. In so doing, solutions found by one of the stakeholders would not become obstacles for another stakeholder; it was a means by which all of them were fully informed of decisions that were being made. Public authorities, such as urban and environmental planners or utility managers, did not participate in such meetings, though.

Perhaps owing to this, several obstacles had to be overcome throughout the design phase, some of which not allowing full achievement of environmental ambitions. In the first place, the building was originally designed to be totally energy independent and even to be able to supply

Figure 5.3   ING Bank headquarters, Amsterdam

energy to the surrounding houses. The energy company, at the time still government-owned, not consenting to this, claimed that the building would thereby become its competitor, which could eventually lead to large-scale consequences in case other buildings/companies started to pursue the same aims. The building is therefore 80 per cent energy independent, something that is achieved via a series of passive architecture measures that were gradually explored throughout the design phase.

One of the first measures regarded wind impact on the envelope. Given that the building complex would occupy one or two whole blocks, an attempt had to be made so as to mitigate the so-called 'cyclone effect' – by which wind speed is significantly increased next to large vertical surfaces – hindering the isolation system and subsequently impinging higher levels of indoor acclimatization. In order to achieve such reduction, the design team proposed the façades not be parallel to the street configuration, but rather curvilinear including irregular shapes to decrease the wind impact (see Figure 5.3). This solution, in turn, caused serious disagreements with the local authorities, which threatened not to issue the building permit, despite the potential environmental improvements. According to the architects in charge of the commission, the permit was only issued because one of the members of the bank's board persuaded a highly positioned city councillor on the occasion.

The second, related, important decision concerning the façade design addressed the need to reduce noise impacts from the road. In order to achieve this reduction, the façade should not be vertical but rather slant in relation to the street. This would in turn imply non-standardized slabs, something that would significantly increase the building costs. The design team, however, managed to meet a solution by which the slabs would be identical despite the external visual difference that gives an effect of indoor and outdoor variation. It was due to this that internal atria were created, on top of which natural lighting elements and cavities for exhaust air were introduced.

Once the external shape was defined, the team started to explore other features such as materials, water elements and greenery. As for materials, the complex was designed to explore a high thermal insulation system, which includes an external brick skin[19] based on a precast concrete inner wall, with a sheath of insulation in between, where all windows are double-glazed. As a consequence, heating and artificial lighting energy is downsized through simple passive solar measures, such as sunlight in addition to internal gains, such as heat emanating from artificial lighting, equipments and from people themselves, a system that is coupled by hydraulic radiators connected to a 100 cubic metre hot water storage tank in the basement. The water in this tank is heated by cogeneration equipment located in the complex and by heat recovery from the elevator motors and computer rooms. There is also a mechanical ventilation system, including a heat exchanger device, which captures the heat of the outgoing exhaust to heat the incoming air. The complex was not projected to have an air-conditioning system,[20] but rather to use the thermal storage capacity of the building's fabric, a mechanical ventilation device and natural ventilation through operable windows for passive cooling.

Furthermore, the spaces dedicated to circulation inside the building complex, the so-called 'internal streets', are filled with diverse works of art, which serve not only to give visual pleasure, but in many cases to also improve the indoor microenvironment. The same applies to certain coloured metals added in the top of the towers' atria reflecting light on the sculptures located on the ground floor, which in turn give light to the surrounding walls. The complex is also equipped with three outdoor gardens and extensive internal landscaping, all irrigated by second-quality water, which is stored in an underground tank. As the water elements are constantly in move, there is no risk of the development of legionnaires' disease.

Finally, by the time the design phase was practically over, another group of opponents to the complex expressed their concerns. These were the investors, directly or indirectly connected to the construction, arguing that the image the building would convey through the organic architectural style would not be of a reliable, solid and serious company. They also claimed that, in two years' time, after the euphoria was over, the board would regret having built it that way. Their prediction, however, turned out to be wrong. Over the following years the building was claimed to have attracted approximately 120,000 visitors per year, more than any Dutch museum at the time, despite its doors not being open to the public; still nowadays it receives some 40,000 visitors annually, who have to have special permission to be allowed in. Public opinion, therefore, has been favourable, helping the bank to secure its image *vis-à-vis* the market.

In addition, the building complex also proved extremely cost-efficient. Despite giving the impression of being rather costly, the complex was in fact rather low-cost to construct on the occasion (50 million guilders,[21] 1987 prices), due to the economies of scale provided by the repetition of elements – that visually speaking do not seem to be repetitive – and to the downsizing of building services' equipments (cooling, heating, lighting, and so forth). On the occasion, and as compared to the previous headquarters occupied by the bank, this complex consumed proportionately one twelfth of the energy (only 0.4 GJ/m² annually). As compared to an adjacent bank constructed in the same period in a nearby site (actually an ABN AMRO building), the NMB was claimed to be five times more economical in terms of energy use per square metre, and its construction costs were slightly lower. In this respect, the extra construction costs attributed to the complex's energy saving systems was estimated to be around 700,000 dollars, a cost that was recovered in just three months' time, as the annual energy savings in electricity bills amounted to 2.6 million dollars (Vale *et al.*, 1991; Wilson *et al.*, 1998). The building was also claimed to have the lowest energy costs among Dutch office buildings at the time, where absenteeism levels among bank employees, in addition, dropped significantly (by 15 per cent), due to the better working environment the building provides, leading to an overall improved productivity.

Despite winning several prizes, the building has been widely contested, and subsequently analysed and evaluated, bringing to the fore other stakeholders, such as researchers, advisors, appraisers. Among these Novem, the Dutch Agency for Energy and Environment, was also involved as an advisor and evaluator not only in the building's early design process (Novem, 1991) but also during refurbishments or occasional increases in the number of staff so as to ensure the building to remain within the ceiling energy consumption put forward by the EPN.[22] However, no further significant environmental innovations have been pursued in the building's operational phase, except for the installation of an energy monitoring system.

This said, it is important to bear in mind that while the building's greening process was originally initiated by the NMB-Postbank board of directors – of course largely supported by the expertise of the design team and influenced by other stakeholders – current decisions regarding its operation (including environmental implications), are made by the ING Group of today. The building is run by ING's internal facility managers, who take care of the general maintenance services. These managers have direct contacts with the local energy and water utilities, particularly through the payment of bills. However, more complex issues such as energy audits or other environmental themes involving local policy networks are decided and coordinated at a higher administrative level, that is, by the Group's Executive Board.

In this respect, the Group's Executive Board is responsible for issues regarding the (worldwide) properties of ING and their environmental features, deciding upon the launching of programmes, which in their turn are to be implemented by the executive committees, the latter including ING Europe, ING Americas, ING Asia/Pacific and ING Asset Management (see Chart 5.1). The Executive Board is therefore the bank's main division dealing with the operational issues of the buildings, including establishing financial as well as environmental policies, and for making final decisions, including those regarding the Group's properties. It consists of six members who are controlled 'from a certain distance' by a Supervisory Board (see ING 2000a, 2000b). It is difficult, however, to establish with precision where the role of one ends and that of the other begins, although in general terms overall – local and global –

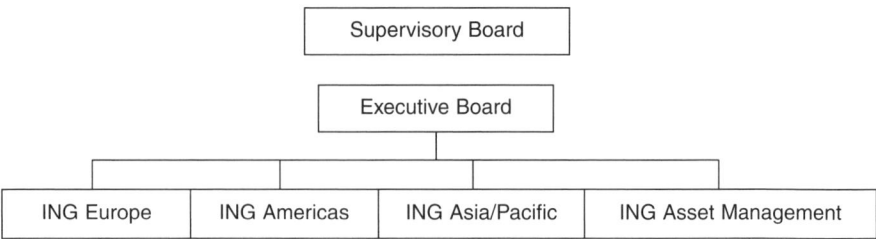

Chart 5.1   Management structure ING
            (based on ING, 2000b, p. 8)

corporate strategies, policies, communication matters and environmental affairs are initiated and decided upon by the Executive Board, which is located in Amsterdam.

In 1995, the Executive Board introduced an environmental report, including a corporate environmental policy regarding the Group's performance *in the Netherlands*. Such policy consists of internal guidelines – concerning particularly waste and energy use processes (including its commitment with the Dutch long-term agreement – LTA – for the reduction of energy consumption, see above) – and external ones, by which the Group is committed to developing products that contribute to a better environment. In the same year the bank also endorsed the International Chamber of Commerce Business Principles (Charter for Sustainable Development), mostly due to the process of internationalization that the bank was undergoing by then, for which such a charter would ease its credibility as a global institution. In 1999, the Executive Board approved the ING Business Principles offering its employees a 'framework for high ethical standards of code' (ING, 2000b).

More recently, the Executive Board has established objectives to homogenize, not only in the Netherlands but also worldwide, the environmental aspects of the Group's properties. So far, the process has begun to be implemented in the Netherlands alone, where central energy-monitoring systems have been installed in the majority of the Group's Dutch offices and an internal energy awareness campaign has been launched, which is claimed to have led to a significant reduction of energy consumption. It seems correct to suggest that much of what the bank has accomplished so far in terms of energy management stems partly from the privatization of the Dutch energy market (which demands a detailed energy monitoring system within the offices), and partly from the Group's commitment with the Dutch government, by which all banking and insurance sector companies have to decrease their energy consumption by 25 per cent, based on 1995 levels until the year 2005 (part of the LTA or long-term agreement, for which Novem is assisting the bank to achieve reductions).

A last word should be said regarding the Group's new headquarters building, which was recently completed in the Zuidas, becoming a landmark on the A10 highway (see Figure 5.4). With a total gross floor area of 19,500 square metres, and designed by Dutch architects Meyer and van Schooten, this building is a horizontal structure expressing some (new) characteristics of the Group, including transparency, decentralization, flatness. Unlike the NMB-Postbank building, this one is very high-tech, designed, however, to be energy efficient as well. It fully exploits

Figure 5.4   ING Group new headquarters, Amsterdam

daylight and windows are openable via a double skin system (cf. chapter 3). In addition, working areas are equipped with an air-conditioning system which is operated by using whenever possible water from an aquifer as well as heat pumps (hot and cold storage in the soil) to reduce energy consumption for both cooling and heating needs. In a way, such decisions have been originally instigated by the Dutch government (through its active policies of energy efficiency, such as the energy standard) and further developed by the ING's Executive Board, which is additionally also trying to convey through the architecture the image of an energy-conscious organization. And successfully. Even before the construction was completed, the building had already become another ING landmark, but this time symbolizing the transparency of the company in the globalized economy, much in opposition to the Dutch-oriented, somehow introverted bank of the 1980s.

Andersen

Arthur Andersen, the American accountancy company established in 1913 and head-quartered in Chicago, was present in 85 countries, where it employed around 85,000 people. Andersen's services included business consulting, corporate finance, human capital, as well as legal procedures, outsourcing and taxation. By 2001, Andersen was still auditing 2300 firms worldwide. Since its extinction the company has been taken over by other accountancy firms. In the Netherlands it has been taken over by Deloitte Touche Tohmatsu.

Andersen had been in the Netherlands since 1961, where it employed around 1600 people and maintained three headquarters: Rotterdam, Eindhoven and Amsterdam. The latter was in fact situated in a site bordering the municipality of Amsterdam so that the building was considered to belong to the Amsterdam South business district, despite being under the jurisdiction of another municipality (Amstelveen, see Figure 5.5). This building complex is another worldwide landmark in environmental

Figure 5.5   Andersen headquarters, Amsterdam

design. Completed in 1996, it is the outcome of a project that was not initiated by the company itself, but by a group of developers and consultants. Its owner is the German investment bank Trinkaus & Burkhardt GmbH, with whom Andersen had a long-term lease contract (originally supposed to expire in 2009).

Decision regarding this building started in 1994, when the president of the Multi Vastgoed bv – a multinational development company of Dutch origin, which operates abroad under the name of Multi Development Corporation – was approached during a seminar on office markets and the demand for 'people-friendly' buildings at the Technological University Delft in the Netherlands by an environmental consultant from DHV AIB, who proposed a joint development for an environmental and human friendly pilot building, to be incorporated for a commercial client. It was in this context that the search for both a client and a site for the implementation of the idea started, a process that lasted roughly one year.

The preliminary design process was initiated during this period, before the client or the site were defined. Similarly to the ING Bank headquarters, the design of the building was also done in a participatory way, via a system called 'holistic participation method'. This methodology, created by the DHV consultant, fosters stakeholders to raise and overcome difficulties in the implementation of environmental projects, by assigning each of them to approach the ideas from another person's point of view: where the financier, for instance, plays the role of the architect, the client of the builder and so forth. This methodology was introduced during a three-day workshop in Eindhoven – organized by the consultant and chaired by Professor Peter Schmid, a pioneer academic and practitioner in the sustainable building field – also involving lectures regarding sustainable building techniques and group discussions. It was attended by a group of stakeholders, among which the developers (Multi Vastgoed), the architects T+T Design (from Gouda, a branch of Multi Vastgoed), the DHV consultants, a feng shui expert, financiers, constructors and a fictitious client. The main opponents during the design phase were the builders, who refused to participate in the workshop and raised several objections throughout the design process. However, ideas regarding the project were clear after the workshop, as well as the envisaged environmental ambitions of the building and how these would be implemented. As in the ING case, public authorities did not participate in this exercise.

Andersen joined the project in 1995. On the occasion, the company was looking for a building to relocate its staff, which was scattered in four office storeys in other buildings in the city, and to explore thereby its own corporate identity via a new architecture. Its main requirement was that the building should have a total of 7500 square metres of office area, where the floor templates should be cellular (standardized in 3.60 × 4.50 metre rooms for two staff members the smallest rooms) so as to provide privacy for the confidential work the company carried out. In addition to this, the building should offer parking facilities, a storage place in the basement, a restaurant and an auditorium. The only architectural guidelines regarded the use of indoor colours and communication logotypes, which were in fact worldwide standards of the company. The staff would select the location where the building would be constructed; the last prerequisite was a bus station to be located nearby the building, something that the municipality of Amstelveen is claimed not to have delivered.

Nothing was expected regarding the building's energy or water consumption from the company's side. When approached by the developers, Andersen had originally no interests whatsoever in occupying a building that would address sustainability issues. The developers allege that it took a long time to fully convince the company of the project. (One of the directors reacted, for instance, when informed that no air conditioning would be installed, saying that in this case he would prefer to work in his car.) This opposition changed, however, with time, and Andersen eventually turned out to be enthusiastic about most of the ideas.

The municipality of Amstelveen did not impose specific environmental regulations beyond those set forth at the national level, such as the energy performance standard (that was just emerging on the occasion). Nor did it have well defined sustainability policies that would interfere with the way the building would be designed. It was, however, very much in favour of having an environmentally friendly landmark building in its territory, thus willing to facilitate the legal procedures. The developers proposed in fact a whole master plan designed according to ecological criteria for the site, to be occupied by different companies, which was never realized due to economic impediments coupled by the difficulty to convince clients about the benefits. Apparently the energy and water utilities did also not interfere in the building's design.

The building complex has undergone several evaluation processes. The first one was during the initial phase, when issues such as location selection, energy, materials, water and green elements were analysed, as well as indoor environmental quality (including the electromagnetic radiation of the site). According to this initial evaluation, the developers proposed three environmental concepts: the 'basic', the 'plus' and the 'eco' packages. Obviously the third was the most ambitious and expensive one, and it was the option chosen for the pilot project. Nevertheless, pressures that arose from schedule and budget constraints during the construction phase are claimed to have led to some changes that were somehow not really ideal from an environmental point of view (Hal *et al.*, 2000). In this sense, although the environmental ambitions as put forward in the 'eco' package were not fully implemented, the complex was estimated to consume on the occasion 30 per cent less than the EPN standards required. In addition, according to evaluation conducted in 1996 when the building was inaugurated, it had the best performance in energy use (energy

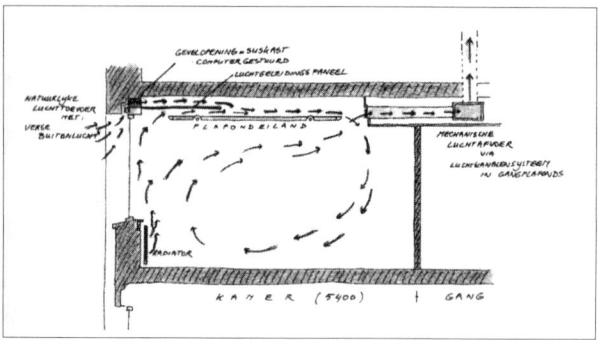

Figure 5.6   Andersen headquarters night cooling system

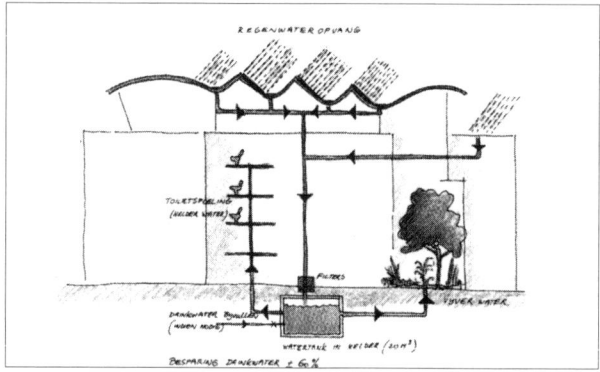

Figure 5.7   Andersen headquarters water management system

efficiency) among European office buildings (at the time of writing, the evaluation was still being carried out by DHV consultants).

In terms of architecture and construction techniques, the complex consists of three buildings interconnected by conservatories. It exploits thermal mass during summer so as to operate without air conditioning in addition to night ventilation through small openings in the glazing (see Figure 5.6). During winter, heat is supplied via a warm water radiation. It also has solar cells in the roofs – in total 270 square metres, being able to supply 15 per cent of the whole energy demand of the building complex – and a system of sunscreens in the conservatory and stairwells. This was another pilot project supported by Novem, in which the combination of self-generation capacity and the use of the mains grid of electricity was explored. In terms of lighting, daylight is exploited to a maximum degree complemented by low-energy lighting fixtures with individual controlling systems. The complex also has a quite effective water management system, using rainwater to flush toilets, irrigate roof planting and wash down semi-open paving (see Figure 5.7). The greatest possible use is made of natural materials, such as brick and timber. The structure applies concrete due to an LCA analysis, which indicated high environmental impact implications if the complex had a steel structure.

According to the chief architect in charge of the project, the complex's construction costs were about ten per cent higher than a conventional structure; the German investor, however, was on the occasion granted subsidies from the Dutch government for the implementation of environmental features. However, its rent fees are considered to be average according to the region's standards.

Andersen, in its turn, did not add to the building's environmental change, neither during the design nor in the operational phase. To begin with, there were no incentives coming from the world headquarters (Chicago) indicating environmental rules or principles, or the like, to be followed, nor did a corporate environmental report as such ever exist.[23] In this respect, although it seems that Dutch employees tried to keep up with high levels of good housekeeping, there were no written commitments or written policies in that regard. Apparently Andersen used the building because it liked it, not because of its environmental characteristics. In that sense, no further environmental solutions have been introduced during the building's operation, such as monitoring systems for energy or water or a sustainable waste management system. On the other hand, and despite complaints regarding overheating in summer, no air-conditioning equipment has been installed either.

The story of the former Andersen building in Amsterdam clearly indicates that environmental initiatives were originated, decided upon and implemented by the local economic network mainly, amid developers, financiers and architects. The role of the state was mainly limited to facilitating the issuing of the building permits as well as to providing financial incentives. The involvement of the global company did not add in this respect, leading one to conclude that Andersen largely occupied such building by chance. However, the company also seemed to be consistent with its overall poor environmental conduct and apparently did not use the building as a pretext to promote itself as an environmentally-friendly institution.

ABN AMRO

ABN AMRO Holding N.V. is currently the main financial services institution in the Netherlands and one of the largest in the world, serving retail, wholesale and private and asset management clients through an extensive global network. Founded in 1991 after the merger between the Algemene Bank Nederland (ABN) and the Amsterdam-Rotterdam Bank (AMRO), ABN AMRO presently owns approximately 500 billion dollars in assets and employs more than 100,000 professional staff in around 76 countries.

ABN AMRO maintains regional headquarters in Singapore, Chicago, São Paulo, London and New York. In the city of Amsterdam the bank owns two main buildings – one in Amsterdam-Zuidoost (completed in the mid-eighties, nearby the ING Bank headquarters) and the other on the Zuidas, in front of the Amsterdam Zuid-WTC metro station,[24] the bank's world headquarters (see Figure 5.8). Ranked by the American Institute of Architects among the ten best green construction projects in 2001, this building has been receiving a lot of attention since its opening in 1999. The objective of this building is to offer not only a pleasant working environment for more than 3000 staff members (ten per cent of the Netherlands' total) but also to

Figure 5.8   ABN AMRO headquarters, Amsterdam

reflect the bank's environmental ambitions, which have significantly changed since the merger in 1991. In this regard, it is seen as a large-scale demonstration project of how a contemporary environmental – though modern-looking – building should be, probably representing the highest achievement of the bank's environmental and sustainable building goals. As environmental innovations have been introduced in the design and operational phases we will provide an account of both.

In the first place, the bank considers that its relationship as a financial institution with the environment is twofold. First, as an organization maintaining around 3600 offices worldwide, it consumes a tremendous amount of raw materials, energy and water, and generates significant loads of waste and wastewater. It also contributes to urban atmospheric pollution issues due to its staff commuting and to the transportation of its required goods. Secondly, by acting as a financial intermediary, the bank has a strong power in steering choices towards specific directions, given that the economic activities conducted by the bank's clients may pose a burden on the environment. In this context, ABN AMRO formulated its environmental policy after signing the Charter of the International Chamber of Commerce in 1992, with a core objective to integrate environmental considerations into all business decisions so as to contribute to the sustainable development of society (ABN AMRO, 2000b).

Approved in 1995, the environmental policy paved the way for the implementation of the first environmental management system, which focused mainly on in-house environmental management – such as waste management, goods purchasing, transport, energy and environmentally sound offices – and financial products and services. As a result, it is the objective of ABN AMRO since this period to reuse 75 per cent of its waste and to seek to include an environmental section in all contracts with suppliers.

Concerning the Dutch premises, the bank introduced in 1997 an 'energy project'. This was done so as to comply with the Dutch government's long-term agreement, previously mentioned in this chapter, by which energy consumption of existing offices have to decrease by 25 per cent until 2005. This project has been implemented in three steps. First, and in accordance with – but not only because of – the required adaptation to the energy market liberalization, a detailed monitoring system was introduced. Based on data logging devices located next to the energy meters, this system counts pulses of energy, electricity and gas use every 15 minutes. The data is accessible by any staff member through the intranet so that abnormalities can be easily identified. Secondly, an energy management system was implemented, controlling energy use for instance when the office is closed or occupants are absent. Thirdly, the energy project fosters an overall reduction of energy consumption, focusing on both new and existing offices. For that the bank has a fund of two million euros per year, to be spent within the Netherlands in addition to other normal activities, such as maintenance. The only condition is that these projects, as well as environmental projects in general, have to amortize within five years, which is an exception to the bank's policy of investing in projects whose payback time lasts at the most two years.

The bank has also developed a sustainable housing policy applicable to all its *Dutch* premises, including among others systems of smart lighting control, efficient heating and cooling, waste management, efficient glazing and where applicable heat exchange. The bank has been carrying out some pilot projects so as to gain experience in the sustainable building field, beyond compliance with the standard requirements dictated by the Dutch legislation. As such, energy consumption and opportunities for natural cooling are taken into account when evaluating air-conditioning equipment. Natural lighting is encouraged in the premises whenever possible and suppliers are required to meet the terms of some additional norms.

The construction of the new headquarters in Amsterdam Zuid consisted, in this context, of a main pilot project for sustainable construction and management. With a required floor area of 90,000 square metres to accommodate 3000 staff members, its challenge was to realize a design that would produce a healthy and comfortable internal environment while maintaining a high level of energy conservation. It should, in addition, express the character and identity of one of the world's leading banks, which is to say, of a 'powerful, reliable, experienced, professional, dynamic and international' financial institution (Pei Cobb Freed and Partners, 2001). The commission was given to the architecture firm Pei Cobb Freed and Partners based in New York.

At an early stage in the project, the bank and Amsterdam's department of physical planning signed a covenant defining some methods of cooperation (ABN AMRO, 2000c). This agreement concerned, among other things, an optimal integration of the building with the surrounding environment. This resulted, for instance, in the incorporation of a public square in front of the building, which was designed by municipal landscape architects in consultation with their American counterparts. Another covenant was also signed with public transport authorities, by which the building would be able to provide only 750 car parking spaces (for the 3000 staff members), so as to encourage the use of public transport. In return, the municipality had committed to work to improve the public transport links. The bank claims to encourage thereby the use of bicycles for commuter traffic and for this purpose it provides appropriate facilities on the premises for parking. No agreements were made with the energy and water companies, yet the building consumes green energy supplied by Nuon. An environmental audit was conducted regarding issues like energy use, waste disposal, water conservation and encouragement of use of public transport.

In terms of environmental features, the building provides in the first place a system of 'climate façades' – constructed with a ventilated glazed panel system – which extract the stale air from the offices via a cavity between the internal and external glass layers, so that less energy is needed for cooling. The façades, in addition to providing protection against traffic noise from the A10 highway, also have a sun protection function. The sun's radiation is directly reduced through these cavities by means of intermediate sunblinds. In winter, the situation is reversed, as the high thermal insulation prevents from heat losses so that there are no heating devices necessary along the façade (European Commission Thermie Project, 1998a). The building does not apply natural ventilation as a cooling strategy, but windows may be opened in offices. (In reality, these windows had originally been designed to be fixed, but a group of employees' representatives demanded that they should be openable as they regarded it as an important feature for their well-being, cf. Meel, 2000). With respect to well-being, the air inside offices is constantly renovated and humidified. Moreover, cooling, heating, lighting and sunshading can be individually controlled in offices.

Another important feature is the system of 'climate ceiling', which operates the cooling and parts of the heating systems of the building (European Commission Thermie Project, 1998a). These are made of perforated aluminium panels with separate connecting pipes for warm and chilled water, which are in turn supplied to the offices as required. The cooling is based on the coldness of an underground aquifer, which is much more efficient than a conventional system,[25] coupled with night ventilation in summer. As for heating, the complex tries to use waste heat to heat the underground garage, which by itself also helps the rest of the building by being less cold. The building is connected to the district-heating network, which in turn covers the basic demands. Additional requirements are generated by a system of boilers.

In terms of lighting, use is made of high efficiency direct/indirect fixtures with metal reflectors and high-frequency electronic ballasts. Daylight is also explored to reduce the energy load, benefiting from several atriums and a generous use of glass. The lighting system is smart and louvres are automatically shut when human presence is not detected to avoid overheating.

However, despite the environmental features implemented and the related achievements (for instance the building tries to consume ten per cent less energy than the EPN), the building also presents several drawbacks, particularly due to its high technology, which makes it also more vulnerable. There were several complaints regarding overheating as the heating and cooling system using a liquid medium might get clogged from time to time. In addition, an extensive use is made of granite imported from the United States, implying not only high costs but also an unreasonable use of energy for transportation ('grey energy', cf. chapter 3). As for water conservation, for instance, the building does not have any special device except for water-saving taps, which are quite normal for the standards of this building. ABN AMRO, however, intends to make water one of its main projects in the future.

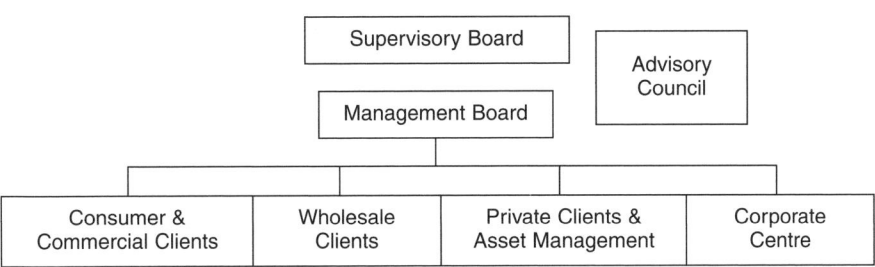

Chart 5.2   Management structure ABN AMRO
(based on ABN ANRO, 2001, pp. 119–120)

Finally, with respect to its office-stock in the Netherlands, the bank has been facing difficulties in achieving the required reduction regarding the implementation of the EPN, 850 MJ/m^2/year, since it has introduced the desk-sharing scheme in its premises making the offices always fully occupied. Of course, the greater the number of people, the higher the consumption of energy, but in so doing the bank also saves on property land and optimizes energy consumption. With regard to the energy performance standard, which is expressed in terms of energy consumption against area (not taking into account number of persons), there is a process going on at the moment to see how this issue can be renegotiated and if the number of users should also be stipulated in the standard. The Dutch government, on the other hand, is convinced that energy consumption in office buildings can be reduced much more, down to or even below 500 MJ/m^2/year, of course without considering the new working routines.

Environmental decisions at ABN AMRO, such as the bank's environmental policy, are primarily initiated by the Health and Safety Department – which operates under the Consumer and Commercial Clients business unit – and confirmed by the Management Board (see Chart 5.2). Decisions regarding the bank's properties, in contrast, are initiated by the Housing and Real Estate Department – which also operates under the Consumer and Commercial Clients business unit. The Housing and Real Estate Department is also responsible for developing proposals concerning sustainability issues of the *Dutch* premises, such as technologies, monitoring systems, and so forth.

The environmental decisions regarding the bank's world headquarters in Amsterdam were, in this respect, primarily proposed by this department and approved by the Management Board. However, despite this initial drive towards the building's greening, environmental innovations were of course deployed against the backdrop of other (local) practices of environmental management, such as the EPN and the covenants signed with the municipality of Amsterdam and with the public transport authorities, so one cannot say that ABN AMRO was the main environmental carrier in the story. When it comes to its foreign premises, for instance, where the local infrastructure for dealing with environmental management is most likely weaker, particularly in economic capitals located in developing countries, the bank expects the local branches themselves to come up with such environmental management proposals, which in addition, if incurring great expenditures, should be approved by the world headquarters in the Netherlands. In addition, as mentioned before, the amortization period of five years for environmental projects does not apply to foreign branches, which instead have to meet a payback of only two years. Such financial decisions are made by the Management Board in the Netherlands, which, for instance, decides on – global and local – amortization periods of investments in certain technologies, following the proposals made by the Housing and Safety Department (Netherlands) or by the foreign branches.

Within this framework, environmental investments of ABN AMRO have much to do with the following formula: maximum environmental gain = maximum environmental impact reduction with a minimum payback time. Some of the environmental investments are made to comply with legislation, others to ensure a clean record and many to make sure financial savings can be achieved. In this respect, the bank spends almost 20 million euros annually in energy bills for its Dutch premises, which are now constantly being monitored. In terms of savings, the world headquarters building alone, by having 20 meters installed with its detailed monitoring system, in addition to other low-energy techniques, saves about one to two million euros per year (the building's total cost was approximately 280 million euros). Water technologies, for instance, have not been installed in the building as water is still a rather inexpensive resource, as far as the Netherlands is concerned, and investments in water-saving devices are claimed not to meet the amortization period as mentioned above (five years for environmental projects).

IBM

IBM, the American IT multinational, employs around 316,000 people in 100 countries. Its total market share is estimated worldwide at 30–40 per cent. Its global annual revenue is around 88.4 billion dollars.

In the Netherlands, IBM has no production facilities but maintains four main headquarters buildings in addition to four smaller ones. In the city of Amsterdam, the company has an office complex recently refurbished in the Zuidas (see Figure 5.9) and has recently finished the construction of a new one in the same district, a building designed by American architect William McDonough, an environmental design expert, and developed by the same company involved with the Andersen building, the Multi Development Corporation.

The design concept of this building originated again from the architectural firm T+T Design, a branch of Multi Development Corporation, the same initiators of the Andersen building. The investor is Westland Utrecht Hypotheekbank (73 million euros). The building complex has a total area of 34,000 square metres, spread throughout a series of different buildings, which vary in height, where the highest has thirteen storeys (50 metres high), and offers 224 underground parking spaces. IBM leases the building on a long-term contract.

Decisions regarding this building have been made jointly by the developers and IBM, mainly pursuing two main features. The first is an idea of 'urban environment', offering a contrast to the isolated office towers that have been sprawling along the highway A10, dominating the landscape. Second, the building is focused on creating a healthy, pleasant and especially a flexible work environment by offering access to daylight and natural ventilation. In order to approach these features, a series of narrow office buildings encircle an exterior courtyard, allowing access to abundant fresh air

Figure 5.9   IBM headquarters, Amsterdam

and daylight, and providing a contextualization with the surrounding housing. This composition, in addition, allows people to be easily connected to the outside through a courtyard in the lower levels and through a series of terraces, balconies and winter gardens for upper floors, regardless their location in the building.

In terms of environmental management, however, the building cannot be considered to be extraordinary despite complying with the Dutch government's regulations. Unlike the Andersen building, for instance, this one does not use PV cells,[26] passive cooling elements, sustainable water management, and so forth. The selection of materials, however, has been made on the basis of durability, energy performance, maintenance and environmental friendliness. An orange-red brick was selected for the cladding, alternating with grey stone with a ceramic layer. It is important to note that in the case of IT companies, computer floors not only consume lots of energy due to their equipment but also require high cooling loads (due to the heat generated by computers), usually being the main energy users of the building. These rooms have to be cooled all year round; a fact that also applies to dealing rooms of banks. The building's curtain wall, in this sense, uses a recently developed coating, so that the building is significantly protected against heat gain, minimizing cooling loads while external visibility and access to daylight is ensured. The building also exploits the use of internal landscape architecture, water elements and greenery to provide a 'people-friendly' atmosphere. In addition, it also offers proper access to bicycle routes, frequent bus service and a train/metro station 850 metres away.

IBM has a longstanding global environmental management policy, which also applies to its facilities. Some of the strategies – for instance concerning work safety and health, as well as environmental, energy and natural resources conservation – started to be formalized already in the 1970s, and have been evolving ever since. In this respect, IBM's buildings are in general terms *stakeholder*-oriented, in the sense that the company seeks, by offering a comfortable and high-standard office environment conveying an appropriate image, to get the best out of its personnel as well as to sensitize clients looking for its advice and consultancy. Floors are usually open, flexible and the 'e-place' (desk-sharing) work culture is encouraged.

In terms of environmental policy, IBM's current approach sets forth, among other things, the following objectives, which are also decisive for several features regarding energy and water management in its buildings: (i) to meet or exceed local standards and regulations concerning the environment; (ii) to continuously improve its environmental management system and performance, and periodically issue progress reports to the general public; and (iii) to conduct rigorous audits and self-assessment of IBM's compliance with its policy (IBM, 1999). IBM also has a system of in-house environmental management covering, for instance, waste, water and energy management. These apply to buildings both leased or owned by the company worldwide.

Regarding the first objective, the general rule is to comply with the most stringent standard, either the local one or that set by the company. In this sense, and in terms of energy and water efficiency, the buildings in Amsterdam do comply with the local norms – for instance the EPN, the Arbo rules, legionnaires' disease management and other local prescriptions. As for the LTA (long-term agreement) with the Dutch government to reduce energy consumption by 25 per cent until 2005, nothing has been done so far but the company expects to meet these requirements within a few years' time. Since IBM encourages the 'e-place' concept, a similar constraint as found at ABN AMRO regarding the status of the performance standard is taking place at this company as well. Although its policy fosters best techniques to be cost effective, IBM does not buy green energy, unlike ABN AMRO, despite the possibility of having tax abatements.[27] In terms of energy monitoring, the buildings have installed a comprehensive energy monitoring system since 2002, based on Erbys data logging devices, similarly to ING and ABN AMRO.

Concerning the second objective, the company strives to achieve reductions in energy and water consumption in the order of four per cent and one per cent per year respectively in all its worldwide offices and facilities. In terms of energy, this figure is easily achieved particularly by downsizing server areas – which as mentioned above, are heavy energy consumers – in addition to installing new techniques, such as smaller computers requiring decreased cooling loads, as well as by promoting behavioural campaigns to save water and energy. As the Dutch environmental policy framework is fairly advanced, the company's global policies usually are below the Dutch standards regarding environmental management.

The third objective is accomplished by regularly conducted audits regarding waste, water and energy, at least as far as the premises are concerned, which lead to the issuing of constant reports, usually provided by the Real Estate & Site Operations Department, which the Environment/Health and Safety Division belongs to. In the case of unusual, detailed investigations, external consultants are outsourced. Special teams commanded by the United States headquarters periodically check the result of these audits in the local headquarters. Therefore, staff involved in the above-mentioned departments strive to keep up with the local and global requirements.

Such global environmental policy is established at world headquarters level (USA) and is (largely) controlled by the regional administrations. The Netherlands, in this case reports to the EMEA (Europe, Middle East and Africa) region, which in turn is subdivided into more local administrative bodies, the North and Nordics region being the one to which the Netherlands belongs (see Chart 5.3).

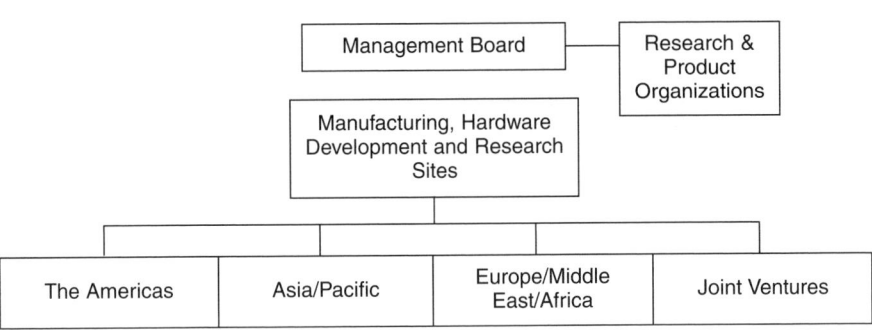

Chart 5.3   Management structure IBM
(based on IBM, 1999, p. 33)

The pursuit of this global environmental policy is claimed to be carried out so as to ensure IBM's leadership in relation to other companies of the sector, a clean record for its corporate image, as well as cost-benefit issues in a rather pragmatic way. This policy is coordinated via intranet, so that it is homogenized in worldwide terms; local branches do not have any decision-making power regarding its formulation. Since the policy requires local branches to deliver data and facts annually in the format of an intranet report, the Senior Management is ultimately responsible for environmental matters. However, decision-making processes regarding the company's properties are quite independent country-wise, whereby external consultants are frequently hired to offer strategic advisory services on property-related affairs. But when in comes to budget approvals to major projects, IBM-Netherlands needs to have the consent of the European North-Nordic region, headquartered in London, and ultimately of the main headquarters in the USA.

Conclusions

While Amsterdam's office-stock has seen a large expansion since the beginning of the 1990s, as the city became one of the main headquarters locations in north-west Europe, it has also been subjected to a growing number of environmental management practices. At the national level various covenants have been issued and standards introduced, particularly since the energy sector liberalization onwards, and following international pressures regarding carbon dioxide emissions, bringing into focus a new need to address environmental issues in office buildings. The municipality of Amsterdam, in turn, largely – but not exclusively – due to its land tenure system, has also been establishing covenants with or requiring environmental audits from companies, developers or other actors interested in building in the city, so as to attempt to control the environmental performance of its stock of office buildings.

Where companies are concerned, these new environmental management practices are in general terms smoothly assimilated. As a matter of fact, and with the exception of Andersen, all three other companies analysed in this city are even primary players in driving environmental innovations in their buildings. ING Bank, for instance, not only initiated the environmental ambitions of its headquarters in the mid-1980s but also *pushed* for their materialization – in view of the impediments posed at the time by the energy company and the urban planning department. Although the approach of Amsterdam's planning authorities has changed since, this building is still a good example of the city's early office-stock ecological restructuring process.

More recent developments have now taken a different route, moving away from 'self-sufficiency' goals (such as proposed by the ING Bank building) to solutions approaching more environmental 'efficiency' (cf. chapter 3). ING, for instance, is now seeking sustainability goals by applying advanced monitoring systems, dematerialization and substitution of certain technical systems, as well as high performance technologies and materials, as the new headquarters of ING Group illustrates. The same applies to ABN AMRO with the development of a high-rise pilot project addressing mostly energy conservation, and IBM which, following its global standards, seeks to achieve annual reductions in the energy and water consumption of its premises worldwide mostly in the operational phase of the buildings. Other examples that corroborate this trend are the European headquarters of Nike in the Greater Amsterdam area which, despite not being a property of the company, was also largely 'greened' after the company expressed its wish for an environmentally efficient building (Bouman, 2000). One should also mention the former European headquarters of Nissan (now occupied by the company Mexx), which was designed to have its parts totally reused after dismantling, thus implying environmental conservation at the demolition and recycling phase.

The environmental restructuring of Amsterdam's office-stock seems thereby to be proceeding in the light of two (converging) tendencies: one of them regards the efficiency of the local environmental management, which has been providing enabling conditions for the market to pursue environmental innovations, such as the covenants (based on the National Packages for Sustainable Building) and the energy performance standard with its related subsidies schemes in energy advisory services. The other regards the global environmental management stemming from the multinational companies, which mostly attempt to go *beyond* the prescriptions set forth by the government being, indeed, major environmental reform triggers in the city of Amsterdam. The result of such interactions is leading to somewhat synergistic solutions, which may be described in terms of dematerialization of the use of resources, through for instance natural ventilation instead of air conditioning (ING and Andersen), substitution of technologies (such as use of green energy), monitoring (particularly of energy and through the energy performance standard), as well as monetarization (through tax incentives for the use of green electricity provided by energy suppliers).

The two spaces of social action are therefore mutually enforcing, clearly not competing with each other, to the extent that they are pursuing basically the same discourse of environmental policy: promoting more efficiency, and not self-sufficiency. A more detailed evaluation of these features of Amsterdam's ecological reform, also with regard to ecological modernization theory, will be presented in the conclusive chapter of this study.

Notes

1   This fact in turn has a historical background, as the country's administrative geography and economic policy have been based on physical *heterogeneity* rather than cohesion (Taverne, 1994). Nowadays, as several Dutch large companies including those of the financial sector and transnational companies emanate not only from Amsterdam but also from other Dutch cities, the Dutch economy is fairly scattered throughout the country, particularly in the Randstad area. There are of course some exceptions, such as Philips, which recently relocated its headquarters from Eindhoven to Amsterdam.

2   The Dutch Randstad can be understood as a polycentric urban system consisting of the four largest Dutch cities – Amsterdam, Rotterdam, The Hague and Utrecht – together with a number of smaller cities in the western part of the Netherlands linked by an extensive green heart. Its physical constitution is rather unique for it has no centre and is instead a pluricentric urban conglomerate consisting of a ring of cities in a diameter of almost 80 kilometres, whose core is a large green area. It also has no hierarchy and is thereby frequently designated as an 'inverted metropolis' or a 'ville sans agglomération' (Taverne, 1994).

In political terms, the Randstad results from a strategic institutionalization taking place in the Fourth Report on Spatial Planning (1988) so as to enable the Netherlands to hold a strong urban system to compete with other large capitals for businesses, meeting therefore the new challenges set by the globalized economy. Other similar urban systems can be found in Germany (Ruhr), in Japan (Kansai) and in Italy (Po Valley). Its total population is about five million inhabitants, 1.45 million of whom live in the municipality of Amsterdam – the largest among the four, with 730,000 inhabitants in the inner city alone. Yet, even though the Dutch economy – and subsequently head office locations – is fairly scattered throughout its area, in general terms one can say that The Hague remains the seat of the Dutch government, at the same time being a leading international bureaucratic centre, while Utrecht is a city mostly oriented towards education; Rotterdam mainly a trading capital, as a major world seaport, and Amsterdam the country's financial centre.

3   According to Sassen (1994), in 1990 Amsterdam ranked seventh most important European global city due to the number of top head offices location entries (banking, industrial and commercial firms), after London, Paris, Frankfurt, Hamburg, Brussels and Copenhagen.

4   However, the three other major Dutch financial institutions – Rabobank, VSN and General Bank – are headquartered either in Utrecht or in Rotterdam.

5   This is due to the fact that companies have started to realize that property ownership implies high fixed costs, which could be allocated otherwise. As an example, KPN telecom, the Dutch leading telecom company, has recently decided to sell all its properties in order to invest in further information technology. By outsourcing office space, companies also become somehow more impartial regarding their liabilities with property issues, in addition to being freer to allocate, or shift, their investments where and how they wish.

6   Still the first 'miniature skyscraper' of Amsterdam came to be located in the city centre (the Utrecht office building, constructed in 1905). This building began Amsterdam's high-rise tradition, a tradition that mostly consists of unrealized plans and in which the term semi-skyscraper has become more suitable (Kloos, 1995). In this respect, although favouring high-rise buildings, several objections were clearly expressed against their construction in the city centre, particularly by the architect H.P. Berlage, who proposed such building typology for the outskirts of the city instead, through his celebrated Plan Zuid of 1917.

7   For this matter Meel (2000, pp. 129–147) provides a detailed description.

8 According to Amsterdam's department for the environment (Milieudienst Amsterdam), the general infrastructure in the city of Amsterdam is rather good, with the exception of the energy supply which, due to the increasing presence of information and communication technology companies, has started to present some shortcomings in recent years.

9 In terms of energy supply, the Netherlands's total primary energy demand, in 1996, was as follows: natural gas (51 per cent), oil (32 per cent), coal (13 per cent), nuclear (one per cent), and others (including renewable energy sources, three per cent) (CBS, 1997). Most of the energy consumed in office buildings in Amsterdam thus derives from fossil fuels, with consequent climate change emissions implications. In fact, the country is estimated to emit about 50 million tons of carbon dioxide per year (Milieudienst Amsterdam, 1998).

10 This is also related to the aim of decreasing motorway traffic congestion, particularly in the southern region.

11 The geopolitical importance of the Zuidas region leads to a contradiction with the overall decentralist administration of Amsterdam.

12 According to Amsterdam's water supply company (Gemeentewaterleidingen Amsterdam), the act specifies water use, particularly for heavy consumers such as car washing facilities, but contains very little regarding the use of water in offices.

13 Concerning grey water, the Amsterdam City Council in conjunction with the Amsterdam Water Supply company is launching a programme to supply grey water (not drinkable but suitable for washing machines and toilets) to a new housing development in Ijburg district (Gemeentewaterleidingen Amsterdam, 2000).

14 While the *energy policy* remains under the MINEZ, the implementation of the EPN has been passed to the VROM. The VROM, in turn, maintains an *environmental policy* that includes both a climate change and a sustainable building programme, the latter recognized, in Dutch, as Duurzam Bouwen.

15 Since the ALARA principle suggests that environmental impact reductions should to be as low as reasonably *achievable*, it leaves enough room for negotiations among interested parties.

16 According to Amsterdam's water supply company, a temporary law passed by VROM in early 2002 compels buildings or housing complexes (larger than ten households) to undergo risk analysis, so that most attention is currently given to this issue.

17 NMB became ING in 1992.

18 In which Middenstands is the Dutch word for shopkeepers and retailers' class.

19 The brick skin underwent a whole refurbishment as since the walls are slanted, they were starting to develop algae growth due to problems of infiltration, particularly next to the windows. This was solved by introducing a kind of glue in the cement that holds the masonry together.

20 At one point in time the number of employees increased by 60 per cent, requiring the installation of air conditioning in some areas. Nowadays it is occupied by around 1500–1600 people.

21 Approximately 23 million euros.

22 In one of such studies, for instance, Novem detected that the number of staff could increase as long as all computers became flat screen ones, so that the EPN would be met (Novem, 1999).

23 For this reason the organizational chart of Andersen is not presented.

24 ABN AMRO's total office-stock in the Netherlands consists of approximately 700 buildings, whereas ING has a stock of about 400 buildings.

25 According to the Dutch law, the water used from the aquifer has to be subsequently replenished (Netherlands National Team, 2000).

26 Decisions regarding the installation or not of energy saving equipment have been made on the basis of cost-benefit estimates.

27 IBM energy supplier is Nuon, from whom the company buys conventional energy.

Chapter 6

São Paulo

Figure 6.1   Paulista Avenue

São Paulo's growth into the leading business capital of the Southern Hemisphere started in the late 1970s and early 1980s. Since then, the city has been expanding sharply, a process that has been accompanied by numerous transformations in its physical setting and environment. A paradoxical city, the size and economic importance that São Paulo has achieved are contradicted by a general absence of official urban and environmental planning. As a result, haphazard changes in the urban space – and their environmental side effects – have made São Paulo a cacophonic cityscape, or, as many say, a 'bomb primed to go off'. The assimilation of corporate headquarters contributing to the city's verticalization and expansion has taken place at the interface between the rush to achieve a competitive edge over other cities for the setting up of businesses and, on the other hand, widespread disregard for the environment.

As I will suggest in this chapter, however, the ecological restructuring of São Paulo's office-stock is in its *status nascendi*, an embryonic process. Although the office property market grew to be highly speculative in the city, seeking short-term profits (usually at a cost to the environment), some developers have recently started to introduce the concept 'green building', indicating that a more efficient use of resources is about to be triggered. My argument starts with an overview of the main characteristics of the urban setting, describing the geographical distribution of the office districts, some characteristics of the property market and the typology, environmental profile and general regulatory framework of buildings. Subsequently, I will shift the discussion to the two 'spaces' of environmental management, analysing the (emerging) strategies first advanced by local utilities and environmental management agencies, and secondly by the companies ING, Andersen, ABN AMRO and IBM. Although these two social spaces seem to provide little evidence that an ecological reform of São Paulo's transnational buildings is under way, this chapter concludes with some general observations and other evidences that point toward an emerging greening process, discussing thus the conditions and actors that are favouring it.

The Urban Setting

São Paulo was founded by Jesuit priests in early 1500s on a hill near the confluence of the Tietê and the Tamaduateí rivers. This location would later reap benefits from its proximity to the Serra do Mar and the harbour of Santos, and develop into an intermediary point for transportation routes between the coast and inland plains. Remaining among the poorest rural centres of the colonial period, and mostly colonized by adventurous settlers coming from the south of Portugal, São Paulo's early origins provided few clues of what the town would look like in the following centuries.

It grew slowly until the end of the nineteenth century, a period during which coffee plantations started to spread throughout the state of São Paulo (of which São Paulo city is the capital city) conferring on the city a new role, that of the world's main coffee export centre. São Paulo has since then grown at an extraordinary rate, attracting investments into industrial sectors and urban infrastructure, in addition to a strong migratory influx. A population of no more than 30,000 inhabitants in the late nineteenth century surpassed one million in the 1940s (EMPLASA, 2000), quickly altering the city's topographic constitution with the development of residential and industrial complexes, the canalization of rivers and streams and the construction of dams for energy provision. In this process, a gap in environmental preservation started to widen, as public services – such as waste collection, sewerage disposal, street cleaning, paving and urban drainage – have too often failed to cope with the speed of the city's growth.

Nowadays, São Paulo has become a high-rise city, with a strong trend towards urban decentralization and high levels of pollution, with a total metropolitan area of more than 8000 square kilometres inhabited by around 20 million people (Ibid.). With an intense economic dynamism supported by governmental incentives to further attract industries and the services sector, Greater São Paulo[1] has become not only Brazil's 'command centre' – generating about half of Brazil's gross national product – but also the economic and financial capital of the Mercosul, as well as Latin America's main industrial and service pole. Thus, unlike the predominantly industrial and nationally oriented centre it had been for decades, São Paulo has been increasingly involved in the globalized world economy and has become a predominantly services capital – a shift currently considered to be irreversible. As a result, it represents the link between the national and international economies, concentrating the headquarters of numerous national and multinational corporations, decision-making institutions, banks, as well as telecommunication and service firms. São Paulo's GDP and income distribution are comparable to those of Italy.

São Paulo's stock of office buildings has historically originated in the old city centre, particularly with the construction of the Martinelli building in 1929, the city's first skyscraper, a building which in fact triggered the city's verticalization process. For decades the old centre remained the city's financial nucleus, growing from the capital accumulated by the coffee industry and boosting São Paulo's industrial-ization and modernization. As its area became packed with high-rise buildings by the late 1950s and early 1960s, new developments started to move south, first to Paulista Avenue, on the highest topographical point of the city, afterwards to the Jardins region.

Still in the 1960s, service activities (such as information technology, advertising and consultancy) started to develop along Faria Lima Avenue, an avenue at the southern edge of the Jardins neighbourhood. As this region also became saturated with high-rise buildings by the late 1970s, other service sector nuclei were founded further towards the south – first in the Berrini region, including the Centro Empresarial complex and Berrini Avenue, where the World Trade Centre building would be constructed in the mid-1990s, and later on in the Marginal Pinheiros (also referred to as Nações Unidas) and Verbo Divino regions, the latter being the latest vertical occupation of the city. Profiting from Brazil's economic stabilization since the mid-1990s, these new regions saw an escalation in the number of commercial buildings and service sector establishments, a trend that took place alongside the growing specialization and digitization of the urban economy contrasting the downturn in industrial activities. Table 6.1 demonstrates this economic shift.[2]

Table 6.1   Changes in the distribution of establishments in São Paulo, 1986–1997

SECTORS	1986	1990	1994	1997
	(in percentage)			
Industrial/manufacturing	17.9	18.1	**16.2**	14.6
Commercial	32.7	33.2	**35.1**	36.2
Services	**35.5**	**35.6**	**38.9**	**44.7**
Others	13.9	13.1	**9.8**	4.5
Total	100.0	100.0	**100.0**	100.0

Source: Brazil Ministry of Labour, 2002

São Paulo's office-stock today totals more than 4000 square kilometres (CB Richard Ellis, 2002b) and is concentrated on two main regions – a 'centralized' one, including the old centre and the Paulista, Jardins and Faria Lima regions, and a 'decentralized' and expanding one, comprising the Marginal axis which links the old centre to the Verbo Divino region (see Figure 6.2). The old city centre, in this context, although still concentrating around 40 per cent of financial activities of the city and remaining an eminent financial hub, has been losing its importance due to a strong deterioration process, where an obsolete office-stock, unsafe and difficult to reach, has been further beset by a poor environmental quality. Paulista Avenue, in contrast, has in recent decades taken on the role of the city's (as well as of the country's) most influential

Figure 6.2   Distribution of São Paulo's office-stock

economic centre due to the high concentration of high-rise buildings mainly maintained by banks. But it is especially the southern business districts along the Marginal axis that have been drawing attention during the past years due to the speed at which they expand, requiring in turn massive adaptations in the urban infrastructure, particularly concerning the road network.

In this context, the city has become home to the main national and foreign business groups. Major national and international market research agencies, operating for decades in Brazil, are now based in São Paulo – including Nielsen, Ibope, Marplan and Gallup – and the twenty largest advertising agencies in the country have their head offices in São Paulo. São Paulo is also home to large international IT companies, the world's most important auditing firms, in addition to the country's largest publishing companies. Financially, the city is not only Mercosul's largest consumer market – concentrating ten per cent of South America's shopping malls and responsible for over one third of Brazil's purchasing power (having a consumption potential larger than Rio de Janeiro state, or that of the states of Paraná and Rio Grande do Sul together) – but also Brazil's economic core, where 16 out of the 20 largest multiple, commercial and savings banks in the country are headquartered, four of them being among the largest national business groups. São Paulo has also South America's largest stock exchange – Bovespa – and the world's fourth largest futures and commodities exchange – BM&F. In addition, it also maintains sophisticated and diversified health, education, culture, leisure and tourism service networks, comparable to those found in major metropolises of the developed world. It also has the highest number of executives and specialized labour available in the country as well as hospitals, best hotel chains, restaurants, in addition to Brazil's most important universities and research institutes. Geographically, São Paulo also benefits from being a mandatory route for any connection between the North, North-east, Centre-west and Southern states and other cities of the Mercosul.

It has two of the three main airports of Brazil in terms of number of passengers in addition to being a distribution logistics centre – located nearby the Tietê-Paraná waterway system (one of the largest of Brazil) and the port of Santos (Latin America's main exportation terminal and largest container port) – further benefiting from a high quality road and telecommunications network, exceptional by Brazilian standards.

It goes without saying that São Paulo's property market is a highly dynamic one, characterized as being a developer-oriented market where a wide range of local developers and a growing number of foreign ones participate.[3] Yet, most of the commercial developments are still carried out by local developers, too often using local architects, which mainly reproduce examples carried out in the USA responding to a market influenced by American culture. In terms of architecture, much value is given to the façade design and large open layouts, seeking the optimization of use of space, where new developments too often lead to an extremely dense land use as well as an indiscriminate demolition of existing buildings long before the end of their useful lives. Building designs are frequently elaborated from the outside to the inside, where the 'glass box' concept is highly praised, and where environmental performance issues are only marginally considered. In addition, being a car-oriented city, buildings offer an impressive rate of parking facilities (one parking space for every 30 square metres of rentable area) so as to respond to the commercial demand. In fact, a high rate of parking space is one of the most important prerequisites for the building to be labelled as grade A (top segment) in the city, so that commercially developed buildings which do not comply with this condition inevitably face market constraints.

This international orientation of São Paulo's stock of office buildings has of course been eradicating the local architectural tradition, while leading to a chaotic ensemble, where the imposition of global influences on the urban space make of São Paulo a prime example. This imposition constantly reaffirms São Paulo's condition as a developing country's global city, as the social divide between capitalists inside the buildings and a large third world crowd outside has grown impressively. This condition is also exacerbated by the vulnerable economic context in which São Paulo's property market operates, continuously exposed to economic fluctuations. While overrated after 1994, the period that brought about the dollarization of Brazil's economy, the market has significantly devalued since 1998 due to the economic downturn caused by the Asian crisis, coupled to a surplus in office space. Recently it has started to present a vacancy of around ten per cent, proving an increase of vacancy as compared to the 1990s, with a (decreasing) prime rental basis of 390 dollars m^2/year (CB Richard Ellis, 2002b).

As part of this condition, too, São Paulo's office buildings are located in an extremely polluted environment. As in any large city in a developing country, the city suffers from high levels of urban atmospheric pollution due to its large car fleet. Back in 1995, the fleet already consisted of 5.16 million vehicles – 3.3 million gasohol-fuelled light-duty vehicles, 1.5 million ethanol-fuelled light-duty vehicles, and 360,000 diesel-fuelled heavy-duty vehicles – a number that has grown approximately at five per cent annually (World Bank, 1997). This fleet is responsible for nearly all CO, HC, NOx, SO_2 and particulate matter emissions in the city, making urban atmospheric pollution one of São Paulo's environmental priorities. This is particularly so during the winter, when these gases are trapped in the atmosphere due to thermal inversion, reaching highly toxic concentration levels (Secretaria do Verde e do Meio Ambiente do Município de São Paulo, 1998). Indirectly, the fleet also brings about economic losses of more than six million dollars daily due to the city's intense traffic congestions. (These congestions are, in turn, giving rise to a large alternative helicopter fleet, currently estimated the second largest after Tokyo, also promoting another distinctive infrastructure feature of the city: the large number of helipads in office buildings.)

Ecologically, São Paulo's metropolitan area is surrounded by a green belt with a broad hydrological network, including the rivers Tietê, Tamanduateí and Pinheiros, and the Guarapiranga (27.2 square kilometres) and Billings reservoirs (37.9 square kilometres). Although constituting one of the city's most important ecosystems, serving energy generation purposes at the same time, this hydrological network has been seriously affected by untreated urban sewage and industrial wastewater emissions. Nowadays, the water that used to be pristine suffers from severe eutrophication (an algae bloom following a high increase in nutrient concentration in water), making water scarcity a recurrent environmental problem, which affects a significant share of the population with related diseases and periodic rationing. In terms of energy, the city is predominantly supplied by hydropower sources with an additional oil-fired thermoelectric plant, which is occasionally used to provide peaking or emergency power for water pumping. This network of hydropower supply is deemed to have caused a regional environmental impact, as the reversal of rivers towards the reservoirs has contributed to their pollution and degradation.

Moreover, as a 'global city', São Paulo is continuously undergoing a verticalization process coupled to an urban expansion trend, where more and more high-rise towers are being constructed as the city grows further, placing massive pressure on the existing infrastructure, such as the road network, water and energy distribution and sewerage, and also affecting the urban microclimate. As a result, São Paulo has increased urban runoff levels and serious flooding problems due to a diminished absorptive capacity of the soil and impermeability of the clay – following the high level of impermeabilization of the city with the excessive use of asphalt, concrete and constructions, among others, and decreased green areas – particularly during the summer when heavy rains occur. There are 400 areas identified within the city as being at risk from flooding, where around 75,000 people are periodically affected. This problem has become so serious in São Paulo that the local government has instituted an 'Urban Drainage Management Plan', with a budget of five billion Brazilian reais (1998 prices) to be spent over the next 30 years (Secretaria do Verde e do Meio Ambiente do Município de São Paulo, 1998).

In addition, the temperature differential between the centre and the periphery is five degrees Celsius, thus proving the existence of a heat island effect (EMPLASA, 2000), a phenomenon related to the excessive use of low-albedo surfaces (that is, surfaces with low reflective capacity) such as asphalt in addition to the decline in green areas. This puts a growing burden on the existing urban infrastructure resulting, among other factors, from a significant increase of the cooling demand of buildings, with increased energy consumption implications. As a result, São Paulo is increasingly threatened by an energy scarcity problem, parallel to the recurrent problem of water scarcity, and had to undergo a rationing programme in 2001. São Paulo also presents excessive levels of noise pollution, with over 80 per cent of its population continuously exposed to it; a significant part of which derives from the construction and demolition of buildings. Visual pollution stemming from the number of construction sites has also become another serious environmental problem in the city, and the areas surrounding construction sites also present an increased presence of ambient dust and street rubble levels. Finally, forestland has significantly decreased in São Paulo between 1930 and 1990. São Paulo has therefore low indexes of green land per capita, with no more than 4.5 square metres of green area per inhabitant – a figure that is continuously decreasing. Nowadays only about two per cent of the city's area is assigned for agricultural purposes.

The general regulatory framework governing the growth of São Paulo's office-stock has three main local governmental bodies responsible for urban planning and regulation. First, two municipal secretariats – Secretariat of Urban Planning (SEMPLA) and Secretariat of Housing (SEHAB) – lay down laws and norms (in turn to be approved by the municipal chamber), and issue building permits for commercial buildings above 250 square metres of area, as well as factories, hospitals and schools. Building permits for residential buildings and commercial buildings below 250 square metres of area are issued by the regional administrations of São Paulo (the city has around 20 in total).

Secondly, the Metropolitan Planning Company of Greater São Paulo (EMPLASA), an entity created in 1975 linked to the State Secretariat of Metropolitan Transports, coordinates policies in the three metropolitan regions of the state of São Paulo (São Paulo, Santos and Campinas), which altogether constitute the 'megalopolis' of São Paulo. Its objectives are to assist public and private entities in the decision-making processes by generating statistical and cartographical data, to provide technical assistance to the metropolitan municipalities and to serve the general population. It also develops projects concerning land use and occupation, urbanization and urban revitalization, master plans and socio-economic studies.

Despite being traditionally characterized by the lack of official urban planning, the city has, however, a complex set of instruments for the regulation and enforcement of urban construction activities. These govern the physical standards of buildings, through the São Paulo building code, last updated in 1992, and land use issues, above all through the city's zoning legislation, first introduced in 1972, and expected to be modernized in the coming years. Yet, their effectiveness is fairly ambiguous. According to urban planner Raquel Rolnik (1997) there seems to be a contradiction between the space composed within a meticulous urban legislative framework in São Paulo and infringement of the law where property development is concerned. Construction activities in São Paulo, partly owing to such extensive legislation, partly to corruption itself, are all too often circumvented.

Further to this contraposition, another trend that can be remarked in São Paulo is the 'institutionalization of law infringement', a practice that takes place following the local power structure, where economic interests too often prevail over the urban legislative framework. In certain cases, municipal agencies issue new laws to allow alterations in the city's existing construction and urban planning regulations. As an example, the recently passed Lei de Operação Urbana (Law of Urban Operation) legitimizes 'alterations' in the zoning code – such as the verticalization of new areas. These 'alterations' are negotiated with developers during the application of building permits that in principle would be irregular (for example, the application for a commercial building to be constructed in a residential area) implying the payment for the irregularity, implying in turn an amendment in the local regulatory framework. This fact of course further favours the speculative trait of São Paulo's property market, while reducing the possibility of preserving the city's environmental quality.

Local Environmental Management

To the same extent that São Paulo's zoning legislation and building code are comprehensive and complicated to follow, finding effective environmental management practices promoted by local public institutions targeting São Paulo's office-stock is also a hard task. Environmental policy in the city is determined by a wide range of actors – including the federal government, state authorities, municipal government agencies, private sector enterprises, non-governmental organizations, the communication media and informal sector enterprises – and is characterized by a problematic coordination, poor enforcement and frequent infractions, resulting largely from the extensive, complicated legislative framework that exists in the country.

At the national level, the main institutional body dealing with environmental issues is the Ministry for the Environment. At the state level, the main agencies are CETESB (the state agency for environmental protection), SABESP (the state company for drinking water supply and sewerage) and DAEE (the state department of water and electric energy). At the local level, the main institutions are the department for the environment (Secretaria Municipal do Verde e Meio Ambiente) and the metropolitan council with representatives of the state and the mayors of the municipalities that altogether constitute São Paulo metropolitan area (38 in total, including São Paulo city). In addition, there are also the above-mentioned EMPLASA, which conducts studies and has certain responsibilities for implementing environmental rules at the urban development level, the secretariats of planning and housing, which are responsible for issuing norms that may also have an environmental character geared to the building level, as well as the energy and water utilities Eletropaulo (acquired by American firm AES Corporation after its privatization) and SABESP, which are responsible for the implementation of rules set up at higher governmental levels.

Policy guidelines, basic laws (concerning, for instance, minimum emissions, environmental standards, licensing requirements for new projects, in addition to overall policies regarding energy and water efficiency), as well as budgetary decisions are generally controlled by the federal government; pollution control, water supply, sewerage and power supply are under state government control (with certain exceptions, such as with firms operating in the private utility market that follow federal regulations). The role of the municipality itself centres on solid waste management issues, noise pollution control, streets, parks and recreation, education, health care, intra-city public transport and cultural preservation. The legal instruments available for urban environmental management include legislation and regulation (for example, licensing), economic and fiscal measures (such as fines, pricing of resources and user charges), planning and direct investment (including water, pollution control, sewage, and so forth), in addition to a set of environmental standards and zoning legislations. The efficiency and effectiveness of such instruments, however, are too often regarded as limited owing to the fact that, as environmental protection and general environmental services are provided at different levels, inter-sectoral and inter-governmental coordination for environmental management is considered to be problematic in Brazilian cities. In many cases environmental responsibilities (including the deployment of policies, instruments and their enforcement procedures) are transferred from one governmental agency to another, resulting in the end in a poor overall environmental regime.

In terms of local environmental management of construction activities, São Paulo's office-stock is primarily influenced by the municipal legislative framework, comprising a building code and a zoning law, which have, however, a limited environmental content. The latter, for instance, includes environmental protection norms for certain areas of the city, such as environmentally or culturally sensitive neighbourhoods, which nevertheless frequently tend to be breached due to economic pressures. The former, the building code, includes some norms with an environmental character – particularly concerning (mandatory) levels of natural ventilation, lighting, water capacity, ratio of green area, and so forth – which are nevertheless considered not to go beyond what can be considered 'reasonable' in terms of environmental comfort, and therefore do not really promote an environmental upgrading of buildings.

Ironically enough, instead of a greening process, an opposite trend can be noticed in the city of São Paulo. In addition to the above-mentioned Lei de Operação Urbana, which by itself prompts the intensification of the environmental pressure of the city, the city's overall property market focuses too much on the marketability and construction efficiency of buildings from the investor's viewpoint (for example, capitalization over land values, gross-to-net ratios, occupation efficiency, and so on), so that little is achieved in terms of bioclimatic design approaches, which demand certain 'losses' of space, through, for instance, buffer zones, uneven shapes or use of vegetation. In this regard, and in order to attain an optimal occupation proportion, office spaces tend to be rather deep, requiring therefore more and more the use of artificial lighting and acclimatization with their energy consumption implications.

Moreover, traditional local bioclimatic solutions such as the *brise soleil* (sun-shading devices) and the use of concrete for the purpose of thermal mass, much celebrated during the 1960s' and 1970s' architecture, are nowadays considered to be practically non-marketable. This is due to the fact that these devices are claimed to be about three times as costly to acquire or are too troublesome to maintain as compared to a curtain wall. And curtain wall, in its turn, is too often used as an environmentally friendly material. In general, architects practising in the city claim that as this technology evolves, curtain walls are indeed becoming the best solution for external cladding, even in tropical climates like São Paulo, as they allow good luminance levels but prevent the penetration of solar rays, which would in turn heat up the indoor space. This is of course debatable if one takes into account the net energy balance consumed inside buildings applying the technology.

Finally, there are restricted incentives by the local governmental toward the implementation of energy or water efficient (office) buildings. In terms of energy efficiency, some proposals have been made during the past few years for the construction of self-sufficient buildings with the introduction of co-generation equipment. But with no governmental subsidies of any kind, however, some of them proved to be economically unfeasible, such as the Villa Lobos shopping mall, while others have managed to be carried out, for instance, the Plaza Iguatemi building, completed in 2002, in fact the most expensive office space currently available in the city. The same limitation of public incentives applies for water issues. Buildings that use underground water resources – and thereby contribute to reducing the over-burden of the mains grid – still have to pay the water company a fee for the use. The decentralization of wastewater treatment, in this respect, also receives few, though increasing incentives; but sometimes the contrary can also be seen, as biotech-nologies, for instance, in wastewater treatment systems are apparently forbidden.

Certain environmental management programmes are, however, being instigated from within local policy networks. These are promoting the beginnings of an ecological restructuring process of São Paulo's office-stock. To begin with, São Paulo's department for the environment, although not developing specific programmes directly targeting the environmental efficiency in office buildings, plays an important role in the city's overall preservation of green areas, indirectly affecting the activities of the building industry, eventually also influencing the way buildings use energy and water. Recently it has been seeking to promote a better management of both public and private green land, the latter through the rein-forcement of existing laws – such as the zoning legislation – or concession to fiscal benefits, and the former by maintaining quotas for the implantation of green areas. The department for the environment has also expanded the access of urban farmers to better technologies and trade structures, created a 'green incentive', benefiting sponsors of environmental education, research, documentation and preservation actions. It has also developed a report on Local Agenda 21, including a series of environmental ambitions, tackling the issues of water resources, solid waste, hazardous waste, pollution (air, noise and visual) and green areas, among others (Secretaria do Verde e do Meio Ambiente do Município de São Paulo, 1997). In addition, environmental impact assessments are now mandatory for constructions on sites within protected areas, stipulated by the zoning law, and mostly concern general environmental preservation (such as trees, natural topography and contami-nation of aquifers), but do not extend to water and energy efficiency in buildings. The projects, which aim to be located in environmentally sensitive areas, have first of all to comply with formalities of the department for the environment, before applying to SEHAB for a building permit.

In addition, São Paulo's energy company, AES (formerly Eletropaulo) has a pact with the Brazilian government determining that one per cent of the utility's net annual income has to be spent on energy conservation projects.[4] For the company, this represents around 50 million Brazilian reais (approximately 21 million dollars, 2001 prices), a volume that is distributed into two kinds of projects. The first are 'research and development' projects, consisting of different programmes such as the expansion of transmission lines' capacity and development of electric energy plants to be run on solid waste, among others. The second is termed PACDEE (Programa Anual de Combate ao Desperdício de Energia Elétrica – annual programme to combat electric energy wastage) involving projects to improve the efficiency of public lighting and of the energy supply chain, and projects related to the distribution of low energy lamps to low-income households, among others. The selection of programmes is decided by the population at large and eventually approved nationally. Besides these projects, the company has also started an environmental management system to ensure the continuous improvement of its operations.

But like the department for the environment, AES-Eletropaulo has at the moment limited specific programmes targeting energy efficiency in office buildings, despite the critical energy rationing programme instituted during 2001,[5] and neither energy advisory service is being offered so far. Despite the overall privatization process, consumers are still captive in the sense that they still rely on one single company within the municipality of São Paulo, to whom they directly pay their related bills, sometimes intermediated by facility managers. Yet, the utility initiated several informative campaigns to alert consumers as to how energy can be saved, also including the office building sector, indicating that energy waste in offices may reach up to 15 per cent of total consumption, leading to increased bills, infrastructure overload and compromising the efficiency of office equipment. It also called attention to the fact that, on average, air conditioning takes up around half of the total energy consumption of the office space in São Paulo, while lighting accounts for 24 per cent, pumps and elevators 13 per cent, and office equipment 15 per cent. But these information campaigns have so far not yielded substantial results from the consumers' side.

Accordingly, the energy rationing of 2001 mentioned above did not result in radical behaviour changes or significant, large-scale technological improvements. But it did, however, initiate an awareness-raising process among the overall population as early indications demonstrated that a voluntary reduction was having a surprising impact on the elimination of wastage, through for instance the replacement of incandescent bulbs by energy-saving ones (ABN AMRO, 2002). And it did also lead to an opposite direction, as many companies, office building complexes and other large facilities started to achieve the required reduction by turning to on-site generation equipment, usually powered by diesel, which not only consumes energy excessively but also contributes to urban pollution. As apparently no monitoring was done during the period in terms of avoiding such behaviour, new office buildings dedicate nowadays a significant space in the machinery rooms for the possibility of a future energy generator.

Finally, São Paulo's water network includes the companies CETESB (the state agency for environmental protection) and SABESP (the state company for drinking water supply and sewerage treatment, which is in fact among the largest sanitation companies of the world in terms of consumers served). While the former is responsible for the regulation, enforcement and monitoring of the raw water supply and treatment cycle, the latter deals with the distribution and treatment of commercial water, operating eight water production systems within the metropolitan area of São Paulo. Both companies are government-owned. Consumers, as within the energy network, are also considered to be captive.

In terms of environmental protection programmes, while CETESB has been seeking to better monitor the illegal occupation of areas near water sources so as to avoid their contamination[6] (Secretaria do Verde e do Meio Ambiente do Município de São Paulo, 1998), SABESP has been investing in the expansion of the collection and treatment systems, although both companies work in close cooperation. SABESP is also promoting the partial removal of pollutants through on-site installation in certain buildings, industries and public facilities. At the treatment stations, attempts are made to separate pollutants from the water before they are returned to the environment, where the treatment is conducted in two cycles, a solid and a liquid one. Today there are five stations in São Paulo metropolitan area, treating nearly 91 per cent of all wastewater volume (SABESP, 2002).

Regarding the water supply, SABESP has also been developing programmes to optimize the system. The first one is related to the reduction of water loss (given that around 22 per cent of the volume of water is lost through leaks and around 21 per cent through illegal consumption) through which it intends to control water losses throughout the supply chain. The second, the water reutilization programme, currently involves only the industrial sector through the encouragement of on-site secondary water quality treatment and reutilization. The third programme, concerning also office buildings, is the rational use of water (referred to as PURA – Programa de Uso Racional de Água). It has been initiated in collaboration with the IPT (Institute for Technological Research of the University of São Paulo), where a series of pilot-projects and action plans have been implemented in certain hospitals, public schools, industrial kitchens and commercial and residential buildings. Although this programme is still in its infancy, the objectives are to maximize the supply of water in São Paulo in view of the existing capacity, thereby reducing investments in the expansion of the capturing capacity of the water sources, the volume of water to be treated and the city's aggregate energy consumption. These objectives are to be achieved primarily through the elaboration of laws, regulations and norms towards the rational utilization of water in buildings, including, among others, the technological development of sanitary devices (and eventually their standardization in the building code), the implementation of modern monitoring techniques, as well as the intro-duction of educational programmes in the curricula of public schools (SABESP, 2002).

Global Environmental Management

Since its beginnings in the mid-20th century, São Paulo's office-stock has always had an international orientation. For this reason, several multinational companies are long established in the city, most being owners of their office spaces. More recently, however, the increase in interest rates in Brazil during the past decade has prompted companies to shift their investments from property markets into other kinds of funds, a fact that has induced them to be tenants, rather than owners, of their offices in São Paulo. In this sense, the spaces are commonly property of investors, including foreign investors, whose participation in the city has been growing substantially.

As the following accounts will demonstrate, as with the local environmental policy networks, the multinational companies analysed in this study seem to add little to the greening of São Paulo's transnational spaces. As owners, their involvement in the design phase of the building during which environmental inno-vations such as substitution of inadequate technologies and dematerialization may emanate, usually took place long ago, at a time when related policies were also more limited. As tenants, their contact with local public organizations is usually restricted to the utilities, to whom energy and water bills are paid. Yet, in view of the trend of outsourcing facility management services to external providers, such companies usually have limited contact with local urban and environmental planning agencies as well as utilities of energy and water. As will become clear, it seems that to the same extent that local environmental management in São Paulo is in general at an early stage, the environmental management strategies prompted by global corporations are also just beginning. For this reason, and as only limited environmental innovations can be detected, the following descriptions will provide an overview of how such innovations *are not* materializing in São Paulo's transnational spaces in view of this local-global interplay.

ING Group

ING first opened its branch in Brazil in São Paulo, in 1985, where it started to operate in the field of investments for corporate clients under the name of ING-Barings. At the time the bank consisted of 20 staff members, renting one office floor of a building located on Paulista Avenue. By 1991, it already had 100 staff members. Nowadays there are around 180 people working for ING in São Paulo, in addition to a small team at a representative office in Rio de Janeiro. ING's head office in São Paulo consists of three office floors (totalling 3750 square metres) in the HSBC Tower, a building previously named L'Arche building, located on Faria Lima Avenue.

ING's relocated its staff from Paulista Avenue into this building in 1991; the process was totally decided upon by local managers and intermediated by the property firm CB Richard Ellis. At that time, the bank pursued three main criteria in terms of property selection. First of all, large slabs were necessary to accommodate the staff in the maximum of three office floors. Secondly, the building should offer state-of-the-art technology and infrastructure, such as optic cables, separated telephone centres, raised floors for cabling, central air-conditioning system and security. The third criterion was that the building should be well located and transmit a strong image of modernity. Nothing was demanded in terms of environmental efficiency, neither stemming from local managers nor from global ones. ING moved into the L'Arche building in 1995.

The L'Arche building (see Figure 6.3), in turn, a building whose architecture has been much criticized, was originally commissioned by the CCF Group, an investment bank of French origin.[7] CCF aimed to bring its staff together in a single facility, which was to comply with the following criteria: large slabs, best installations for employees, updated equipment and an underground parking facility.[8] In this sense, this building was initiated with fairly high technological ambitions, where decisions were mostly made through online meetings (for the first time in Brazil). Being a French bank, the architectural design should also resemble its country of origin one way or another. The commission was given to Architect Julio Neves; the building was designed following the proportions of the French monument La Défense, using a large doorway portico and extensive curtain wall. As can be noted, environmental criteria were not pursued at this stage.

Another aspect that should be mentioned is that the L'Arche building was designed prior to the expansion of Faria Lima Avenue, at a time when the surrounding neighbourhood was occupied by small houses and shops, and at a time when the zoning legislation prohibited the construction of office buildings in this region. Nevertheless, approvals were granted, turning this building into one of the most speculative and marketable undertakings in São Paulo of the 1990s, the first to inaugurate on Faria Lima Avenue's expansion.[9] Nowadays, after the CCF has

Figure 6.3   ING headquarters, São Paulo

worldwide been taken over by Hong Kong Shanghai Banking Corporation (HSBC), the building has been renamed into HSBC Tower.

As for ING's decision-making process regarding this building, it is important to bear in mind the fact that the bank was on the occasion still NMB: a small, young bank internationally speaking. At the time, foreign branches had total freedom to select their premises, as well as the related architectural and techno-logical features, also including environmental issues. The bank's operational system has today become more centralized at the global level, that is to say, in the Netherlands. The Brazilian branch, in this respect, reports to ING Real Estate in New York, which is the head office of the Americas, which in its turn reports to ING in the Netherlands. According to ING's premises manager, no environ-mental issues are checked through such contacts, however.

In this context, ING's head office in Brazil implements only a limited environ-mental management framework so far, which is mostly related to the recycling of waste, such as paper (intermediated by an outside company that collects scrap paper in São Paulo for recycling) and bottles. Local managers claim that it is difficult to implement the same environmental ambitions as compared to the Dutch premises when it comes to property options in São Paulo – for example, those concerning energy, water and overall environmental efficiency – as the bank *rents* its properties in the city.[10] No specifications are required from the global headquarters; local managers apparently have neither a particular motivation (nor receive subsidies) in this regard. In addition, ING also has little contact with local utilities, except for the fact that it pays energy bills directly to Eletropaulo, while water bills are interme-diated by a facility manager Cushman Wakefield Samco, which does the facility management for the whole building. Again, contacts related to the environmental and urban planning agencies are practically non-existent, first because the company did not get involved in the design phase, during which contacts regarding approvals are established, and secondly as these contacts during operational phase are rather limited, except for cases of major refurbishments (which was not the case).

In turn, as energy and water efficiency were practically not considered throughout the design process, the building falls short in terms of passive environmental control and high-performance technologies or materials, although it has water-saving devices and a smart air-conditioning system, which had been decided upon during the construction phase as part of the building's specifications (standard to all floors).[11] During the energy rationing programme of 2001, ING's policy was to switch off certain lamps in the three office floors, to install a smart lighting system in lavatories (decision made by the local premises manager) and to initiate a behavioural campaign among staff, for example, by promoting the switching off of computers during lunch hours. ING also used energy from a diesel-powered generator three hours daily to supply energy for one of the floors. Since this was polluting equipment, producing a considerable amount of noise and odours, special filters were also installed so as to curb the generator's environmental impact. In this respect, the bank did not receive any instructions from Amsterdam in terms of how to proceed with the energy rationing. Decisions were all made locally, and the use of such equipment was also *not* monitored by local environmental planning agencies. With the exception of the smart lighting system installed in the lavatories, the other energy-saving strategies were discontinued after the end of the rationing programme.

Andersen

Andersen began operating in Brazil in the 1930s, first in the port of Santos and subsequently in São Paulo in the 1940s. At the end of the 1990s it merged with Coopers and Lybrand in the country. In 2002, it was taken over by the consultancy firm Deloitte Touche Tohmatsu. The account given in this section corresponds to Andersen's policies prior to 2002.

Beyond São Paulo, Andersen had a vast network of branches in Brazil, including Belo Horizonte, Curitiba, Rio de Janeiro, Porto Alegre and Salvador. It offered services in the fields of fiscal and financial auditing, as well as business consulting, among others. In the 1970s, Andersen's branch in São Paulo was located on Rebouças Avenue, in the Unibanco building, a rather small office at the time. Since the 1980s onwards, Andersen started to use two main buildings in the city. One of them – totalling 2500 square metres of office space – was located at the Centro Empresarial, where the company's administration, treasury, accountability and human resources departments were located, and where around 300 employees used to work. The other, considered to be the Brazilian head office of Andersen, was situated in the Verbo Divino business district, totalling 4500 square metres of office space, and accommodating around 800 staff members, including 51 out of the 75 senior associate members in Brazil.

As a matter of fact, Andersen's head office in São Paulo (see Figure 6.4) was rather commonplace in terms of architecture or building technologies. The construction, completed in 1986, was in reality commissioned by Fundação Previdenciária IBM (one of IBM's foundations), an institution which owned the building and rented it out to the consulting company ever since. The property company CB Richard Ellis acted as an intermediary between Andersen and the Foundation. With no architect in charge of the construction, the building was designed by the builders themselves, constructed by the firm Hochtief, and supervised by a technical advisor. The building was also constructed in the least expensive manner, providing only essential infrastructure such as a basic telecommunication system, air-conditioning equipment operating on

Figure 6.4   Andersen headquarters, São Paulo

water condensation and two water cisterns and fluorescent lighting on a circuit of 220 watts. It had neither a stabilizer for the IT department nor an energy generation equipment. Despite the aim of decreasing all construction and operational costs as much as possible, nothing was considered regarding energy or water efficiency issues, besides the regular standards set forth in the municipal building code.[12]

In 1998, the building underwent a refurbishment process, which mostly redefined its indoor structure, such as layout, furnishing and elements of decoration. Again, in terms of energy and water efficiency nothing was considered or mentioned besides the standards of the building code, although an energy generator powered by diesel (Mercedes engine) was installed in addition to two no-break stabilizers.[13] During the energy-rationing programme of 2001, Andersen's policy to reduce energy consumption was to use the energy generator from two to four hours daily, to be coupled with the switching off of certain lamps. All decisions regarding energy rationing were reached locally between the facility manager and main local associates of the company.

In this respect, and in terms of decision making, major changes regarding Andersen's head offices in Brazil were to be approved by the company's global headquarters, located in Chicago, through the property department, while minor ones could be decided locally. Budgetary issues, nevertheless, required approval by the global headquarters. Yet, the global headquarters apparently dictated little as far as Brazilian premises were concerned. No specifications about the architecture, facility management or anything similar (such as energy or water efficiency) of São Paulo's offices were given from Chicago, except for those relating to space use or occupation – such as size of rooms according to employee hierarchy – clearly indicating an overall aim to optimize the occupation efficiency, thereby saving costs on property space and, subsequently on issues regarding energy and water expenditures. In this sense, partly owing to this and partly to a lack of local initiatives, energy or water efficiency equipment had not been installed, despite the willingness of local facility managers to improve the energy and water performance of the building –

issues that were rejected time after time by the local management board in view of other priorities. Voluntarily, however, local facilities managers fulfilled an environmental management system that mostly involved the recycling of waste and indoor air quality control. These initiatives were clearly locally raised, as Andersen did not have an environmental policy whatsoever.

Interactions with local environmental, urban planning and utilities managers were in this sense limited. Andersen paid its energy and water bills directly to the related companies, Eletropaulo and SABESP, and as these did not have specific programmes regarding office buildings, no environmental innovations could be established through this interception. However, no contacts whatsoever ever took place between the company and the department for the environment or urban planning agencies, as Andersen was not directly involved with the design phase of the building and the related procedures for construction approvals, during which such contacts mostly take place. In addition, the use of the energy generator was also not checked or monitored by the responsible environmental agency (CETESB). In this sense, as local environmental management programmes launched by São Paulo's public agencies are fairly limited as far as office buildings are concerned, and as Andersen itself, as a multinational company, did not contribute towards improving the building's energy and water performance, this building does not present any environmental innovation.

Yet, before the company's dissipation, the central headquarters in Chicago had apparently planned to standardize the premises Andersen maintained worldwide in terms of architecture and building technology. The standardization would take place through Chicago's property department and would start to be implemented in 2002, in a process to last about three years. The overall aim would be to homogenize office layout, visual communication, and so on, but also efficiency issues, such as those related to the applied technologies (such as lighting, water-related devices, air conditioning and heating systems, where applicable). The main ambition would be economic, according to a senior associate member, with however an environmental preservation inspiration.

ABN AMRO

ABN AMRO consolidated its presence in Brazil with the acquisition in 1998 of Banco Real, a bank of Brazilian origin operating in the country for more than 80 years. Although ABN AMRO had already been in Brazil for some years by then, its activities in the Brazilian market underwent a substantial transformation after the acquisition. Initially, the bank started to operate in several segments and through a network of companies – including ABN AMRO Bank, Banco Real, Bandepe and Real Seguros – an administrative system that was in turn restructured in January 2001. From this date onwards, ABN AMRO's management started to operate on a globally defined basis, including three main business lines of services: wholesale clients, consumer and commercial clients, and private clients and asset management (ABN AMRO 2000a, 2001). Despite this global homogenization, however, and following local market influences, ABN AMRO has in fact become a 'hybrid' in Brazil. It explores the image, visual marketing appeals, as well as the name of the former Banco Real when it comes to private, retail clients – such as through the

**Figure 6.5   ABN AMRO headquarters,
São Paulo**

bank's retail shops and related marketing campaigns – while appealing to the international experience of the Dutch institution regarding wholesale clients and large-scale investments.

Before the acquisition, ABN AMRO held a representative office in São Paulo, which was located in the Verbo Divino region, in which around 200 employees worked. As the acquisition involved all of Banco Real's assets, ABN AMRO became consecutively owner, in terms of property, of not only around 3900 retail shops in the country but also of the former Banco Real headquarters on Paulista Avenue (see Figure 6.5), a building where around 4000 staff members nowadays work. This building, in this respect, had been commissioned by Banco Real in the 1980s, constructed by JHS Construção e Planejamento Ltda., and designed by a local architect. Following Banco Real's visual marketing approaches, the building's architecture makes use of a series of slim arches clad by curtain wall, employing sober materials and colours such as beige and brown (such design features are in fact Banco Real's visual symbol, trying to convey an image of seriousness and tradition). Energy or water efficiency do not exceed the standards put forward by the local building code at that occasion.

After the acquisition, ABN AMRO's new Brazilian headquarters in São Paulo went through a refurbishment process. Following prescriptions of Dutch managers from the world headquarters in Amsterdam, this refurbishment took place mostly at decoration level, including the replacement of furniture, carpeting and internal cladding, by other materials that would yield an image closer to the one the bank pursues in the Netherlands. It also improved the air conditioning equipment, as well as the building's security and fire protection systems. As can be noted, nothing was considered in terms of improving the building's energy or water efficiency, environmental performance or anything alike, and no specifications in this regard were either put forward by Dutch managers from the Netherlands or raised by those based in Brazil. Respectively, nothing was demanded from the local policy or economic networks (such as energy or water utilities or the planning department) to improve the building's efficiency.

In fact, environmental management carried out in São Paulo's premises – including the headquarters – do not go much beyond a somewhat commonplace environmental management routine, which mostly covers basic environmental topics such as waste recycling and basic indoor air quality issues. This is probably due to the fact that there is no interest on the part of world headquarters to pursue such ambitions abroad,[14] but also partly due to the fact that local managers are apparently also not much concerned with such question in Brazil. The building is administered by the facility management firm Cushman Wakefield Samco, which, besides carrying out environmental management issues, is also the intermediary between the bank and energy and water utilities for the payment of bills.

During the energy rationing programme of 2001, ABN AMRO also did not go beyond conventional measurements to improve the energy performance of its premises in São Paulo, and only initiated a campaign through which unnecessary lamps were switched off, elevators were more efficiently used (two of them were kept in disuse) and air conditioning systems were kept at 25 degrees Celsius during the summer months despite external conditions. (Unlike the other two companies above described, ABN AMRO did not use a generator powered by fossil fuels to achieve the required energy saving standard). The head office also had the lighting system switched off during the night (it used to be continuously lit), which by itself allowed the bank to achieve the mandatory reduction of 20 per cent as stipulated by law. Here no specifications or instructions were given by the Dutch headquarters. The campaign was discontinued after the end of the rationing.

According to a local director, decisions concerning ABN AMRO's Brazilian branch, including environment-related ones, are, in principle, exclusively made by Dutch managers from the Amsterdam's head office. Exceptions are made to minor refurbishments or small-scale projects. Budgetary issues are also to be approved by the Dutch head office. However, if Brazilian branches should wish to improve their environmental performance, the initiatives are to be raised by local managers, and the budget to be approved by the Dutch ones. One of the criteria for such approval is that, in terms of energy management, investments should amortize within two years. Contradicting the bank's policy in the Netherlands, which states that energy-related internal projects can amortize within five years (cf. chapter 5), ABN AMRO clearly serves as an example of the environmental management divergences that a multinational company may have worldwide.

IBM

IBM established a representative office in Brazil in the early twentieth century, operating first under the name Computing Tabulating Recording Company and subsequently under IBM since the 1920s onwards. By the 1930s IBM inaugurated one factory in the state of Rio de Janeiro – Benfica, in fact the first production unit IBM ever opened in South America – followed by another one in the state of São Paulo in the ensuing decades, in Sumaré.

Nowadays, IBM comprises two main groups in Brazil – Personal System Group and IBM Global Services – through which it offers practically the full line of products of the multinational company. It develops, in addition, products for the banking sector in the country, such as those related to information and communication technologies.

Figure 6.6   IBM headquarters, São Paulo

In terms of property, and besides the two above-mentioned production units, IBM also owns several retail shops in the country's main cities and three main buildings, in Rio de Janeiro, Hortolândia and São Paulo, the latter being the company's head-quarters in Brazil (see Figure 6.6). This building, located on 23 de Maio Avenue, was designed in the 1970s by the architectural firm Croce, Aflalo e Gasperini. It is considered to be one of São Paulo's main architectural land-marks, totalling 26,400 square metres and accommodating around 2000 employees, about 42 per cent of IBM total staff in Brazil (IBM, 2000).

At an early stage, decisions regarding the construction of IBM's headquarters in Brazil were partly made by the construction company of the occasion, and partly by an American IBM staff, the project director, who accom-panied the whole construction process of IBM's Brazilian headquarters.[15] In this regard, while the construction company decided location issues, the American IBM staff indicated prerequisites for the building's design, among which was a large base to be used for specific services and equipment on the ground level.

According to the architect in charge, what was particularly discussed during the design phase between the IBM staff and local contractors (urban planning and envi-ronmental agencies, as well as utilities did not participate in such decisions) regarded mostly the placing of circulation elements, such as elevators and staircases, as well as issues concerning the air-conditioning system, which was later on defined as a single system located on the ground floor with peripheral shafts and ducts instead of several systems serving the floors. Options regarding the building envelope were also extensively discussed and the choice was eventually made for predominant use of fixed windows (glasses with a refraction coefficient of 30–33 per cent). No suspended floors were applied on the occasion, as this technique was not yet available. For the cladding, simple concrete was extensively used, whose quality would later on prove to be rather low; a fact that is claimed to have resulted from the shift of construction companies in the building course. In this regard, several other finishing problems were also detected over the years. The envelope, for instance, presented serious problems of infiltration, especially on the ground floor base. As a consequence, the building underwent two important refurbishments and is still constantly being upgraded.

Issues of energy and water efficiency, as understood today, were not considered during the design and construction phases, although options favoured the selection of best performance equipment available on the occasion. Feasibility studies were also carried out for the installation of an underground natural ventilation system, which was in the end not implemented. Eventually, a full acclimatization system was opted for, requiring the building envelope to be hermetically sealed with the exception of a few openable windows placed strategically for the external cladding's maintenance. As a result, the building is intensive not only in terms of air-conditioning use but also in terms of artificial lighting, given that floor plans are rather deep. All decisions were made between the IBM staff and local contractors; contacts with local planning agencies were only held for the approval procedures. In this regard, no specific environmental issues were required by planning or environmental agencies, and none stemming from the energy and water utilities on that occasion.

IBM headquarters consumes 8000 cubic metres of water monthly from underground resources – enough to supply 500 houses – and 850 MW of electricity, equivalent to the supply of a 17,000-inhabitant town (Infra, 2001). Concepts of energy and water efficiency are apparently emerging in the building, however, although still mainly related to the updating of the obsolete technology of the 1970s building. In 1996, IBM initiated studies which led to the implementation of energy- and water-saving programmes including the updating of technologies – such as lighting, IT equipment, sanitary devices and air conditioning – towards their rationalization, as well as occupancy densification. In this respect, retrofitted fluorescent lamps were applied to enhance the lighting potential per light unit, using the same energy load. In terms of water use, taps with controlled flow and digital sensors for certain sanitary devices have been installed. All of this has been initiated and coordinated by the local facility management department and monitored by IBM's department for Real Estate & Site Operations located in the USA, although paid for through local budgets.

During the 2001 energy rationing, IBM complied with the 20 per cent consumption reduction by switching off certain bulbs as well as the external lighting and by decreasing the functioning hours of building, of its cafeteria, as well as of its air-conditioning system (the latter normally operated 24 hours daily). Unlike ING or Andersen, however, and like ABN AMRO, IBM did not switch on the building's energy generation equipment. After the rationing programme, some of these strategies continued to be applied; for example, the reduction in the opening hours of the cafeteria, the reduction of the opening hours of the building and the external lighting are only be turned on from 19:30 until 21:00 (whereas prior to the energy-rationing phase it used to remain on throughout the night).

An interesting point raised by a facility manager was that since the beginning of the energy-rationing programme, the concern for water efficiency was also reinforced. Water consumption started to be monitored daily since the beginning of the energy-rationing programme, leading to the detection and repair of several abnormalities, such as leaks in the water supply system. This resulted in a decrease in water consumption of about 25 per cent. Water consumption in the building has been monitored on a daily basis ever since.

In terms of decision-making processes, worldwide standardization of technological features, and so forth, IBM has a global environmental policy that applies to all its premises worldwide. According to local facility managers, nothing is really standardized in terms of energy and water technology or efficiency per se, although the company stipulates technologies to be selected from the most restrictive policy, either the company's internal one drafted in the global environmental policy guidelines, or the local ones, that is, the local legislative framework.[16] The company also determines in the global environmental policy that all IBM's properties need to reduce their consumption of energy and water by four and one per cent per annum respectively. Although little attention is given as to *how* local facility managers will achieve such targets, they are checked monthly by IBM's department of Real Estate & Site Operations, located in the USA, which allocates no special budgets for this purpose, however. In this regard, the driving force for saving energy and water is economic, that is, to achieve financial savings on energy and water bills, rather than ecological, which is to say, to protect the environment.

Besides these programmes, IBM's facility management department has a subdivision dealing with the environment. This subdivision takes care of the monitoring of indoor air quality, by checking the air-conditioning system every six months (which is in fact mandatory according to the Brazilian legislation), as well as the water quality, by controlling the water quality of the underground aquifer. It also implies waste control and recycling as well as the control of light chemical products, such as those used in cleaning the building. The facility management department is therefore the intermediary between the global company and local planning and environmental agencies and utilities. Direct contacts, however, are mainly held with utilities, as the department is also responsible for the payment of energy and water bills, although no specific energy- or water-saving innovations are introduced in view of this interaction.

Finally, although IBM's headquarters in São Paulo has nowadays a fairly high degree of autonomy to maintain the building, limited to this framework however, budgetary issues are strictly controlled by the global headquarters in the USA. Local environmental innovations taking place in São Paulo, limited as they may seem, can be considered to be located somewhere between local ambitions and concerns set forth at a transnational level.

Conclusions

The aim of this chapter was to assess how the environmental restructuring of São Paulo's office-stock is taking place at the interface between management practices advanced by local agencies and utilities and global companies. First we outlined the main characteristics of the place and then described the spaces of environmental management, the local and the global.

As the case studies demonstrate, ING, ABN AMRO, Andersen and IBM seem to implement limited environmental innovations in their offices. No particular dematerialization or substitution of unsustainable technologies or advanced monitoring systems (with the exception of IBM to a certain extent) are detected in their buildings. This may primarily be explained as these companies mainly have no direct involvement with decisions made during the design phase (reducing possibilities for the dematerialization or substitution of technologies). Secondly, there are no specifications set at global headquarter level – with the exception of IBM – concerning the environmental performance of the offices in São Paulo in their operational phase, so that possible refurbishing mostly regards decoration features, not dematerialization or substitution of technologies, or the introduction of advanced monitoring systems. Thirdly, the four companies investigated seem to have little contact with local organizations that may potentially influence on their environmental performance – such as the environmental department and the utilities. In this sense, most environmental management systems pursued by the companies of this research are initiated locally, voluntarily and are self-financed, and are therefore rather limited. Their main discourse is thereby based on 'common sense', except for IBM which fulfils a global environmental management regime extending to the energy and water performance of its premises, in its turn following an economic – rather than ecological – motivation.

Conversely, environmental management practices promoted by local organizations such as urban planning and environmental departments, energy and water utilities, seem to be slowly emerging in São Paulo. The water company introduced a programme aiming to demonstrate how water use in diverse kinds of facilities may be practised more rationally, while the energy company, after privatization, has a R&D budget to be allocated for energy efficiency projects, which may be applicable to office buildings. In this sense, although no monetarization of resource use could be detected so far, these programmes seem to suggest only an 'intention' of dematerialization or substitution of technologies, probably initiated for better managing (limited) resources in view of a growing number of consumers. However, at the moment there seems to be a mismatch between such intentions and the environmental dimension of the offices of multinationals, as the former are too incipient, not to say insignificant, to influence the latter. The environmental department, for instance, still carries out environmental management according to the Local Agenda 21 paradigm, that is, in principle encouraging better management of green areas, solid waste, pollution, and so on, but in reality achieving rather little. Its main instrument to influence the environmental aspect of office buildings is the requirement of environmental impact assessments for buildings to be constructed in environmentally sensitive areas; other command and control instruments such as the local building code and master plans do not go beyond 'reasonable' standards concerning energy and water efficiency. Apparently there are no covenants regarding environmental topics being applied in the city. In most cases the department for the environment *does not* interfere in the daily building practices in São Paulo.

On the other hand, however, local agencies are also not hindering the implementation of environmental innovations: Bank Boston, for instance, has recently completed the construction of its headquarters in the city following the American green building LEED principles, which puts forward a series of environmentally sound recommendations (cf. chapter 3). Decisions have been made at the bank's global headquarters level; locally, the bank is now promoting itself through the media as an institution caring for the well-being of the city. Apparently approvals for the construction, also regarding the electrical and hydraulic projects, were easily obtained, despite their innovative environmental dimensions. Another example is the Rochaverá Plaza, an office complex initiated and to be constructed by the developers Tishman Speyer Properties, working jointly with the local construction company

Método. This building is bringing in the technology utilized by the developers in the Sony Centre and the Messe Turm, located in Berlin and Frankfurt respectively. Although designed by local architects,[17] the Rochaverá is applying in São Paulo the German legislative framework for key environmental issues – that is, relating to natural ventilation, lighting, reutilization of water, high-performance technologies, and so forth – without facing impediments from local planning and environmental agencies or utilities. When completed in the coming years, it will add about 120,000 square metres of green office space to the city.

These two examples seem to provide evidence that certain global economic actors may instigate or induce the ecological restructuring of São Paulo's transnational spaces. In coming years these two buildings may serve as benchmarks of environmental management and performance – in terms of technology as well as legislation – for other commercial buildings and local planning agencies to follow and adopt. If this proves indeed to be the case, environmental innovations stemming from the global sphere may catalyse a new market dynamics in the city towards a self-regulatory paradigm, a paradigm in which the market starts carrying out environmental change fairly autonomously. In this case, globalization will also be serving to do good in the local environmental sphere as is already the case with these two examples. But for this to work it seems correct to suggest that local public agencies will need in the short term to refine their political approaches so as to channel on a large scale such innovations stemming from the global space into the local environment. As will be explained in more detail in chapter 8, this requires a combination of suitable incentives and constraining regulations in order to foster this environmental leapfrog and make globalization and urban environmental reforms two interrelated movements.

Notes

1   Greater São Paulo is the term used to designate the city jointly with its amalgamated municipalities.
2   Table 6.1 shows that a shift in the establishment distribution has intensified particularly since 1994, the year that saw Brazil's economic stabilization with the introduction of the Plano Real and the dollarization of the national currency. While favouring overall commercial activities – and being positively reflected in other sectors of the urban economy – the economic stabilization coincided with the period during which the municipality of São Paulo was administered by the progressive party, which profited from the economic upturn to attract large fluxes of investments (from both national and international origins) into the city's services sector, as well as in its property market, boosting a large number of new office building developments (EMPLASA, 2000). And it was precisely in this context that São Paulo managed to secure its role as an emerging global city, the most prominent in the Southern Cone, offering a wide range of services related to hyper-mobility of information: that is, planning, advertising, marketing, legal, insurance, financial and consultancy, among others.
3   Tishman Speyer Properties (USA) was in this regard the first to establish offices in the city in a joint venture with a local construction company – Método – followed by Turner, Hines, AIG Lincoln (USA), Hochtief (Germany) and Dumez (France). Other recent joint ventures include Brazil Realty – a merger between IRSA of Argentina (in which George Soros has a 28 per cent stake) and Cyrella, currently one of the biggest developers of the

city – and Grupo Multiplan, another major local developer that is now joint with Goldman Sachs (World Architecture, 1997). The participation of foreign design firms has been justified by the so-called 'Brazil cost': the cost of an onerous legal structure, coupled to high interest rates, and heavily levied employees (World Architecture, 1997) – putting local designers at a disadvantage and further propitiating the 'Americanization' of the local architecture. American architectural firms such as RKTL and SOM not only practise widely but have even set up representative offices in the city due to the large number of commissions they have been receiving. These foreign firms generally claim that local developers, having become much more sophisticated with globalization, no longer need to hire Brazilian architects to reproduce American buildings. They also allege that local architects have a certain 'arrogant disdain for clients' which prevents them from responding to market needs; a criticism in reality directed at traditional local architects in the pursuit of local solutions like large concrete slabs (for example, the Museum of Modern Art building), solutions by and large fostered during previous decades. But to build in the city they are required to work in cooperation with local architectural firms, not only to comply with the local legislation (as this is decreed in the Brazilian legislation), but also to obtain necessary expertise to *tropicalize* their proposals, that is, embed their proposals into the local network of suppliers, contractors, approval processes, and so on.

4   This pact, which has apparently been successfully implemented, was a resolution of ANEEL – the national electric energy agency, created during the privatization of Brazil's energy sector to control the activities and operations of firms in order to ensure national interests *vis-à-vis* private ones. It applies to all concessionaires and agents of the energy sector. ANEEL also determined how this budget should be spent – that is, including R&D programmes as well as programmes related to the prevention against energy waste – and is responsible for the monitoring of such programmes.

5   The rationing programme was instituted after a severe drought during the years of 2000 and 2001, the worst in 40 years, which decreased the water capacity of the hydroelectric system. In the city of São Paulo, it compelled consumers to decrease their energy consumption in the order of 20 per cent per consuming unit (for example, a household), as compared to the average consumption figure achieved during the period May–June of 2000, during the period June–December 2001.

6   One of the main water supply problems the city faces is the contamination of water resources particularly by illegal domestic sewage, which renders the overall water quality unreliable. While water supply reaches nearly all the population, wastewater treatment in São Paulo has always been problematic. Back in the early 1990s, for instance, only 70 per cent of residents were connected to the sewer system, and only around 40 per cent of the collected sewage received any treatment (SABESP, 1990). The city only possessed two biological secondary plants in addition to a mechanical primary one and five smaller wastewater treatment plants at the time to process a volume of 621 000m^3 per day.

But with the contamination of water sources and limited availability of underground resources, drinking water has to be brought from river basins increasingly distant from the metropolitan area, such as the Piracicaba river basin through the Cantareira system, and treatment costs at the Guarapiranga reservoir have significantly increased (Philippi, 1990). Water scarcity has thereby become a problem of periodical significance, particularly in dry seasons, when the water levels at the reservoirs are lower. According to the Secretariat of Hydro Resources and Works, the capacity of the Alto Tietê basin, which includes the São Paulo metropolitan area, is 201 m^3/capita/year, a figure one tenth of the indicated value set by the United Nations for all direct and indirect uses. In addition, there are still several waste-related problems such as irrigation without technical criteria and the unsuitable use of industrial, domestic, or public water, causing losses in the supply chain and frequent interruptions in the supply (SABESP, 2002).

7   In fact, ING was approached by the CCF prior to the construction to join the investment, although it turned down the proposal.
8   According to local facility managers, no environmental criteria were raised by CCF.
9   While the commission was given in 1991, approval for the avenue's expansion was only given in 1995. The building's original design is claimed to have gone for the approval process at SEHAB with a 'fake' side entrance, towards a narrow side street, whereby the main one with the portico was hidden.
10 The reason why the bank rents out properties in Brazil is that interest rates in the country are high, therefore investments in properties are not financially favourable.
11 This air-conditioning system switches on automatically when human presence is detected.
12 The air-conditioning system, still in use by 2001, was claimed to be extremely energy-intensive, consuming 80,000 kWh per month, functioning eight hours per day.
13 The construction company was Re-light. According to the facility managers, the aim was again to conduct a low-cost refurbishment in the short term, to the detriment of the building's maintenance efficiency and cost in the long term. This was due to the fact that Fundação Previdenciária IBM, the building's owner, did not intend to further invest in the building, so that major technologies, that were not replaced in the course of the years, became increasingly obsolete. Andersen altered the building's internal layout on a yearly basis, however.
14 Note the inconsistency with ABN AMRO's global office building in Amsterdam.
15 According to the architect in charge, the initial construction company went bankrupt so that the building had to be completed by another contractor.
16 Due to the restrictive character of IBM's global environmental policy, some regional differences are commonly detected. In fact, only carpeting and furnishing are done by the same companies worldwide (Miliken and Global Mobilinea, respectively).
17 This building was designed by Aflalo e Gasperini, the same designers of IBM in the 1970s.

Chapter 7

Beijing

Figure 7.1   Chaoyang district

In 1986, the Chinese government instituted the Land Administration Act commodifying and internationalizing the right of land use in urban China. As a result, profit-oriented property companies have been created in Chinese cities with a mandate to develop commercial estates, rapidly converting the closed communist capital into a metropolis of the globalized economy. While this process has enhanced the local economy, it has also rendered Beijing susceptible to property speculations, resulting not only in physical growth but also in pressures on the urban environment. Although it ranked among the most liveable cities of the world in the pre-communist era, Beijing is among the top ten most polluted today, suffering from decreasing green areas, heat island effect, vehicular atmospheric pollution, water scarcity and, not least, energy inefficiency.

The aim of this chapter is to analyse how Beijing's stock of office buildings is being environmentally managed, by looking at programmes and strategies advanced by local utilities and environmental policy agencies, as well as by global companies occupying office spaces. While the modernization rush after the introduction of economic opening policies has greatly added to the rise of environmental challenges, it has, as will be demonstrated, also contributed to the modernization of the building industry and the introduction of certain environmental management practices. To some extent, Beijing can be considered to be a city enjoying a privileged position due to its strong governance, with environmental protection among the highest priorities.

The Urban Setting

Beijing's historical antecedents date back to around 3000 years ago, but its political importance was mainly established in the thirteenth century, when the Mongol dynasty set up its political base there. Since then, Beijing has developed according to Chinese ancient urban planning standards along a north-south axis, consisting of an external city (with aristocratic settlements), an imperial city (enclosing the most important state bureaus as well as noble settlements) and the imperial palace. It remained the northern capital of the Chinese empire since the fifteenth century.

Since 1949, Beijing attempted to gain a new image, whereby urban planning and architectural styles were directly influenced by early Soviet models. Major efforts were made to give traces of imperial power or symbolism of places and monuments a new function – which was to serve the communist regime (Jianfei Zhu, 1999). The overall focus was on fostering intensive industrialization – rather than urbanization – replacing consumption by production; a transformation that nevertheless resulted in environmental pollution.

The open-door policies and reform initiated by Deng Xiaoping in the late 1970s and early 1980s – with the introduction of market mechanisms and the opening of the country to foreign investment – ushered in a new phase in the city's urban setting, reorganizing its economic regime. These policies included alterations in urban land use, finance and investment structures, which started to include more flexible policies of loaning and capital pooling, attracting foreign investments, among others, into the urban property sector. The property industry grew rapidly, soon becoming the city's leading economic sector (Dianchun Jiang *et al.*, 1998). The result was an ever-accelerating proliferation of local urban developments and property investments taking place in the city in a modernization process without precedents in its history.

As a result, international business enterprises and foreign residents started to thrive in Beijing, also drawn by its status as China's capital enjoying a better urban quality as compared to other Chinese cities.[1] Beijing has thus emerged as a global city which, although in political competition with Shanghai, is no longer only characterized as China's political and cultural centre (carrying out the administrative work for nearly 1.2 billion people) but also as the country's expanding international financial, educational and services capital (Gu and Kesteloot, 2001; Hu Zhaoliang, 1991). In this view, starting in the late 1980s Beijing has been seeing a growth in the concentration of banking, trading and all types of corporate activities in the city, while becoming the headquarters of the main financial, insurance, trade, telecommunication and information organizations present in China[2] (Ke Huanzhang, 1997; Hu Zhaoliang, 1991).

Consequently, in response to the sudden increase in demand for office space starting after the economic reform, Beijing has seen massive urban renewal and old inner-city redevelopment projects, where property investments in the city on average amount to about half of total investments made in the city nowadays (Dianchun Jiang *et al.*, 1998). Another expansion in the property market has been recently triggered after the city received the International Olympic Committee vote in September 2001 to host the 2008 Olympic Games. Hundreds of large construction sites have been opened to bring the 3000-year-old city to a new level of development, implying too often the demolition of traditional settlements and the relocation of their inhabitants.[3] A remarkable 22 billion dollar budget is to be spent on further urban development and reconstruction projects in the coming years – comprising 127 large urban infrastructure works, including the extension of the road, subway and railway flows (Meyer, 2002). Despite the obvious environmental pressures, however, to which we will return later in this chapter, the municipality of Beijing has also stated its intention to convert the city into an ecological one, promoting itself internationally under the logo 'Beijing 2008: Green Olympics'. From the above budget, 12 billion dollars alone are to be spent in projects to clean up the city (Rosario, 2001).

It goes without saying that the Chinese capital historically lacked a central business district. Most of the administrative, financial and business buildings were scattered in areas outside the Second Ring Road, which delimits the old city (Gu and Kesteloot, 2001). With the economic opening, the pressure for more concentrated office, commercial and service zones so as to develop the city into a strong international metropolis led to the modernization of the historical inner city area and the establishment of business districts.[4]

A large part of Beijing's office-stock is therefore rather newly constituted, dating from China's economic opening. This expansion was brought about through a series of municipal development plans, proposing the rehabilitation of the three pre-1949 main central business districts (Wangfujing, Qianmen and Xidan) into new commercial centres, as well as instituting five primary and 30 secondary additional commercial and retail centres including office towers, hotels and other commercial services, scattered regularly throughout the city. In addition, three interrelated development zones were created in the city with distinct functions: the Haidian Special Zone (designated for research and development in high-technology fields), the Shangdi Information Industry Base (IT companies) and the Fengtai Industrial Park.

According to the property company Jones Lang LaSalle (2002a), Beijing's office property (grade A, that is, top segment) is currently blooming in five main locations. The Beijing Central Business District (CBD), the most developed area of Beijing, is a 4Km² section of Chaoyang district with its core at the intersection of Jianguomenwai Avenue and the Third Ring Road. The East Changan Area, situated in central Beijing's Dongcheng with the CBD and Finance Street Area in close proximity, is serviced by several five-star hotels and grade A office buildings. The Third Embassy Area is home not only to several foreign embassies but also to numerous grade A office buildings, privileged also by green areas and comfortable surroundings. The Airport Area, traditionally benefiting from its proximity to the airport expressway, is generally popular among European companies. Finally, the Zhongguancun area, located in Beijing's northwestern Haidian district, has recently become the focus of local high-tech companies, incorporating the Zhongguancun Science, Software Parks and a potentially rich supply of labour from the many nearby universities and research institutes, although the concentration of grade A office buildings still lags behind Beijing's other submarkets (see Figure 7.2).

In total, Beijing's top segment office space currently amounts to about three million square metres, predominantly located in the eastern parts of the city, although standards in Zhongguancun are improving in view of recent and forthcoming completions (Ibid.). Since 2001, office property in Beijing has started to present an increase in vacancy levels with the completion of new supply, where the

Figure 7.2   Distribution of Beijing's office-stock

total grade A office-stock is currently estimated to be vacant at 16.3 per cent (2002 figures). Rentals, in this context, are continuously declining, particularly in the Third Embassy Area, attributable to emerging competitive rents on offer in newer buildings and the softening of some landlords previously attempting to maintain rental levels high (Ibid.). However, China's entry to the World Trade Organization has brought about an economic improvement for the sector since the beginning of 2002, as large financial and insurance corporations stepped up their search for quality office space in the city (CB Richard Ellis, 2002c). The office property market is expected to grow in the coming years.

Beijing seems to be a kind of laboratory of postmodernism in terms of building design. Yet, as China experiences an urban modernization leap of great magnitude in today's world, its architectural products still lack a clear theoretical definition or conceptual framework. On the surface, they appear to be hybrids between foreign technological approaches and national pride, evoking traditional architectural solutions in the conception of modern-looking ensembles. Upon closer examination, however, they seem to be an historical repetition of the period which followed the fall of imperial China (after 1912), appearing thereby to be something like a new learning or cultural process taking place after the country's economic opening and reform.

Post-imperial Chinese architecture had been greatly influenced by the western Beaux-Arts design approach, introduced by American scholars through teaching programmes and design practices in the 1920s and 1930s, producing combinations of traditional elements – especially the Chinese roof profile and some decorative motifs – with modern building types and construction methods (Jianfei Zhu, 1999). Although this movement has persisted throughout the twentieth century, despite the new forms and technologies, it possessed an overall socialist realist trait under Mao Zedong's regime until the economic reform of 1978. During this period, architecture in China was largely proletarianized, following aims that were much more techno-cratic than cultural (Kögel and Meyer, 2000). A return to post-imperial China's architectural practices is currently taking place with the 'commercialization of cultural icons and symbols', coinciding in historical terms with the consolidation of postmodern architecture in the west (Jianfei Zhu, 1999). This period is referred to as the third wave of national style. But the difference as compared to post-imperial China is that it is mostly manifested through high-rise office buildings, whose ensemble is criticized for looking rather like a 'visual cacophony', in which every building strives to be higher, more eye-catching than the other. In Beijing, this is clearly noticeable through the application of roof profiles on high-rises and superblocks, where buildings often present a composition looser and more open than that of previous decades. Office buildings are normally hermetically sealed from the outside environment through isolated (usually glass box) façades and fully auto-mated, seeking above all space utilization efficiency or profitability. (A case in point here is the administrative headquarters of the Ministry of Electricity, designed to have a free space on one street corner to offer citizens a public space, which, during the course of the construction, was built upon following a cost-benefit logic.)

The third wave of national style is thus widespread within a dynamic economy, the growing presence of foreign design firms and the rush of national architects to cope with countless project commissions. Estimates indicate that China has one tenth of the number of architects in the USA. Yet, each Chinese architect designs five times the volume of work in a fifth of the time, and in exchange for a tenth of professional honoraries (Verdú, 1999; Lin, 2001). As compared again to Europe or the USA, the Chinese architectural scene is organized extremely differently, characterized by state planning companies with several hundred employees in multi-specialist teams. Although foreign architects have started to step into professional opportunities in China, they are still relatively few in number. They are not only brought into the country by foreign investors seeking reliable professionals, but in most cases they are literally *imported* by Chinese design companies (including government-owned ones) to supply them with the latest architectural trends, state-of-the-art construction techniques,[5] project management systems and, no less importantly, a celebrated signature (Ruano, 1999a).

In terms of environmental quality, as can be expected, in the process of rapidly turning into a global city, Beijing has become an extremely polluted city. While in the 1930s it was often mentioned in western literature as one of the world's most liveable cities, it has been currently ranked, together with Shanghai, among the top ten most polluted cities in the world by the United Nations[6] (Chang Sen-Dou, 1998; Ruano, 1999a). This is of course partly resulting from the high concentration of heavy industries within municipal boundaries[7] and the rise in living standards, but also largely from the 'commodification' of Beijing's property sector and the resulting environmental pressures, where five main environmental themes now dominate.

First of all, Beijing has since the mid-1980s turned into a large construction site, lacking in green areas and with increasingly frequent dust storms. In an effort to curb the problem, a protective forest system was established in the north of China to prevent the storms coming from the Gobi desert (Li Min, 1997). But while the problem persists, Beijing's residents currently have only 2.3 square metres per capita of green area, a number far below the average figure laid out by the United Nations (which is 60 square metres per capita), a situation in which the galloping activities of the property sector play a key role (Jones Lang LaSalle, 2002b).

Secondly, the heat island effect following the increasing density of land use is a significant climatic phenomenon in Beijing. With a total area of 16,800 square kilometres, with mountains in the west and in the north, and a total population over ten million people, the average air temperature in the inner city in summer months is about three to four degrees Celsius higher than that of the suburbs. Considering the city proper alone, which has an area of 1040 square kilometres, the temperature differential is about four to five degrees (Li Min, 1997).

The heat island effect is further exacerbated by a third environmental problem – vehicular and industrial emissions – as heat released from combustion of vehicular fuels contributes to the formation of an 'urban heat dome'. The use of automobiles within the municipality, in this regard, has significantly risen during the past decade as the city grows, contributing to a drastic increase in atmospheric pollution in Beijing. But it was only in 1998 that the state banned leaded petrol and made catalytic converters mandatory. According to the Beijing Municipal Environmental Protection Bureau, China's vehicle emissions limit is two to three times higher than that of developed countries; as a consequence, 74 per cent of hydrocarbons and 63 per cent of carbon dioxide in Beijing derive from such sources. Besides industrial and vehicular emissions, air quality in Beijing is further worsened by chemical industries located in suburbs in addition to residential coal burning and road dust, the latter coming from the 4000–5000 construction sites scattered throughout the city and, to a lesser extent, from the Gobi desert (Fu-chen Lo and Yu-qing Xing, 1999).

A fourth environmental theme, certainly the most critical problem aggravated by Beijing's urban growth and the rampant activities of the construction industry, is water shortage and the subsequent increase in soil erosion the city has been undergoing. Located near the northern tip of the North China Plain, in a region characterized by a semi-arid temperate monsoon climate, Beijing has only about 600 millimetres of annual precipitation. In addition, the distribution of rainfall in Beijing is inconsistent, owing to its topography and monsoon. In a year of average rainfall, Beijing is endowed with water resources ranging from 4.2 to 4.5 billion cubic metres; in a dry year the amount can fall to 3.3 billion cubic metres (Chang, 1998). The rainfall period from June to September is about 85 per cent of the yearly total and dry years occur frequently[8] (Luo Tingdong, 1993). After the economic opening, which led to population growth and the improvement of living standards, the demand for water in Beijing has increased tremendously in the past decades. There is nowadays an estimated shortage of about 200 million cubic metres annually – for a year with normal precipitations, and 1.17 billion cubic metres for a below-normal year – and estimates still predict a shortage of 900 million cubic metres by 2010 – for a year with normal precipitations, and 1.98 billion cubic metres for a below-normal year – meaning a sharp conflict between supply and demand[9] (Luo Tingdong, 1993).

Finally, in energy use, although considerable progress has been made in the supply of electricity, central heating, gas, coal, and so on, since the introduction of economic opening policies, the rapid urban development and enhancement of living standards have exacerbated energy shortages (Wu Xumin, 1993). Coal still remains the main source of fuel, accounting for 70 per cent of all fuels used in the city (World Bank, 1994b). The constant increase in coal consumption, in this respect, has brought about continuous deterioration of the environmental quality, especially during the heating season, when the total suspended particles – such as sulphur dioxide and nitrogen oxide – in the air exceed the standards allowed by the state, severely worsening Beijing's air pollution problem. Parallel to this, buildings in Beijing, including grade A office buildings, are estimated to consume far more energy for heating than buildings in similar climatic zones in Europe or the USA, and still to be far less comfortable to be in. Designs, materials and construction techniques are deemed to be in general highly inefficient, while energy efficiency standards are still lacking, outdated or poorly enforced.

As regards the overall legislation (therefore not taking into account environmental issues), the Chinese land and property market – thus the country's urban planning framework and the composition of the urban office-stock – have been changing since the economic reform of the late 1970s under Deng Xiaoping. The property market took over particularly since 1986 with the institutionalization of China's Land Administration Act first in development zones and subsequently in Chinese cities (Zou Deci, 1995). While urban land was previously assigned for free, Deng's policies conceived a system of urban land administration through which the state levies a tax on the right to use land. The state continues to be the sole urban landowner, but the right of land use, usually set for a period of around 50 years for office buildings and 70 years for housing, becomes an asset separable from its ownership. The right may thus be transferred, sold, leased, mortgaged or eventually terminated by the government.

Urban planning, in this respect, also developed a new agenda after the economic reform. It had been first introduced in China in the 1950s, under Mao Zedong, following contents and models of the former Soviet Union, then laid fallow during the Cultural Revolution period. In the 1980s, some experiences from developed countries were introduced, leading in 1989 to the approval of the Chinese Urban Planning Act, an international urban planning system, though suitable for the Chinese characteristics, consisting of six chapters and 46 articles[10] (Zou Deci, 1995). The key point of the act is the fact that urban planning in China may be divided into a master plan (city, neighbourhood level) and detailed plan (building level), both of which may be further divided into several sublevels. Urban plans and construction activities should obey principles specified by the Urban Planning Act, thus meeting the standards and technical norms laid down by the government (Zou Deci, 1995). The act is complementary to the Land Administration Act and the (related) Environmental Protection Act, which we will get back to later on in this chapter, and may be locally specified with correspondent regional regulations, for example, the Beijing General Urban Planning Regulation, approved in 1992[11] (Jakubowski, 2000).

As private property companies have been created, foreign investors have started to step up their commercial interests in Beijing, and urban architectural practices have started to be internationalized, with a growing presence of foreign architects. According to Chinese law, foreign architectural firms commissioned in China must work in partnership with a Chinese design company for at least the design of executive plans. While foreign firms may carry out preliminary designs themselves, the Chinese government encourages such partnerships also at this early stage. Constructions, in this sense, must be strictly in line with urban planning and subordinated to the central planning management.

In describing the legislative framework of urban China, it is important to note that together with the internationalization of urban land use, urban land prices have significantly risen, resulting in the increase of land use efficiency by legal means. Urban densification, particularly in terms of increasing the plot ratio issue (that is, the area of the plot allowed for construction, which was previously controlled by strict guidelines), started to be legitimated, and so did a verticalization process (Hamer, 1993). According to Gaubatz (1999), despite the fact that China's urban planners now make use of international practices (for example, zoning regulations, height restrictions and controlled development), numerous concessions to high-profile developments are commonly being permitted as a result of conflicting regulatory frameworks and ill-defined enforcement procedures. This is leading to a mismatch between what is planned and what is built in the city while resulting in a kind of urban planning that seems to follow rather than dictate patterns of development (Gaubatz, 1999). Moreover, the absence of tradition in high-rise construction frequently renders local planners dependent on reviewing American or Japanese building codes, which in turn leads to several discussions and negotiations between interested parties in a process of 'mutual education' (Ruano, 1999b).

Beijing is a clear example of this. As the country's capital and main historical city, Beijing has, at least on paper, strict height and density controls. The General Beijing Master Plan of 1982 stipulates that the maximum height of the inner city is nine metres in the centre and 18 metres in the outskirts (Chang, 1998). As a result, investors are rarely keen to invest in the old city and the construction of low- and mid-rise structures continues to predominate in Beijing. But economic pressures following the commodification of the property sector have increasingly complicated the implementation and enforcement of the city's urban planning laws, often leading to infringements. As a result, the revision of the above-mentioned 1982 Master Plan of Beijing, conducted in 1993, had to reconsider height restrictions significantly so as to legitimize existing structures (Gaubatz, 1999).

In Beijing, urban planning issues (such as zoning regulation), buildings codes (concerning, for example, height and orientation of buildings), their enforcement, and the issuing of building permits are carried out by the Urban Planning Bureau of Beijing. Concerning the design of office buildings, priority is still given to the architectural typology, that is, aesthetics. In terms of the actual building process, regulations seem to be more flexible, as clients and architects may discuss them with the competent authority.

In administrative terms, Beijing is considered to be an 'independent municipality' in China, directly under the jurisdiction of the central government (Chang, 1998). The administrative area of the Beijing municipality consists of four urban districts

(Dongcheng, Xicheng, Chongwen and Xuanwu), four inner suburban districts (Chaoyang, Fengtai, Shijingshan and Haidian), two outer suburban districts (Mentougou and Fangshan), as well as eight rural counties (Mao Qizhi *et al.*, 1997). The People's Congress of Beijing and the Standing Committee of Beijing Municipal People's Congress are the governmental bodies constitutionally empowered to draft and issue municipal rules and regulations.[12]

Local Environmental Management

Nationally, environmental protection was first introduced in China in the early 1970s. The Environmental Protection Act of the People's Republic of China[13] was drafted in 1979 but formally enacted only in 1989. The National Environmental Protection Agency (later to be known as SEPA, State Environmental Protection Administration) has since then been China's national environmental authority, responsible for, among others, the drafting of national environmental laws, rules, regulations, provisions, and guidelines, the preparation of national environmental protection plans and the supervision of environmental impact assessments for cross-regional construction projects (World Bank, 1994b).

At the local level, Beijing first opened its Environmental Protection Bureau in 1974, an entity subordinated to and directly supervised by the Urban Construction Committee. The Bureau, and subsequently the Beijing Environmental Protection Committee, were established to strengthen environmental leadership in the city. The responsibilities of the Beijing Environmental Protection Bureau include the drafting of environmental policies, rules, regulations, provisions and standards for Beijing as well as their enforcement procedures. The Bureau is also responsible for collecting excess pollution discharge fees and penalties, revising and approving environmental impact assessments and environmental protection facilities, as well as assist the National Environmental Protection Agency and the Beijing Environmental Protection Committee in the drafting of (national, urban and rural) economic, social and environmental development programmes (World Bank, 1994b, Beijing Municipal Environmental Protection Bureau, 2002b).

As with overall environmental management in China, environmental protection in Beijing follows the San Tong Shi approach,[14] which refers to the implementation of environmental control measures from source, in other words, the implementation of clean technology. This approach has been strengthened by the Administrative Measures for Environmental Control for Construction Projects – drafted jointly by the State Council, the State Planning Commission and the State Economic Commission – detailing requirements for the design, construction and operation stages of construction projects, and the related responsibilities of the local Environmental Protection Bureaus, construction departments and construction units (World Bank, 1994b). Based on these measures, at the local level, the Beijing Municipal Urban Planning Commission, the Beijing Economic Commission and the Beijing Municipal Environmental Protection Bureau issued the Detailed Rules for Implementation in Beijing Municipality of the Administrative Measures for the Environmental Protection of Construction Projects, thereby specifying requirements for construction projects in Beijing as well as related penalties (World Bank, 1994b).

Parallel to such developments in environmental policy making, the Chinese government has clearly recognized that a deteriorated urban environment acts as a deterrent to further economic growth and that the property sector is 'positively correlated with environmental qualities' (Jones Lang LaSalle, 2002b). In this sense, the Chinese government is now committed to eliminating pollution to further attract foreign investments and boost the urban economy. This implies the environmental upgrading of nearly all industrial sectors, including the property industry and the related practices involving the development of the urban office-stock.

These measures were in turn further promulgated by the State Council into a set of regulations (the Regulation of Environmental Protection of Construction Projects) in December 1998, requiring that an environmental assessment report be submitted to government authorities in charge (Ibid.) – in the case of Beijing to the Municipal Environmental Protection Bureau – for large-scale commercial and residential projects (industrial projects fall under another regulatory category). For smaller scale projects, the Ministry of Construction has drafted a set of guidelines for the implementation of ecological features in the construction of buildings in general, although no specific environmental prescriptions exist yet in this regard. As for Beijing, priority is being given to water conservation issues, particularly in residential buildings and hotels, for which the installation of recycling facilities are becoming increasingly mandatory.

Environmental concerns, in this respect, are becoming an important part of the Chinese construction scene, in which attention is not only focused on the management of local natural resources (such as energy and water consumption), but also on broader sustainability issues. As the feasibility of property development projects must increasingly comply with environmental laws to obtain construction permits, Chinese architects and urban designers have become aware of the issue, reaching consensus on certain points. First, buildings should address the human scale and seek harmony with the environment. Concepts such as green building or sustainable urban development have obtained growing sympathy among them (Xu Anzhi, 2000). A second point currently considered is the fact that tradition deserves due respect and historic buildings and public spaces should be preserved. In this regard, although cases of demolition of traditional settlements are still many, the Chinese government has guaranteed to retain historic public spaces by using legislation, but it is not yet clear *how* this will be achieved (Wei Gaochuan, 2000). In addition, the government has been seriously committed to invest intensively in green areas – the marketing campaign for the 2008 Olympic Games serving as an indicator (cf. above).

But some questions still puzzle Chinese architects. It is still not yet known how the cultural and regional characteristics of Chinese architecture will be preserved in view of globalization pressures, or how a good environmental and architectural quality will be maintained in the course of rapid urbanization. Also, and no less critically, how shortsighted, profit-oriented or environmentally abusive developments will be avoided amid China's shift towards a market economy. The answers to such questions remain unclear, despite the fact that China has officially embarked on a comprehensive urban greening process. The following paragraphs describe how the main environmental policy agencies in Beijing are currently implementing management programmes to improve the environmental impact and the energy and water efficiency of the city's office buildings.

As indicated above, the outset of environmental protection practices in Beijing was linked to construction activities, as the first Environmental Protection Bureau, inaugurated in 1974, was originally subordinated to the Beijing Urban Construction Committee. In a way, this put Beijing's office-stock at a kind of advantage for the eventual start-up of an ecological restructuring process. As environmental protection issues were gradually prioritized in the city, the Beijing Municipal Environmental Protection Committee was established in the late 1970s. The relationship between construction activities and environmental protection were thereby further formulated in April 1980 into directives on construction in Beijing, promulgated by the Secretariat of the Central Party Committee – namely the Beijing Urban Construction Master Plan – clarifying Beijing's status as China's capital, urging thus stronger environmental politics. In addition, since 1994 a Local Agenda 21 was implanted in Beijing as an effort to promote sustainable policies along with action plans, so as to ensure that the coordination between development, resources and environment is met (ESCAP, 2003).

The Beijing Municipal Environmental Protection Bureau has three affiliate institutions (Beijing Municipal Environmental Protection Research Institute, Beijing Municipal Environment Monitoring Centre and Beijing Municipal Technical Training Centre for Environmental Protection), 11 subdivisions, and employs over 100 persons. One such subdivision is the Department of Construction Supervision.

Since December 1998, the Bureau has been officially entitled to control (approve and enforce) the environmental performance of the city's construction activities by requesting different kinds of environmental impact assessments, the parameters for which – spanning from energy and water conservation to overall environmental preservation – were specified in April 1999 by the National Environmental Protection Agency. For commercial property developments, including hotels, offices and residential buildings with a construction area above 60,000 square metres or land area above 30,000 square metres, in all areas, an environmental impact assessment report should be carried out for Bureau approval. Should these developments be in sensitive areas, the requirement for an environmental impact assessment report would be for projects above 20,000 square metres and land areas of above 10,000 square metres. Regarding non-sensitive areas, projects above 5000 square metres should fill out an environmental impact assessment registration form, describing the environmental impact on the surrounding environment. Finally, all renovation projects of old districts as well as the development of new districts, disregarding the total area, are required to submit an environmental impact assessment report for Bureau's approval (Jones Lang LaSalle, 2002b).

In terms of penalties, constructions are to be stopped (and developers to be fined) should they (i) be initiated prior to the environmental impact assessment procedures; (ii) be modified in their scale, nature, location or other important aspects without re-submitting the related environmental impact assessment reports, forms or registration forms; or if (iii) they are delayed by five years after the approval of the environmental impact assessment reports, forms or registration forms, and these are not re-submitted (Jones Lang LaSalle, 2002b).

Moving now to energy issues, the main energy agency in Beijing is the Economy Commission of Beijing Municipality – which is subdivided into five departments, namely Energy Supply, Energy Saving Office, Industrial Management, Safety

Production and Technical Improvements – acting both as the city's energy manager and main policy maker as well as the city's energy utility (the Beijing Power Supply Bureau). The Commission does not have energy-saving programmes directly related to office buildings, which is not yet a priority in Beijing in terms of policy, although its Energy Saving Office manages, to date, the energy efficiency of industrial facilities.

Yet, efforts are being made to render Beijing an energy-saving city, mostly owing to the fact that although significant improvements have been achieved in terms of energy management in the city – including better services – the rapid economic development and the enhancement of living conditions have progressively led to shortages in the supply of electricity, thermal energy, gas and other energy sources as well as to severe deterioration of the air quality due to the extensive use of coal as main energy source (Wu Xumin, 1993).

In this regard, attention has to date been somewhat focused on optimizing the efficiency of new and existing high-energy consuming industries, such as iron and steel, the upgrading or replacement of their obsolete technologies, as well as domestic energy use, for which more and more co-generation facilities are being promoted for central-heating systems. Energy-related policy making has not yet reached the city's office-stock, although the Chinese government has recently started to support energy-saving demonstration projects, both for housing and office buildings (examples include the sustainable housing base in Beijing Elk Garden in southern Beijing's Yizhuang Economic Development Zone and the ACCA21 – Administrative Centre for China's Agenda 21 – building).

Other energy supply programmes that the Economy Commission has fostered in recent years in Beijing include: (i) the expansion of the use of natural gas in Beijing in order to provide a gradual substitution of coal burning for gas (although few further investments are taking place in renewable energies); (ii) the development of a district heating system to gradually replace residential coal burning, which causes much environmental damage; (iii) the decrease of sulphur and ash contents in Beijing's coal; (iv) the security of energy supply to the development of outer suburbs; and (v) the development of energy supply to municipal rural areas according to the principle of 'suiting measures to local conditions, multiply energy complimenting each other, comprehensive utilization and striving for efficiency' (Wu Xumin, 1993).

In terms of water services, the Beijing municipal government has a Water Management Bureau, the city's water utility and policy maker, which is subdivided into three departments: Water Resources, Water Saving Office and Water Supply. Since the economic opening, water conservation in Beijing has been receiving a growing attention, given that shortages in the city's water supply system are a recurrent problem. Programmes date back to 1981, when Beijing carried out a Water Saving Policy in an all-embracing way, achieving reductions in water consumption levels, for instance, about 40 per cent in industrial consumption terms after eight years of the programme's implementation. Similarly, the rate of daily domestic water consumption dropped in percentage from nearly eight per cent during the period 1979–1981 to roughly two per cent during the period 1981–1987. But despite the Water Saving Policy, since China's economic reform daily water consumption has increased tremendously in Beijing. Nowadays it is estimated that each Beijing inhabitant consumes on average about 300 litres daily, several times more than in the pre-1978 period. This increase in water consumption levels in Beijing is also due to the construction of more power plants – such as the Gaobeidian Thermal Power Plant, the Songjiazhuang Thermal Power Plant, the Pinggu Power Plant and the Ming Tombs Power Storage Station, despite recycling efforts – as well as to the agricultural enhancement policy, whose guiding principle states 'serve the Capital, make the farmers prosperous and construct the countryside with socialist modernization', requiring investments in irrigation, although through water-saving systems (Luo Tingdong, 1993).

Nowadays, the Water Saving Office of the Water Management Bureau develops technical guidelines for the use of water facilities as well as consumption parameters – applicable to all types of buildings – implying a raise in water costs proportional to consumption levels (applying the 'use more, pay more' principle). In this sense, while energy efficiency in office buildings is still not such a major concern in Beijing (although energy prices tend to rise), water efficiency is not only a growing political priority but also a major public concern. Office buildings in Beijing, in this regard, with a total area above 50,000 square metres, are required to apply a water-recycling scheme.[15] These technical guidelines are in fact expected to be adopted (with certain adaptations) all over urban China in the future.

Global Environmental Management

Deng Xiaoping's economic opening policies ratified the entry of foreign firms in the Chinese market. Most of such firms established representative offices in the mid-1980s and early 1990s, usually in Beijing or Shanghai, originally to 'explore' economic opportunities in mainland China. As a result, multinational companies tend not to make large investments in the city, and are mostly tenants of their offices they maintain in Beijing thus far, renting space from Chinese investors. Consequently, most foreign firms have limited environmental programmes for their offices in Beijing, claiming that the size of the spaces is rather irrelevant for prompting environmental initiatives. As tenants, they are in addition not involved with the design of the space nor directly connected with the utilities and environmental policy agencies, as such connections are intermediated by the investors, through their facility management departments. As the following accounts will make clear, possible environmental innovations in their offices are largely due to initiatives stemming from local environmental management practices.

ING Group

ING maintains three quarters of an office floor (approximately 560 square metres) of the Landmark Towers complex in Beijing (see Figure 7.3), situated close to the East Third Ring Road, within walking distance of the CBD and 20 minutes by car from the city's airport. The complex is a prominent one, consisting of three office towers totalling 55,000 square metres of office space, in addition to serviced apartments and a hotel.

ING first established offices in this complex (Landmark Building 1) in the early 1990s, the first offices the company opened in the city. Among the criteria for the

Figure 7.3   ING headquarters, Beijing

selection of the Landmark Towers, ING was looking for a building that would be in line with the company's corporate image, easy to access, reasonably priced, and that would offer a good quality of office space (such as good elevators and floor space). No environmental topics were considered during this decision-making process, a process that was coordinated partly by ING and partly by the company's Platform in China, the latter consisting of an internationally composed board of managers. As ING is a bank also involved with property management, there was no intermediate actor – such as a property agent – for this purpose.

The Landmark Towers complex, inaugurated in 1990 (Phase 1, where ING is located[16]), is owned and managed by the Landmark Management Co., which is a Chinese-Singaporean joint venture (shared ownership with the Ministry of Economic Affairs, following Chinese rules). This company collects rents, operates the buildings' technical systems and pays for water and energy bills, among other things, respectively to Beijing Water Management Bureau and to the Economy Commission of Beijing Municipality. ING thus does not interact with these local environmental management networks of environmental management above described, as all such connections are intermediated by Landmark Management Co. (the same applying to the design phase of the building, during which ING had no participation whatsoever).

In 2002, the Landmark Office Tower Phase 1 underwent a refurbishment process to update part of the building's technical systems; initiatives were taken by Landmark Management Co. For the tenants, a major result of this refurbishment was not so much technical, but financial. Not only did rental fees rise by 22 per cent (from 18 dollars m^2/month to 22 dollars m^2/month) but electricity bills started to be paid separately to the building manager, whereas they used to be included in the rent fee prior to the refurbishment. The reason for this shift in the charging system was not only because energy prices are likely to rise in the coming years, but also due to the fact that energy bills can be monitored and differentiated among tenants, as some of the companies consume more or less energy than the others. The same does not apply to the use of water, as water-consuming facilities are communal to each floor (which is in fact typical of office buildings in Beijing). Although the motivation for this shift was purely economic – and not environmental – it can be expected that more attention will be paid to energy saving within the offices as companies start to be charged individually. As for the use of water, although the communal use of lavatories (shared lavatories for each storey, whose standard comprises four units of office) does not in itself lead to water-saving strategies to be launched by the companies themselves (as these are not directly involved with the bills), the building operates a water-recycling scheme, following the standards set forth by the Water Management Bureau.

ING, in turn, considers that the environmental load of its offices in Beijing is too light to call for an environmental management system in their running. There are only about 15 people working in Beijing and the costs for the implementation of energy- and water-saving programmes are claimed not to be cost-effective. In this respect, although common sense is fostered for the use of energy[17] and water, there are no procedures concerning the conceptualization or implementation of more specific environmental programmes. In this sense, and bringing no environmental innovations to its office space in Beijing, the main environmental feature of the space, which is the water-recycling scheme, was introduced by the building owner, following prescriptions set forth by the local water utility.

On the other hand, as a property company,[18] ING considers environmental concerns to be increasingly imperative for the projects that it develops in China and elsewhere. In this regard, ING is at the moment involved mostly with the development of (large-scale) residential buildings in China, for which it is trying to influence decisions regarding the environment. This is taking place from the planning phase (including the selection of the site, as well as decisions regarding the energy supply system and water management, to be negotiated with the government), to the design phase (through for instance better designs and appropriate construction techniques), finally to the building management/operational phase. The company however acknowledges that the steering of decisions towards environmental care is not always easy to achieve as ING is often not the major investor in the project.

In terms of corporate management structure, ING Real Estate's representative office in Beijing (where decisions regarding the selection and running of the offices of ING in Beijing take place) communicates directly with ING Real Estate located in The Hague, which in turn reports to the board of ING Real Estate, reporting to the Asset Management group, which in turn reports to ING's Executive Board.[19] Although ING's management structure is very hierarchical with a type of management style that seems to be rather top-down, decisions regarding the running of the offices in Beijing, including those regarding environmental management or energy or water efficiency, are to be made *locally* in Beijing. There are therefore no channels from the global company to the local management of Beijing's offices regarding the transfer of environmental care concepts.

Figure 7.4   Andersen headquarters, Beijing

Arthur Andersen opened its office in Beijing at the China World Trade Center building (see Figure 7.4) in 1991 and closed it down in 2002, when it was absorbed by PricewaterhouseCoopers in China. Following the profile of Andersen's buildings analysed in Amsterdam and São Paulo, Andersen in Beijing was not a particular case in point regarding global environmental management. On the other hand, the construction of the China World Trade Center building is a relevant account particularly where water efficiency is concerned. As its name indicates, this building symbolizes China's opening up to international trade. Profiting from a good location on the Jianguomenwai Avenue, its architecture is very much in line with global trends, incorporating modern fittings in a 39-storey tower.

Decisions regarding the construction of the China World Trade Center complex started in 1985, initiated by the Shangri-la Group, the building's investor and developer. American architectural firm Sobel/Roth won the bidding for the conceptual design of the building, while Japanese engineering company Nikken Sekkei Ltd. was appointed for the building's engineering design. In 1986 French company SAE started foundation work; construction finished in 1989. Shangri-la Group has ever since been the building owner in partnership with the Ministry of Economic Affairs (in a fifty-fifty contract). The complex totals 42,000 square metres, comprising two office buildings and two hotels, in addition to a subway station, meeting area, mall and parking facilities.

The China World Trade Center is notable for being one of the first buildings in Beijing to install a water-recycling scheme. Although this has become a common practice nowadays in Beijing (cf. above), there were no regulations at the time regarding water consumption in buildings. The idea for installing a water reutilization system was introduced by Japanese engineering firm Nikken Sekkei, although the technology for the whole water equipment was imported from the USA, Hong Kong and Japan (being the most advanced at the time), and the setting of

Figure 7.5   ABN AMRO headquarters, Beijing

standards was done following American ones. In contrast, however, nothing was done for improving the energy performance of the building beyond conventional standards.

Neither the Beijing Urban Planning Committee nor the Beijing Environmental Protection Bureau imposed any specific requirement regarding the building's environmental performance. There was no legislation at the time requiring the submission of environmental impact assessment reports. In addition, at that time China did not have any specific regulations for such scale of building (neither for the architecture nor the engineering) so new standards had to be developed for the China World Trade Center. In this regard, the innovation of the water reutilization scheme was introduced by foreign firms.

ABN AMRO

ABN AMRO opened its first Beijing branch in 1985. In 1999 it moved its offices to the Kerry Centre building complex (see Figure 7.5), located in the Chaoyang district, totalling 921 square metres with 16 employees; all decisions were made by local managers and assisted by the property firm Jones Lang LaSalle. The Kerry Centre was selected among other property options as the building was claimed at the occasion to offer the newest and best foreign-managed office space and to be conveniently located near the main business centres of Beijing. There were no environmental considerations in this process.

In fact, according to the China Architecture Design & Research Group (which participated jointly with Hong Kong architectural firm DLN Architects & Engineers in the design process as the Chinese counterparts), the Kerry Centre, despite being one of the most prestigious office buildings in Beijing, is a 'basic' building in terms of energy and water efficiency, complying with – but not going beyond – standards laid down by the Beijing Urban Planning and the Water Management Bureaux. In this respect, the building has a small water treatment plant to provide secondary clean water for the flushing of toilets but nothing sophisticated in energy efficiency, apart from a smart lighting management system.

Like the China World Trade Center, the Kerry Centre is also owned by the Shangri-la Group (also in partnership with the Ministry of Economic Affairs). It is managed by one of the Group's companies, Kerry Properties, which collects rents and pays for energy and water bills (included in rent fees). ABN AMRO, in this regard, interacts with Kerry Properties in issues regarding the management of the office space – through which environmental topics may possibly emerge – but is not directly involved with the local utilities or environmental policy agencies, such as the Water Management Bureau, the Economy Commission of Beijing Municipality or the Environmental Protection Bureau; nor was it involved with any decisions made during the design of the building.

In this respect, it is for the building managers to save on energy and water. While water is saved through the water-recycling scheme, energy is becoming a growing concern, representing over 20 per cent of the maintenance expenditures, the second largest expenditure after the disbursement of salaries. As such, attempts currently made to save energy include the following: (i) turning on external lighting only from 18:00 until 24:00; (ii) turning on and off lifts and escalators at strategic hours; and (iii) running two of the three chillers on steam during the day while only using a third electricity-powered chiller during the lowest energy fare hours (from 5:00 until 7:00). The managers estimate that energy and water prices will increase by 20 per cent and 30 per cent respectively in the coming years, a fact that will probably initiate an awareness-raising process regarding utility services in the city.

Environmental innovations introduced in the building, such as the water-recycling scheme and the energy-saving options, were totally decided on by local actors outside the company; the first following public prescriptions, the second following the motivations of the building managers. ABN AMRO is not introducing any innovations in this regard, nor is the bank interested in investing in specific appliances for its small office space. The bank claims to have a low budget for the premise, so that the selection of specific environmentally sound appliances or the implementation of environmental programmes, which in the short term might be costly, are easily ignored. Environmental issues, in this context, are not considered, due to short-term money saving – that is, the bank is not interested in pursuing environmental programmes that may be costly in the short term, so that only common sense environmental management issues, such as basic waste recycling are taken into account. ABN AMRO's representative office in Beijing reports to the Operations Department in Hong Kong, which communicates in turn with its Amsterdam head-quarters. According to an ABN AMRO manager in Beijing, topics concerning in-house environmental management are never raised through these channels.

IBM

IBM is located at the IBM Tower of the Pacific Century Place complex (see Figure 7.6), which consists of two office towers and a shopping mall, located in the Chaoyang district. IBM occupies seven office floors out of the 25 office floors of the IBM Tower (approximately 17,000 square metres and 1200 employees). The Beijing branch is the Asia Pacific headquarters of IBM, and is thereby a key branch.

IBM moved to the IBM Tower in 1998, assisted by the property firm CB Richard Ellis, following an 'environmental site assessment' procedure, which in line with the company's global policy was the most important criterion for the selection of the Pacific Century Place for the establishment of its offices.[20] The environmental site assessment procedure consists of an appraisal scheme used by IBM to determine the building's history in terms of (indoor) use of chemicals and hazardous materials (such as halon 1301, which is forbidden by IBM), as well as in terms of the energy and water management system, for instance, if the water quality meets IBM's standards, and indoor pollution. Apart from this assessment, other criteria that applied for the selection of IBM Tower were the building's accessibility and architecture, which should be in line with IBM's corporate image.

Figure 7.6   IBM headquarters, Beijing

IBM Tower is a property of Jing Wei Real Estate Company, from which IBM rents its office space. There is also an independent service provider (Kell) assigned by the landlord for the general management of the building. IBM however pays for its water and energy bills through its property manager, CB Richard Ellis, and these are not part of the rent fee. In this sense, and like the other case studies in Beijing, IBM is also not directly connected to the local utility and environmental policy agencies in its operational phase; nor was it at the design phase of the building.

Yet, unlike the other companies in Beijing, IBM introduced an environmental management system in 2002 which, apart from the application of ISO 14001 standards in its production line in China, also involves the running of the offices. As such, it covers topics such as (i) solid waste management, involving the separation and proper disposal (as well as recycling efforts) of hazardous and non-hazardous waste; (ii) energy saving, through constant behavioural campaigns for example (the building does not have a smart lighting system); and (iii) water saving, also through behavioural campaigns (the building also does not have a water-recycling facility). According to IBM's global environmental policy, offices of IBM China are also expected – and checked (by IBM Japan) – to decrease annually their energy and water consumption by four and one per cent respectively. Energy saving, in this regard, is an important component of the environmental management of IBM, which is achieved, in addition to the above-mentioned behavioural campaigns, through a series of standards laid down by the company: (i) setting targets by floor; (ii) shutting down lighting after 20:00; (iii) strictly avoiding redundant lighting devices; (iv) controlling air conditioning use; (v) lowering hot water temperatures at sinks; (vi) investing in lighting stabilizers; and (vii) promoting mobile work. As local practices of environmental management regarding energy and water consumption are limited (in the case of water consumption, the human resources manager of IBM Beijing claims that the building does *not* have a water-recycling system), innovations are introduced through IBM's global environmental policy.

Environmental as well as occupational, health and safety issues at IBM China Beijing branch are still dealt with inside the human resources department; the company does not yet have a department for the environment in Beijing, although environmental themes are growing in importance at the branch. These activities are reported to the China human resources managers (also located in Beijing), who report to the IBM Japan environmental manager (responsible for orienting and checking the Beijing branch), who finally reports to the IBM headquarters in the United States. IBM Japan – following IBM USA – is therefore the main channel to provide the guidelines in terms of energy and water efficiency set forth at the global headquarters level (IBM USA) to IBM's premises in China.

Conclusions

In this chapter we tried to assess how environmental management is carried out in Beijing's office-stock, by looking at the policies and strategies of local utilities and environmental agencies, and their interception with the strategies of four multinational companies that are occupiers of office space. First we provided an overview of how the rush to modernization since the country's economic opening has aggravated local environmental problems and the use of resources such as energy and water. Secondly we explored the reforms that the local planning and regulatory framework have been undergoing ever since, leading to the institutionalization of environmental directives applicable to office buildings. Among these, we highlighted two of the most prominent instruments: the water-recycling standard for office buildings above 50,000 square metres and, more recently instituted, the requirement of environmental impact assessment procedures for certain kinds of developments.

From the information gathered in this chapter, it seems that the ecological restructuring of Beijing's office-stock pursues an environmental policy framework fostering clean technologies. The above two instruments indicate that the main environmental discourse tends to explore solutions of dematerialization – such as through the water-recycling systems – as well as substitution of technologies. No sophisticated monitoring systems for energy/water-saving purposes could be detected in this research, although the increase in the price of water and energy is a sign of monetarization. The attempt to apply clean technologies is also manifest through the 'environmental campaign' for the 2008 Olympic Games, as Beijing is claiming to make substantial investments in the years to come including the completion of demonstration projects for a green residential complex and an office building. It seems that the environmental reform of Beijing also benefits from the fact that the city's Environmental Protection Bureau has been instituted under the Urban Construction Committee, so that the development of environmental management themes are, or at least to some extent, conceptualized and implemented under the umbrella of the environmental challenges of construction activities (such as the environmental impact assessments, for instance).

At the other end of the spectrum, however, the companies analysed in this research demonstrate that environmental themes applicable to their offices are rather limited to 'common sense' approaches, with the exception of IBM. Their argument is that they are tenants of the spaces, which are often rather small, representative offices only. This justification is further explained as most of them do not receive incentives (authoritative, financial or technological) concerning environmental management from the global headquarter level. In addition, societal connections between the global companies and the local utilities and environmental policy agency are practically non-existent, as these connections are primarily intermediated by the facility managers of their offices, which are usually the owners of the buildings. None of the companies analysed in this city was involved with the design of the building either. Perhaps owing to the fact that its premises in Beijing are larger than those of the other companies, IBM was the only case to have introduced environmental innovations in its offices, such as the use of 'environmental site assessment' and an environmental management system also applicable to the use of energy and water in the offices as part of the company's global environmental policy. Paradoxically, it was also the only analysed company to occupy a building that does not have a water-recycling scheme.

From such evidence, it seems that in general terms the environmental restructuring of Beijing's office buildings is being driven by local policy and economic networks – comprising the water utility and the environmental protection agency, as well as the investors of the buildings (and their facility managers respectively). It also seems that decisions follow both an environmental rationale as well as economic motivations: that is, to use resources more efficiently in the sense of making 'more out of less'. This is perhaps confirmed as so far most initiatives concern the use of water, which is now critical in the city, whereas the use of energy, which is not yet priority, still remains rather unchallenged for the moment. Multinational companies claim not to be liable for the environmental management of the spaces as their offices are rather small in Beijing. In this sense, it seems that the conditions that are mostly favouring an environmental restructuring of Beijing's office-stock is a growing awareness raising by the government and local building owners that resources should be used more efficiently, above all to ensure the future development of the city and the continuity of commercial-oriented property developments. Whether these events correspond to the tenets of ecological modernization theory will be analysed in the subsequent chapter.

Notes

1   Generally speaking, capital cities are usually the most prominent, or at least the second most prominent cities in socialist countries, easily obtaining labour, financial and material support, as well as better infrastructure services.
2   Culturally speaking, in addition, Beijing is also home to over 60 colleges and universities as well as several science and research institutes, in addition to China's main libraries, stadiums, opera houses and hospitals, which as a whole strengthen Beijing's status as China's main economic city.

3 Estimates suggest that about half Beijing's population (or 6.5 million people) will be relocated in the years prior to the Olympic Games (Meyer, 2002). According to the fifth census, Beijing's population comprises eight million registered permanent residents and a five-million floating population.

4 Despite criticisms, municipal authorities claim that this concentration of service activities could not take place in a development zone such as Pudong in Shanghai, as Beijing lacks an appropriate site within municipal boundaries for it (Fan Yaobang, 1994). In addition, residential neighbourhoods from the Ming and Qing dynasties (hutongs) occupying the old inner city area were usually left in a derelict state, requiring costly and fundamental rehabilitation. Their demolition was (and still is) thus many times considered the most cost-effective solution for the creation of commercial and business areas (Gu and Kesteloot, 2001).

5 In terms of construction techniques, while emphasis in the 1950s was laid on the construction of industrial buildings, during the 1960s and mid-1970s, a period during which the country did not have much international relations, the building industry mostly developed in engineering works underground and in mountainous areas. It was only since the late 1970s onwards that Chinese construction techniques met international standards, making rapid progress ever since (Xu Ronglie, 1989).

6 In fact, China already has five of the ten most polluted cities in the world (Ruano, 1999a).

7 Mostly related to material processing, such as iron and steel, heavy chemicals, construction materials, glass-making, pulp and paper, not only environmentally intensive but also requiring a tremendous energy load; in 1980, for instance, about 90 per cent of the city's total energy supply was consumed by the industrial sector. After the economic opening, and despite the call for readjustment of the urban industrial sector of the whole country, Beijing's industrial structure remained largely unaltered (Chang, 1998). Nowadays, Beijing is, after Shanghai, the second largest industrial centre in China.

8 In terms of surface water resources, Beijing mainly depends on rainwater sources and the Yongding River, the Chaobai River and the Juhe River. Today, there are 85 reservoirs in Beijing – the largest of which are the Guantin Reservoir and the Miyun Reservoir – storing a total of 7.4 billion tons of water on which the city is dependant for its residential, commercial and industrial urban water supply (Li Min, 1997). It is known that surface water can provide 1.74 billion cubic metres in a normal year, 1.32 billion cubic metres in a semi-dry year and 1.03 billion cubic metres in a dry year. The average groundwater reserve of the city is 2.45 billion cubic metres, increasing the total amount of water that can be supplied to Beijing to 4.19 billion cubic metres, 3.77 billion cubic metres and 3.48 billion cubic metres, respectively (Luo Tingdong, 1993).

9 Sewerage is also problematic in Beijing, also significantly worsening as the city further grows. By 1992, Beijing only nine per cent of the total volume of sewage was processed (Wu Liangyong, 1992b), and it had 2880 kilometres of sewers (85 times greater than in 1949, though), seven sewerage systems and three domestic sewage treatment plants, with a daily treatment capacity of 250,000 tons (World Bank, 1994b). These figures have not improved, due to the limited investments in the field, resulting, among other things, in the contamination of the soil and of underground water resources.

10 The overall urban planning legislation in China is set forth by the Urban Planning Act, which is the most important legislation base for Chinese urban planning and building activities. It includes the general principles for the preparation of urban planning, development of new areas and rehabilitation of existing ones, the implementation of urban plans and the related legal responsibilities, and emphasizes that the preparation of urban plans should also address social and environmental issues.

11 Although the central government is responsible for policy making, including the formulation of major laws and regulations, the establishment of finance and tax systems, local governments have the authority to draft local regulations and policies, which should not contradict those promulgated by the central government however (Lin Zhiqun, 1991).

12 The system of People's Congress is the basic political system in China, representing the entities through which the Chinese people exercise state power. They are determined at national and local levels, elected democratically every five years. Standing Committees, in this sense, are set up above the level of People's Congresses (Beijing Standing Committee, 2002).

13 This Act defined, among other things, that the concept of environment includes the urban environment so that the assessment of environmental risks should be made also in view of urban development, construction and regeneration practices (Zou Deci, 1995).

14 This approach was first introduced in the 1979 draft of the Environmental Protection Act of the People's Republic of China, specifying penalties for infractions (World Bank, 1994b).

15 This standard was introduced in the early 1990s and is apparently strongly enforced. Smaller buildings, nevertheless, do not need to cope with such standards at the moment.

16 The other towers were completed in 1998.

17 The building does not have an intelligent lighting management system to make sure, for instance, that energy is not consumed when the offices are not occupied.

18 ING operates four lines of business in China, starting in the early 1990s: ING-Bank, ING-Real Estate, Insurance and Asset Management.

19 The other business lines of ING communicate with related managers in the Netherlands.

20 According to a local manager, this environmental site assessment is not carried out to all IBM's branches in the world.

Chapter 8

The Environmental Glocalization of Office Buildings

This book started out speculating on the transformations cities are undergoing in the era of globalization, as 'transnational spaces' are being created within the urban space, building a link between the 'local' and the 'global'. These transformations are instituting a new urban order, as social connections between local and global actors are now intermingling in the urban space, redefining its metabolism and shape. This book reflects on the rise of a *vicious circle* of worsening urban environment and growing consumption of environmental flows such as energy, water and waste thereby taking place. And it suggests that, running counter to this vicious circle, there is also a *virtuous circle* of urban environmental reforms emerging in the era of globalization.

In line with the theory of ecological modernization, it posits that this virtuous circle is arising insofar as the environment is becoming a central theme of global modernity. In this process, new market dynamics are being triggered in which environmental issues emerge as a new and independent set of criteria to be used when assessing and designing industrial performance, parallel to economic ones. This process is leading to a kind of 'reinvention' of environmental policy making in a way forward in modernity, in which the state launches 'enabling' environmental policies to be adopted by market and civil society actors. In the era of globalization and global environmental change, market dynamics acting in the environmental reform of industrial sectors are in certain cases also promoting positive effects on a global, transnational basis, playing thereby an important role in diffusing environmental innovations worldwide. In so doing, global market actors are in certain cases promoting a 'race to the top' of environmental management particularly in newly industrializing countries, or a globalizing, virtuous or even a *virtual* circle of environmental reforms.

In view of these arguments, this book explored how multinational companies are possibly contributing to a worldwide 'race to the top' in terms of urban environmental management. Its enquiry revolved around the environmental dimension of the offices held by such companies in different metropolises, claiming that (parallel to the worldwide diffusion of industrial environmental management practices that multinationals are increasingly compelled to, regarding, for instance, pollution prevention) the environmental strategies applied in their offices in home countries should be also applied in their offices elsewhere. However, it assumed that in order to analyse how multinational companies may be pushing for the environmental restructuring of their offices in different cities it is also necessary to investigate whether the environmental policies of such cities are stimulating or perhaps inhibiting the process of environmental change. In this light, an investigation into 12 case studies of the interception between corporate environmental strategies (of ABN

AMRO, ING, Andersen and IBM) and urban environmental policies (of Amsterdam, São Paulo and Beijing) has been carried out to develop an understanding of the dynamics of urban environmental change under conditions of globalization.

The previous three chapters of this study have provided an overview of the main mechanisms through which the offices of these four companies in the three cities are undergoing environmental reforms in view of this local-global interface of social practices. At this point, a more critical analysis of the environmental restructuring of transnational office buildings is carried out. There is no doubt that in the three cities the different modes and dynamics taking place in view of the local-global interactions are prompting different arrangements of environmental reforms. As will be argued, however, the environmental restructuring of transnational office buildings in these three cities is also developing similarities in certain aspects. To discuss these similarities and differences the chapter recapitulates the events explored in the previous three chapters and investigates among the three cities and four companies which general characteristics are governing the interaction of the two spaces – the local and the global – of environmental management. Based on this analysis it puts forward a conceptual discussion on the mechanisms that are in place and those that should be enhanced to make the global dynamics of urban environmental change work. Subsequently, it explores the hypotheses on ecological modernization theory stated in chapter 4 in the light of empirical events. The chapter finishes by discussing the contributions that this book makes to both ecological modernization and global/informational city theories and by proposing directions for further research.

While the study has largely focused on energy and water issues, the dynamics that will be analysed at this point do also (to a certain extent) correspond to other environmental aspects of office buildings related to the operational phase – such as solid waste streams, transport strategies, and so forth. Therefore, the variations to be explored below may be considered as representative of the general state of play of the environmental management of office buildings at the operational phase in these three cities in view of the global-local interfaces explored.

The Environmental Restructuring of Transnational Buildings

To analyse how the greening of transnational office-stocks is taking place in view of local and global social dynamics in the three cities, the following subsections will review the environmental strategies of the four companies – as actors in the global 'space of flows' – once deployed at the level of different cities, which operate as 'nodes' in the global network society. At the same time, at the level of these cities they also discuss the characteristics of the urban environmental policies and the resulting forms of the global-local, corporate-urban interfaces. After recapitulating such events for each case in empirical terms, each of the following subsections will analyse the interfaces between 'spaces of flows' and different 'spaces of places' from a more conceptual standpoint.

ING Group in Amsterdam, São Paulo and Beijing

ING's commitment to sustainable building dates back to the late 1970s and early 1980s when it started the construction of the NMB headquarters (ING Bank) in

Amsterdam. The greening of this building was exclusively an initiative of the bank, although its ambitions had – paradoxically – to be downgraded due to a number of impediments caused by the municipality of Amsterdam. For instance, the aim of producing an energy-sufficient structure was not accepted by the energy company at that time (a public company), which required the building to use at least 20 per cent of energy from the mains grid (fearing competition if this was to be done on a large scale). Moreover, the building permit was only issued after one of the directors convinced a high-level authority at the municipality of Amsterdam. The introduction of environmental innovations in this case proved therefore to be triggered by the bank, which at the time was not yet a multinational company.

In turn, the environmental management framework of ING Group (the Health, Safety and Environmental Management Systems) was formulated in 1995, when the Group's Executive Board introduced an environmental report and a corporate environmental policy regarding its environmental ambitions in the Netherlands. The framework consists of internal and external guidelines: the former concerning waste processes and energy use in the premises, the latter regarding the development of products that contribute to a better environment. An important feature of the internal guidelines is the commitment to achieve long-term agreements with the Dutch government for energy efficiency, in view of the prescriptions laid down by the Dutch Ministry of Economic Affairs (the main authority in the Netherlands dealing with energy-related issues), aiming to reduce the consumption of energy in the bank's premises in the Netherlands by 25 per cent, based on 1996 figures, by 2006. It is thus correct to suggest that the decision to initiate the programme was directly related to the deregulation of the energy market in the Netherlands. It was during this period that the Dutch government set up its energy programme – consisting of the energy performance standard and the long-term agreement for energy use, in addition to the energy premium schemes granted to energy companies – so as to ensure that energy in the country would be used in an economic way. To a certain extent, this may also be correlated with the endorsement of the Kyoto Protocol at that time, as the Netherlands committed itself to contributing to reducing global warming by decreasing its emissions of carbon dioxide in numerous industrial sectors, including buildings. In this sense, it is the Dutch Ministry of Economic Affairs – more than the Ministry of Housing, Spatial Planning and Environment or the municipality of Amsterdam (or even the bank so to speak) – that was influential regarding the energy saving strategies in this particular case. In terms of environmental strategies at the ING headquarters, the reduction in energy consumption has been accomplished ever since through behavioural campaigns (through an Energy Awareness Campaign) and the installation of advanced energy monitoring systems (through an Energy Monitoring Programme), the latter being initiated in conjunction with Novem, the Dutch agency for energy and environment (cf. ING, 2000b). According to a local manager, these internal guidelines are mainly developed for financial and marketing reasons, the latter by ensuring a clean record to the public. Regarding the installation of the advanced energy monitoring system, another argument is that this was done mainly due to the privatization of the energy market in the Netherlands which made it necessary for the users to monitor flows of energy more precisely.

In view of these internal guidelines, most of the bank's current achievements in terms of sustainable building are related to energy consumption, through advanced monitoring, although the environmental report also demonstrates a slight reduction in water consumption in the building as well as a concern regarding commuting energy and related expenses. ING Bank's (former NMB) headquarters, constructed strictly according to environmental and health criteria, introducing innovations of radical dematerialization and substitution for both energy and water, is exceptional for the bank's current environmental ambitions, whose approach has not been replicated. The construction of the ING Group headquarters, for instance, has followed a different path to achieve environmental efficiency, favouring mostly energy-related issues. An inconsistency that can be noted in the Netherlands, in this regard, is that governmental as well as corporate programmes tend to target energy use in buildings much stronger than water-related issues.

Also in 1995 ING endorsed to the ICC Business Principles (Charter for Sustainable Development), the most widespread voluntary international code of conduct, known for its generic codes of environmental conduct, which more than 2000 companies have already endorsed. According to a local manager, this step took place mostly to increase the bank's international credibility and thereby facilitate its access to international markets. In 1999, the bank's Executive Board finally introduced an environmental management framework applicable on a global basis, valid for both the internal and external guidelines described above (cf. ING 2000b). One of its aims was to standardize the environmental aspects of the Group's properties worldwide, such as in the field of energy and waste streams.

So far, however, the process of worldwide standardization of the bank's internal environmental guidelines has started to be implemented in the Netherlands and, according to the environmental report, in Australian branches. The Energy Awareness Campaign and the Energy Monitoring Programme are not being implemented in either São Paulo or Beijing at the moment. Local managers report that environmental criteria were not given explicit consideration during the decision-making phase regarding the selection of the premises in both cities. Nor are environmental criteria being applied in the running of the offices, except for basic environmental management systems based on common sense – which are being carried out according to local initiatives, which is to say, voluntarily. Thus the only environmental innovation that is in place regards the use of a water-recycling system in Beijing's office, a standard of dematerialization launched by the Beijing Water Management Bureau. In São Paulo, ING's office does not display any environmental innovations, and this is also attributable to the fact that local environmental policy networks only have incipient programmes targeting office buildings, with rather limited effects. During the city's energy rationing programme in 2001, the bank's policy was to decrease the amount of redundant lighting, start a behavioural programme, switch on an energy generator to cope with the required reduction and to introduce a smart lighting system in the lavatories. While the latter strategy consists of a long-term solution of dematerialization, the other three were discontinued at the end of the energy rationing period.

In both São Paulo and Beijing, decisions regarding environmental issues at ING are raised, decided and financed at the local branch. Therefore, and in spite of the bank's global environmental policy, there is an apparent mismatch between the planned and the implemented as no channels of environmental management stemming from the global headquarters are influencing the environmental dimension – at the operational phase – of the offices in Beijing and São Paulo. The offices in

Beijing and São Paulo only cope with space and conventional (not environment-related) technology efficiency, in addition to issues regarding location and architectural image, where ING is a tenant of the space. In both cities, ING has little contact with local institutions dealing with environmental policies applicable to office buildings, so that possible partnerships for the deployment of environmental innovations are also more limited in these two cities. In Amsterdam, in contrast, the bank is more ambitious in terms of environmental management, which seems to be attributable to the fact that authorities in this city take a much stronger stand regarding environmental issues, where in addition ING is the owner of its properties.

In this sense, the environmental restructuring of ING's office buildings in the three cities is showing more diversity of policy arrangements, than a global homogenization of environmental policies or strategies. In Amsterdam the interface between global and local management of environmental flows is mutually constructive, implemented and enforced. Both spaces of social action are gearing towards synergistic effects, in which the local introduces constraining policies and incentives (such as the energy standard and subsidies) and the global, based on these, responds with environmental management strategies, including an energy awareness campaign and energy monitoring system, among others. In São Paulo, in contrast, the picture that emerges is quite the opposite. There, the management of environmental flows conducted by local and global actors is mutually discouraging, as neither actor is prompting environmental change. Only basic environmental management systems are being carried out there, contradicting the statements of the company's global environmental report. Urban environmental policies are also incipient, and ineffective, providing no incentives or norms of environmental conduct. Finally, the case of Beijing demonstrates that the environmental restructuring of ING's office is dependent on local policy agencies and is exclusively geared towards the dematerialization of water consumption. In this situation, since the company shows inconsistency with its global environmental policy, the environmental restructuring of ING's offices is a process constructed, implemented and enforced unilaterally by the locality.

In view of such observations, one can conclude from the Amsterdam situation that a nation-state in cooperation with a multinational company tends to get environmental policies started also at the level of the 'space of flows', with the company also referring to transnational codes of conduct such as the ICC charter. In other words, the strategies arising from the Amsterdam-ING interception tend to be translated – at least on paper – into global company strategies. However, the expectation of seeing these policies implanted and implemented in similar ways at the other nodes of the globalized society involving ING as a company does not turn out to be realistic. One might conclude that the environmental management strategies of ING in the other cities prove to be driven primarily by local actors and policies, resulting ultimately in environmental strategies at a lower level as compared to the regime ING is striving for in Amsterdam.

Andersen in Amsterdam, São Paulo and Beijing

As the premises of Andersen in Amsterdam, São Paulo and Beijing indicated, this company is not an example of a global network of environmental management practices. The numerous environmental innovations introduced in the (former) Andersen building in Amsterdam South were primarily triggered by local developers and building companies. These innovations exceeded the requirements laid down in the building code, as the building was a pilot project to set benchmarks for environmental performance. Yet, its construction received support from the municipal government (the municipality of Amstelveen), which facilitated the procedures for delivering a construction permit. In addition, the investor (a German bank) also received subsidies from the Dutch government for the environmental features of the building. Novem, the Dutch agency for energy and environment, also participated in enhancing the energy aspects of the building. The Andersen company, conversely, did not have specific environmental ambitions regarding the building and seemed to occupy such green building 'by chance'. Nor did it have any specific environmental policy framework, either at the global headquarters in Chicago, or locally in foreign premises. In Amsterdam, local managers report having conducted basic environmental management systems voluntarily, mostly based on common sense, that is, good housekeeping, although no written commitments were ever available. In this sense, the greening of this building in Amsterdam was mainly influenced by local economic networks (the developers and investors), with the support of local policy networks (through subsidies and other forms of facilitations), but with no direct interference of the multinational company. The main environmental strategies of these local actors are in the energy area again and they consist of dematerialization and substitution of technologies through, for instance, the introduction of solar cells. There is no advanced monitoring in place, however.

Against this background, it will not come as a surprise that Andersen's offices in São Paulo were rather poor in terms of environmental management. In this city, local facility managers claimed that the company only pursued basic environmental management practices, mostly regarding the cleaning of air-conditioning systems and waste recycling, where decisions were made and financed with local budgets. As a tenant, Andersen did not have any involvement in the design phase of the office in São Paulo, and therefore argued that it was not liable for the selection of certain energy and water intensive technologies. Yet, the building underwent a major refurbishment during which period Andersen did not introduce any specific environmental innovation either. Local facility managers report they suggested the installation of energy and water efficiency technologies several times – for cost-reduction reasons mainly. These recommendations were rejected by Andersen's local management board. During the energy rationing of 2001 the building did not incorporate any long-term strategies, such as those related to dematerialization or monitoring, instead achieving the required reduction in energy consumption mostly by deploying a diesel-driven generator.

Andersen's involvement with local agencies regarding environmental care was limited in São Paulo to energy and water companies, for the payment of bills through the facility management department. In this context, and as environmental strategies introduced by local public organizations were also weak in this city, the building does not present any relevant environmental innovation. In Beijing, in contrast, although Andersen could be expected to have shown a similar code for environmental management as in Amsterdam and São Paulo, the building where it maintained its offices (the China World Trade Center building) uses a system of water recycling. This system is interesting in that it had been introduced during the design phase of the building (mid-1980s) by the engineering firm responsible for the construction (a Japanese company, hence a global economic agent), following the available international, state-of-the-art standards and technologies. Although it has now become a standard being applied – and strictly enforced – by Beijing's Water Management Bureau, the China World Trade Center building was one of the first in China to make use of this solution of dematerialization.

Andersen considered itself as a multinational 'partnership', rather than a multinational company, and as such all units worldwide were fairly autonomous, including decisions on the environmental management of the premises. However, before the company's closure, the global headquarters in Chicago had stated a wish to homogenize the environmental performance of the worldwide premises of Andersen, to be coordinated by the real estate department located in Chicago. Although the company did not last long enough to see this homogenizing process taking place, the aim was both economic (to save on energy/water bills) and ecological (to protect the environment).

The interfaces of Andersen in the three cities leave little doubt that the environmental strategies of the company's offices are, irrespective of the location, dependent on the local environmental management, either from policy networks or economic networks, or both. In Amsterdam, the management of environmental flows materializes because local networks of environmental change are rather strong, and as such the building Andersen maintained in this city represented a breakthrough in terms of environmental standards. The company itself, however, did not contribute to this greening process. In Beijing, the local networks are rather strong in terms of water management, so the building Andersen occupied in this city had a particular system of water management. Both in Amsterdam and Beijing, the main company strategy of environmental change was dependent upon the unilaterally constructed, implemented and enforced environmental management frameworks as put forward by local agents. Finally, in São Paulo the situation again turned out to be different because of the virtual absence in this city of effective local environmental policies. In this city, the building Andersen occupied also can be said to provide proof of this general absence of local environmental care, as was already concluded from the case of ING in the same city.

By evaluating the Andersen cases in the three cities, the crucial role played by local actors in the environmental reform strategies of transnational buildings comes to light. Such local actors can either be economic or political actors. The environmental strategies they deploy reach the company and its local facility managers either directly, or via the (representative experts of) local infrastructural networks involved in the provisioning of water, energy or waste services, or via both. As the Amsterdam case clearly shows, local actors might use environmental strategies to attract transnational actors to their local nodes – for instance, the German investment bank via subsidies for green projects. In this sense, by predicting the top environmental priorities to attract such transnational actors to do business, local actors are possibly also laying out a kind of 'green carpet' for companies which – now or in the near future – would prefer certain nodes in the global network for their good environmental performance. In view of this theoretical possibility, the local green office-stock of company X or Y can either be the result of incidental or ad hoc local environmental policies, or the result of a global company strategy aiming to pick a green-equipped node in the global network of cities. The Andersen case indicates that the green building it occupied in Amsterdam must be seen as the result of the former – ad hoc, incidental – type.

ABN AMRO in São Paulo, Amsterdam and Beijing

ABN AMRO endorsed the Charter of the International Chamber of Commerce in 1992, committing itself to integrating environmental considerations into all business decisions. In 1995 an environmental policy was formulated and approved, eventually paving the way for the implementation of the first environmental management system, concerning in-house environmental management (such as waste management, goods purchasing, transport, energy and environmentally and people-friendly offices) and more sustainable financial products and services. In 1997, following the energy performance standard and the long-term agreement introduced by the Dutch Ministry of Economic Affairs in 1995, the bank launched an energy project for its Dutch premises, consisting of three components: the installation of advanced energy monitoring (counting pulses of energy every 15 minutes to detect and correct abnormalities), the introduction of energy management (through intelligent devices, to make sure that lights are off when human presence is not detected) and the reduction of energy use (by investing in technological substitution). As in the case of ING, the introduction of an advanced energy monitoring system is to a certain extent related to the liberalization of the energy market, which requires a detailed monitoring of energy consumption in the building. An important component regarding the energy project is the fact that the bank has a fund of two million euros to be spent annually in the Netherlands, for which investments should have a payback period of five years, thus being an exception to the bank's policy for investing in two-year amortizing projects.

So far, the global headquarters in Amsterdam is the greatest achievement of the energy project, and is a kind of pilot project that introduced numerous environmental innovations, going beyond prescriptions set forth by the government. In addition to energy monitoring and management, it has also advanced technologies for acclimatization, including climate façades and climate ceilings, thus employing dematerialization solutions. The municipality of Amsterdam, in turn, also played a significant role in the greening of the building as it established covenants or methods of cooperation that resulted in the decrease of single car use by employees in commuting, as the building would offer a limited number of parking spaces (this was done through Amsterdam's transport authority, which committed in turn to improving the public transport system). On the other hand, however, neither the bank nor the municipality of Amsterdam influenced the decrease in water consumption. ABN AMRO is thus not pursuing the same ambitions it has for energy when it comes to water use, following the claim that water is not yet an environmental priority, and therefore still a rather inexpensive resource in the Netherlands. These decisions are made by the Health and Safety Department and partly by the Housing and Real Estate Department, which operate under the Consumer and Commercial Clients business unit, and are supervised by the Management Board. Issues regarding sustainable building are ultimately under responsibility of the bank's Management Board, although it is clear that the greening of this building is a combination of efforts made by both the company and governmental organizations at different levels.

In turn, the bank's environmental report states that in-house environmental management, unlike the energy project, is applicable on a global basis. This regards environmentally and people-friendly offices, thereby encouraging improvements in energy consumption, waste, purchasing and transport throughout the building life-cycle, that is, from raw material extraction, transport, construction, use and demolition (cf. ABN AMRO, 2000b). At the moment, however, when analysing the local premises of ABN AMRO in São Paulo and Beijing this policy is not yet in place. In São Paulo, a local manager reports that the procedures during the acquisition – and renovation – of the properties of Banco Real in 1998, decided by Dutch managers, concerned mostly decoration elements, and did not regard the in-house environmental policies as such. In its running, only basic – and voluntary – environmental management systems are fulfilled, concerning the cleaning of air-conditioning systems and basic waste recycling; no specifications are in fact stemming from the global headquarters. During the energy rationing period in 2001 the building employed a few energy-saving solutions, such as the switching off of redundant lighting, but nothing was pursued in terms of longer-term strategies (related to dematerialization, substitution or monitoring). Since local networks of environmental policy also do not have specific prescriptions to prompt environmental innovations in office buildings in São Paulo – nor did they during the energy rationing – the building ABN AMRO maintains in the city is fairly limited in this regard.

In Beijing, ABN AMRO is tenant of a small office space, which was selected because of its location and standards of architecture and building services, not taking explicitly into account environmental criteria. Only standard or mainstream environmental management is taking place, as the local managers argue that the branch is rather small, and the budgets too limited to make up for any long-term investment. The environmental innovation that exists has to do with the water-recycling system, introduced following prescriptions of Beijing's Water Management Bureau, and an energy-saving system (including a smart lighting system) introduced by the facility managers of the building. While the former solution consists of a standard used by the Water Management Board (to ensure that water resources are managed in a more sustainable way), the later is related to the increasing energy prices in the country, prompting facility managers to use electricity more economically.

Decisions regarding the in-house environmental strategies of ABN AMRO in both cities need (at the moment) to be raised locally, by local managers, although budgets have to be approved by the headquarters in Amsterdam. With regard to ABN-AMRO's environmental strategies, two specific characteristics should be discussed. First, the energy project in use in the Netherlands does not apply at a global level. Therefore, in the case of energy projects outside the Netherlands (possibly suggested by local managers at foreign branches), the payback period would have to be two years (unlike in the Netherlands which is five years), thus reducing the scope for investing in technologies that might be costly in the short-term. Second, the in-house environmental strategies, though stated in the company's global environmental policy, for various (also local) reasons are not yet in use in São Paulo or Beijing. These topics demonstrate that while much is being accomplished in Amsterdam – notwithstanding the fact that the bank aims to apply some or most of the Amsterdam elements of environmental management at the global level as well – the bank is at this very moment not (yet) contributing to the greening of its offices in São Paulo and Beijing. Environmental innovations at the offices of ABN AMRO in Beijing and São Paulo thus turn out to be strongly dependent on local policy and economic networks. Finally, both in Beijing and São Paulo direct contacts between the company and local environmental policy networks are too limited to make the global company strategy work.

As can be noted, the environmental restructuring of ABN AMRO's offices in the three cities has much to do with the greening of ING's offices. In Amsterdam, both urban environmental policies and corporate environmental strategies are mutually constructed, implemented and enforced. Local actors launch standards and forms of incentives (such as covenants) for environmental change and the global company responds to these by elaborating a pilot project for sustainable building and an energy project, among others. As in the case of ING, the environmental innovations tend to start with energy issues, with energy policies constituting a hybridization process between urban policies and corporate strategies. In São Paulo and in Beijing, the bank's global environmental policies regarding in-house management are not being implemented, while ABN AMRO's facility managers in both cities turn out to be heavily dependent on local agents and actors.

In this regard, the ABN-AMRO case shows how environmental policies that are to be applied to the companies' housing strategies were originally developed at the local level, these policies resulting from an active interplay and mutual rein-forcement of local strategies and company strategies. While the company intended to generalize (part of) these local experiences into a company-wide environmental strategy to be applied in the space of flows, this pro-active stance does not automat-ically result in worldwide successes. When local actors at other nodes of the global network of cities are not willing or able to unfold a 'green carpet' and are even unwilling to respond to the companies' global strategies in green housing, there results only a selective or partial strategy of environmental reform at these nodes.

IBM in Amsterdam, São Paulo and Beijing

Of the four companies, IBM has the longest-standing environmental policy, including strategies introduced back in the 1970s. This is probably due to the fact that IBM, also having production facilities, has been more compelled than the others in imple-menting environmental regimes. In this sense, its global environmental policy is also more solid in terms of scope and enforcement procedures as compared to those of the three other companies, and also applicable to the running of its offices. Its main rule is to follow the most restrictive standard, either the local or the one set by the company regarding the design and operation of premises, such as concerning issues related to indoor environmental quality, fire safety, energy/water use, and so on. In addition, another rule is that all premises worldwide need to reduce consumption of energy and water annually by four per cent and one per cent respectively (to achieve cost reductions) as well as carry out periodical environmental audits.

In the Netherlands IBM has currently finished the construction of an environmen-tally-friendly building, designed by an internationally renowned environmental architect, where most environmental features follow Dutch prescriptions. As in the case of ING and ABN AMRO, IBM has also installed an advanced energy monitoring system in its premises in the Netherlands, claiming to have done so to facilitate the reading of energy meters in view of the liberalization of energy markets. To achieve the targets of energy and water reduction, IBM in the Netherlands makes use of behavioural campaigns, downsizes server areas, and replaces obsolete technologies. The environmental performance of the premises of IBM worldwide are annually inspected by the Real Estate and Site Operations Department located in the USA. As indicated above, IBM's rule regarding in-house management is to follow the most restrictive environmental policy, either that stemming from its global environmental policy or that introduced by local authorities. In the case of its offices in the Netherlands, the most restrictive rules are those set forth by local authorities, such as the energy performance standard, the long-term agreement, indoor disease-management prescriptions (such as legionnaires' disease), and so forth. In this sense, the greening of its new headquarters as well as the greening of the operations of all its offices in the country are being considerably influenced by local policies.

Both in São Paulo and Beijing somewhat similar environmental standards, albeit achieved through different strategies, are being applied in the premises of IBM. In São Paulo these strategies include a study of energy and water saving initiated in 1996, to update the technologies used in the building original from the 1970s (originally constructed by IBM itself), leading to the retrofitting of lighting systems, the installation of water-efficient sanitary devices and occupancy densification, among other things; all decisions made locally but eventually supervised by the Real Estate and Operations Department based in the USA. They also include an environmental management system for the control of the indoor environment, waste management and water quality. Local facility managers report that the global environmental policy does not impose energy and water efficiency standards as such, but the building is annually inspected for the reductions of four per cent and one per cent of the consumption. Unlike in Amsterdam, as local environmental policies do not have a significant influence on the environmental performance of office buildings in São Paulo, all the environmental management innovations (such as the substitution of the above-mentioned technologies) are being introduced by the company.

In Beijing, IBM's strategies to comply with the global environmental policy include the application of an environmental site assessment for the selection of the office building, through which the indoor environment as well as the management of energy and water are assessed to ensure that, for instance, water quality meets IBM's standards. They also include an environmental management system consisting of waste management (through separation), water saving (through behavioural campaigns) and energy saving (through behavioural campaigns, in addition to saving strategies like avoiding wasteful use). The building is also checked annually for the reduction of energy and water consumption, by IBM Japan, which is in turn inspected by IBM USA. While in São Paulo IBM has a facility management department with an environmental subdivision reporting to the global headquarters in the USA, in Beijing environmental issues are still within the domain of the human resource department, and are reported to IBM Japan. As was the case in São Paulo, all environmental innovations taking place at IBM's premises in Beijing stem from the company. In this respect it is noteworthy that, unlike the buildings occupied by ABN AMRO, ING and Andersen in Beijing, the IBM Tower does not have this specific (local) water-recycling system. So local networks turn out not to have a determining influence on its greening.

In this context, the environmental restructuring of IBM's offices in the three cities again can be said to illustrate a specific local-global hybridization process. This is particularly the case of the buildings in Amsterdam and Beijing, as their greening processes is constructed, implemented and enforced by both the global company and the local agencies. A difference that emerges is that, as the company's environmental policy is to follow the most restrictive rule, in Amsterdam urban environmental policies surpass to some extent the company's environmental strategy, becoming thus the prevailing factor in the greening process. In Beijing, the company's environmental strategies surpass the local policies, although the local also has policies of sustainable building (that is, of water management, which paradoxically do not apply to the IBM Tower, cf. chapter 7). Finally, in São Paulo the environmental restructuring of IBM's offices is exclusively dependent on the company's strategies, as urban environmental policies are incipient. In this case, the greening is a process unilaterally conceptualized, put into practice and reinforced by the global.

IBM thus illustrates the following obvious picture. As a pro-active and global actor, IBM can be regarded as a front-runner in developing environmental policies in the space of flows. This not only implies that corporate environmental strategies at the worldwide level are accommodated with global standards for sustainable housing strategies, but also that companies 'learn' how to deal with the interaction between the space of flows and the space of place. In the case of IBM, this results in the company guideline to always follow the strictest regimes in place, whether originating from local level actors and dynamics or from company strategies as developed in the space of flows. Therefore, to be a pro-active company at the global level, it requires making environmental policies work at *all* nodes in the world network society, despite any lack of incentives or synergies from local-level actors and dynamics.

In a Global Matrix of Urban Environmental Change

By highlighting the main dynamics that may or may not be prompting environmental change, it becomes clear that there are different social dynamics and triggers towards the greening of transnational buildings as well as various types of arrangements of environmental restructuring in the different cities. Environmental policies stemming from the global are in some cases easily adopted or absorbed by the local. In some cases, environmental policies deployed by the local may actively trigger or seek to further policies of the global. At certain times environmental policies of the global may also activate policies of the local and in some cases even bypass local actors and infrastructures by implementing company strategies more or less autonomously. In no single case, however, are environmental policies of the local actively hindering or obstructing policies of the global, or vice-versa. After interpreting the local-global interface of environmental management for the four companies in the three cities, we will now move beyond the sphere of empirical factors and attempt to interpret the above findings in a more general and theoretical way. In so doing, a focus will be given to the opportunities and possibilities for boosting the implementation of environmental reforms in a transnational perspective.

When exploring environmental change in office buildings, the above findings leave little doubt that two different realms of management practices are being dealt with. On the one hand there exists a local urban perspective, comprising the realm of environmental *policies* above all, while on the other hand one identifies global corporate perspectives comprising primarily the realm of environmental *management*. In general, local environmental policies are elaborated with the ultimate aim of influencing the behaviour of both local and global actors in order to realize or maintain the use of natural resources in a more sustainable way. In general too the degree of institutionalization of environmental criteria is positively correlated with the degree of importance attached to the environment by a society at large, that is, the weight and political priority given to environmental protection in the local culture surrounding the nodes of the global network society. In this context, the environmental restructuring of office buildings is primarily one among long-term solutions that are deployed to ensure the sustainability of the local environment and infrastructure in the first place. The dominant discourse in this realm is therefore that of *optimizing the use of limited resources* or environmental flows, such as the physical streams of energy and water. And the dominant means of influencing the behaviour of stakeholders range from constraining policies (such as standards), to monetarization (including increases in energy prices, introduction of eco-taxes, and so forth), incentives and forms of cooperation or negotiated agreements (such as covenants), among others. This also applies to the case of private utilities, as such companies do also want to sell more out of less to ensure the survival of their business. It is self-evident that in different societies environmental interests are given different priorities. Where other priorities dominate or monopolize the political agenda – such as poverty and economic downturns – the environment (and its protective policies) is severely jeopardized, limiting the local urban influence in greening office-stocks.

In contrast, the global realm of corporate management has as its dominant perspective maximizing profits and business continuity. Environmental strategies are only viable if they do not (structurally) jeopardize these dominant goals. By the same token, environmental protection also goes hand in hand with the long-term survival of the company, so that the underlying discourse of corporate environmental management is that of *preserving the environment within conditions of continuity and profit maximization*. For companies, the greening of their offices is sometimes welcomed as an opportunity to improve productivity and increase revenues, by for instance reducing the running costs of the premises (such as through energy and water bills). In addition, it can be used as an opportunity for the company to perform as a (socially and environmentally) responsible company and as such attract clients and satisfy customers. As observed in the case studies, the main corporate strategies as they are developed to realize goals of dematerialization of resource use in corporate offices are based on management principles – such as environmental management systems, environmental audits, environmental site assessment, energy saving projects, monitoring, environmental reports, and so forth. These strategies may further comprise corporate standards (such as reducing energy consumption annually, following the most restrictive rule, among others), which may in turn also push for technological substitution.

As can be noted, the two realms of global corporate environmental management and local urban environmental policies, respectively, do not conflict in principle.

However, a major contradiction in corporate environmental management lies in the increase in short-term capital expenditure due to the investments involved, which sometimes goes against the profit component of their management discourse. Therefore, it is correct to say that the institutionalization of environmental care in the corporate sphere has to a certain extent to be *activated* or encouraged by urban policies or by a specific branch of pro-active corporate strategies, such as those discussed above. Local policies do play a role in overcoming the exclusive dominance of profit maximization strategies, for example when taking the primary steps to trigger environmental change in a specific location. This explains why in cities with a well-developed environmental management structure, such as Amsterdam, companies are more induced to pursue environmental change. On the other hand it can also be seen that global network based environmental institutions and regulations (ICC, WTO) 'directly' trigger actors at the global level as well.

In addition, transcending the dichotomy of local environmental policies and global environmental management, two other mechanisms can be noted with regard to the greening of transnational buildings in major cities: transnational urban environmental policies and local corporate environmental management. Local urban environmental policies are increasingly transnationalized via various mechanisms, spreading to various cities. Local Agenda 21 initiatives, Sustainable Cities Program, renewable energy targets strongly affected by, for example, the Kyoto Protocol, best practice standards in energy efficiency, international transfer of building codes are all policies that started originally with policy makers at the local or national level, but managed to become part of a global political space of environmental policy making. Via international conferences, international information systems (such as journals, the Internet), global meetings such as those in Rio de Janeiro in 1992 and Johannesburg in 2002 and numerous meetings in between, but also via international economic and civil society interactions and exchanges, local policies, strategies and activities become part of a global flow of environmental reform, to feed into and land in other localities. Thus it should not come as a surprise to find to some extent similar initiatives of local policy makers and utility sectors in different major cities.

At the same time corporate environmental management tends to 'localize'. Local branches of multinational firms develop their own initiatives in dealing with the environmental dimensions of office buildings, and the central headquarters of multinational companies give them room for this manoeuvring, albeit to a different extent for different firms on different environmental issues. Andersen is a typical example of a multinational firm that allows greater degrees of freedom to local offices in designing environmental care systems, making the final result of environmental performance in the office buildings more dependent on the local urban environmental policies and local corporate environmental management, than on the transnational environmental management of Andersen as a global firm. 'Localizing' policies in this case can also mean that in the end relatively little activities result. Within the local branches of IBM the degree of freedom to develop a local corporate environmental management is more limited, but is still there. In this case localizing also takes on a specific meaning, namely adapting to local standards only if they are stricter when compared to overall company strategies. Another illustration of local corporate environmental management is the case of Andersen in Beijing, which (incidentally) used the water-recirculation system originally launched by a Japanese engineering firm in the building it occupied in Beijing, which became a standard later on for other buildings in that city. Other economic actors (such as developers, architects and construction products manufacturers) could also articulate and implement greening strategies in local office buildings that might subsequently internationalize via the transnational corporate structures.

As shown above, most dynamics can be accurately described within the interface model, that is, the interface between urban (local) environmental management and corporate (global) environmental management, as proposed in this volume. However, the last two mechanisms in particular have further consequences for this original model. It is not so much that this approach is incorrect, but rather that reality turns out to be more complex. The greening of transnational buildings is not just dependent on and influenced by global corporate flows of environmental management and local spaces of environmental policy and utilities. The 'space of flows' and the 'space of places' both show combinations of political and economic dynamics working simultaneously. Transnational urban policies and local corporate environmental management do play a role, which depends strongly on the local environmental capacity and profile of the cities, the structure and corporate image of the firm and the kind of environmental issues that are being dealt with. This trans-lates into a combination of local or global (urban or corporate) mechanisms and dynamics – as suggested by the quadrants of the matrix in Table 8.1 – which tends to predominate in the greening of transnational office buildings in metropolitan cities in this era of transnational urbanization.

Table 8.1   The matrix of urban environmental change at the local-global interface

	Local/space of place	Global/space of flows
Urban environmental policy	x	x
Corporate environmental strategy	x	x

The Ecological Modernization of Transnational Buildings

This book largely applied the theory of ecological modernization to frame its empirical enquiry. Reverting to the hypotheses elaborated at the end of chapter 4 we should now see how the theory, in its descriptive dimension, fits when exploring globalization and the environmental restructuring of transnational urban spaces. Along these lines I will also reflect on how this study may contribute to the advance and/or refinement of the theory's core propositions in the light of our empirical and conceptual findings and propose lines for further research.

As its adherents have made clear, ecological modernization theory is primarily a theory on social change. One of its core hypotheses is that besides economic criteria, production and consumption processes are increasingly being designed and eval-uated also against ecological criteria. These ecological criteria are eventually devel-oping as an 'independent' rationale of global modernity, inducing transformations in the processes of production and consumption towards an ecological *modernization* logic. In the light of these transformations, the economic rationale of modernity is being ecologized whereas an emerging ecological rationale is being economized while assuming an emancipated status in modernity.

When applied to office buildings, this assumption suggests that in line with other production and consumption processes, office buildings are increasingly designed and operated according to an ecological logic. In chapters 3 and 4 we tried to grasp how this logic is taking place and put forward that the emerging ecological criteria for the design and operation of urban/transnational office-stocks is developing in an undeniable *modernization* process, favouring more efficient – rather than self-sufficient – use of resources. Environmental innovations are emerging in a combination of locally embedded techniques, such as passive solar design, with global technologies provided by global suppliers, such as saving equipment (energy, water devices) and high-performance materials (such as cladding, windows, and so forth), fostering a partial dematerialization in addition to a substitution of technologies and monitoring of resource use. Finally, these environmental innovations are emerging as a means to reduce the expenses of the companies that occupy the office space as well as an asset for marketing the environmental performance of such companies.

The information gathered during the preceding three chapters confirms that, though not to the same extent in all its aspects or in all places, ecological criteria are playing a growing role in the design and operation of urban office buildings worldwide, and much along the above lines. Moreover, the data also leave no doubt that ecological arguments are consolidating as an important factor of urban development as well as of corporate agendas, a fact that applies, though in different degrees, to most of the transnational buildings analysed in this book. Information raised throughout the book suggests that environmental innovations triggered at the interface between urban policies and corporate strategies are indeed fostering a modernization process, comprising solutions of monetarization, monitoring, technological substitution and dematerialization. These developments leave little doubt that ecological arguments are indeed ascending in public and private agendas, particularly when it comes to urban policies where a clear concern regarding the sustainability of using limited resources becomes increasingly obvious. This hypothesis is therefore helpful when studying the environmental transformation of office buildings in different places.

However, the processes through which such ecological criteria are emerging in the urban office-stocks in different locations vary, according to the information gathered in this volume. In line with ecological modernization theory, a second, fundamental hypothesis that we stated in chapter 4 regards the transformation of the institutional order when dealing with environmental protection with the changing roles of both the state and the market in carrying out environmental reforms. Whereas in earlier periods of environmental policy making (such as the 1970s) the state had a crucial role to play in instigating environmental reforms – usually through top-down, command-and-control policies – nowadays the state is rather 'delegating' environmental care tasks to the market via appropriate, enabling policies. When looking at the role of the state in the environmental management of transnational office-stocks, this proposition is in turn entangled in another theoretical discussion as, in an era of transnational urbanization, the role of the state in managing transnational urban spaces also becomes ambiguous (cf. chapter 2).

When assessing the role of the state – in (i) governing the environmental challenges of transnational spaces and (ii) launching enabling policies – the evidence raised in the previous three chapters seems to add more to divergence than convergence. This is probably due to the different economic and political regimes of the cities (deliberately) selected for the research. In a highly developed, democratic and relatively state-controlled market economy city such as Amsterdam, for instance, it is clear that the state – through both municipal and national governmental bodies – plays a key role in controlling the environmental challenges emerging with the rise of transnational spaces as well as in launching a combination of enabling and constraining policies. In a newly industrialized and socialist market economy city such as Beijing it is also clear that the state exerts a great deal of control over the rising transnational spaces, through for instance being a partner in every development that is taking place – although breaches of the building code are being reported. However, its role in managing the urban environment seems to be still approaching mainly command-and-control strategies, as the requirement of environmental impact assessments and the water-recycling standard for large buildings indicate. Finally, in a newly industrialized, democratic and relatively free-market city such as São Paulo the state is still fairly lax regarding the general management of transnational spaces, favouring (economic) growth but allowing a rapid environmental transformation of the city, by for instance modifying zoning regulations and issuing policies that allow growth and – paradoxically – environmental abuse. On the other hand, the state, through different government levels, seems to be slowly launching enabling policies of environmental management, by for instance developing pilot projects in the rational use of water (including for office buildings, launched by the water company) and also by requiring private energy companies to optimize the consumption of energy (launched by national energy agency during the privatization process). Yet, these enabling policies are (still) not effective, calling into question their value in a city where the environment is a topic that is neither prioritized in policy/economic circles nor in societal values. The role of the state in governing environmental change deserves therefore a more careful interpretation when applied to urban spaces on a global scale as we witness that the predictions of ecological modernization theory are not leading to similar consequences in other locations than Europe.

In contrast, however, although these differences are clearly observed, the third hypothesis that comes to the fore regarding the role of the market in implementing environmental reforms is confirmed throughout our case studies. While environmental criteria are emerging differently in political circles, they are being incorporated by economic circles worldwide, although in different intensities, when analysing office buildings. That is, besides the evidence raised in the three cities analysed in this study, market actors – developers, companies, banks, construction products manufacturers, and so forth – are often indeed playing a crucial role in promoting an environmental shift in urban development and building practices. In addition, there is no doubt that market actors are in certain cases not only complying with constraining policies or assimilating enabling policies launched by the state, but are also furthering the development of environmental technologies for office buildings as well as environmental management approaches to be applied in offices. Information gathered in this volume indicates that market actors are in a number of cases – and in all the three cities analysed – indeed going beyond the prescriptions of the government in the carrying out of environmental change.

In this sense, this hypothesis put forward by the ecological modernization theory is certainly helpful when analysing the dynamics of the environmental restructuring of office buildings. However, there are differences between places with a well-developed environmental care capacity – such as Amsterdam, Frankfurt, Tokyo and Sidney – and those where the environment is not a highly prioritized topic. In the former, market actors prompting environmental change are more numerous, hence more influential. In the latter, though they also exist, they are much scarcer. This discrepancy brings us back to the discussion on the role of the state in activating the environmental change of market actors, due to the issue of overcoming the financial short-term obstacles that usually accompany environmental innovations. Therefore, while valid, this hypothesis is still intertwined with the hypothesis of the role of the state in activating environmental change above discussed when analysing different cities.

This said, a culminating hypothesis raised in this study in the light of ecological modernization theory is that, if market actors indeed play a role as environmental reform carriers, in the era of globalization, they may play a role in diffusing environmental innovations worldwide. In so doing, they may prompt a race to the top in environmental management for particularly newly industrializing countries. Although in this book we looked at the contributions that multinational companies may be giving in this regard – claiming that once they start to play a key role in influencing the environmental restructuring of office-stocks in their home countries (cf. above, chapter 3) they should do the same elsewhere – this hypothesis also applies to other global market actors, such as international developers and investors.

Throughout this book we often found information on global economic actors that are favouring a virtuous, virtual circle of urban environmental reforms. The evidence is that such actors are indeed prime catalysts of an ecological modernization process, forming a bridge from locality to locality in the transcending of environmental change: distributing new solutions of environmental management, new technologies, new approaches in urban policies, and so forth. There is no doubt that global and local economic agents are among the main drivers in the environmental restructuring of transnational urban spaces. Although not always acting to transnationalize such environmental innovations (as some of our case studies demonstrate) they are valuable and potential social triggers of urban environmental change. In this light, therefore, the global virtuous circle of urban environmental reform does indeed seem to have been triggered. Yet, to be thoroughly efficient this still needs to be further ignited by adequate public as well as private policies, in line with the discussions above.

Epilogue

The ecological modernization theory taught us that environmental care can be and is in several cases promoted within the framework of a globalizing capitalism. The capitalist structures and dynamics are not jeopardized in advancing the greening of office-stocks. Yet, a consideration that should be given regards the time frame that this transformation process requires, and the degree to which the greening process takes place or might take place within the framework of global capitalism: does it fit the planet's carrying capacity? Information raised in this book indicates that urban environmental reforms are long, intricate processes, which depend on the ability of the various stakeholders involved. In the Netherlands, for instance, the institutionalization of environmental criteria started mostly during and following the energy and environmental crisis of the 1970s. Although 30 years later this institutionalization has led to the incorporation of environmental criteria in different (public, private) agendas, there is still a long road ahead. Nowadays only five per cent of commissioners require a so-called environmentally friendly office building in the Netherlands. This means that governmental policies have to keep evolving and that further stimuli need to be applied to the market. The virtuous circle has been triggered but is not yet surpassing the effects of the vicious circle of environmental disruption.

In terms of theory, the contribution of the study to this field is twofold. First, this study shows that the dynamics of urban environmental change are developing much in line with the propositions of ecological modernization theory, despite the different circumstances analysed in the research. This applies in particular to the emerging ecological criteria and to the role of market actors as catalysts of environmental change, issues that are valid to the three localities explored – albeit not to the same extent in each location. In addition, this study, being among the first to analyse the role of globalization processes in the environmental restructuring of different localities, is also among the first to move beyond the Eurocentric background of ecological modernization theory. For this reason, it contributes to the theory's development above all by showing that despite the many similarities with the theory's core propositions, some social dynamics of environmental reform diverge between the three cities, with different consequences for environmental change. This applies in particular to the role of the government in facilitating environmental reforms (such as the effectiveness of enabling and constraining policies). As discussed above, there is no doubt that in societies where the institutionalization of environmental care is still a somewhat embryonic process – or above all where environmental considerations are completely overruled by economic growth priorities – certain mechanisms still need to be evoked to trigger the dynamics of environmental change. In this sense, the global reach of ecological modernization theory is somewhat dependent on the working out of a number of parallel mechanisms of environmental reform. For this reason, the theoretical contribution of this volume is that it reveals that the dynamics of environmental change put forward by the mainstream elaborations on ecological modernization theory still deserve a more careful deliberation when looking at regions outside north-west Europe or (arguably) the OECD.

Secondly, this volume is also helpful in informing the debates on the global/ informational city or transnational urbanization. These debates, advanced by scholars such as Manuel Castells, John Friedmann and Saskia Sassen have been multiplying since the early 1980s, bringing a whole new research agenda into urban theory. While discussing the impacts of globalization on the spatial, social, economic and political dimensions of major cities, these debates also converge in the idea that globalization has indeed turned into a dominant reference point for interpreting contemporary urban change. The contribution of this study in this respect is to highlight the environmental dimension of major cities in such an agenda, by analysing the links between globalization and the environmental disruption and restructuring of the urban space. Globalization also affects the 'sustenance base' of urban centres. In doing so, the study also makes the link between such research agenda with the one of ecological modernization theory.

In turn, on a practical level, this study also provides insights to (urban) policy makers, corporate managers, local-global interface organizations (such as those developing codes of environmental conduct) and practitioners in general. For the first group of actors it demonstrates, in a comparative way, the mechanisms for environmental reform that may be in place in different localities as well as their effects, in view of the different circumstances of different places. With this information, policy makers may be in a way better equipped to formulate adequate policies to activate and facilitate these dynamics of environmental change. Corporate managers may also make use of the information in this study to better understand the modes, opportunities and constraints for in-house environmental strategies worldwide. Interface organizations may learn from it, particularly regarding the procedures of compliance with voluntary codes of environmental conduct (which should be better monitored and more strictly complied with). Finally, practitioners such as architects, urban planners, developers, and so on may also learn from this study when designing buildings/urban spaces in view of the kinds and shapes of environmental innovations that may be applied, such as technological substitution, monitoring, dematerialization. For this latter group of actors, this study may be of particular use for complementing the mainstream literature on 'sustainable building' by adding to it the societal dimension – exploring how technologies or environmental innovations are in general being selected and decided upon – which is usually so overlooked.

This study is an exploratory exercise. Consequently, there remains much to be done. Further research on this topic may find fruitful fields by shifting the analysis, for instance, from the operational phase of office buildings to other phases – such as construction – for which a whole new research programme should be elaborated in view of the different stakeholders involved (such as commissioners, designers, policy makers, and so on). In an enquiry into the construction phase, perhaps the participation of multinational companies would be more restricted whereas other global market actors would come to the fore, such as product manufacturers, foreign investors, architects and developers, carrying with them probably numerous environmental innovations. Another research line that could be developed is on different types of buildings in transnational urban spaces between local and global actors. Probably research into commercial facilities such as shopping outlets, airports and hotels will find abundant information on environmental innovations in this regard. Such enquiries can seek 'how' and 'why' answers, as in this volume. Conversely, they can also be conducted in a quantitative way, seeking in turn 'how many' sort of answers. This latter group of studies could involve, for instance, a larger number of major cities and look at the emergence of environmental innovations at the local/global interface by focusing on one particular company, one particular foreign investor or one developer. Or, alternatively, it could select a large number of companies, foreign investors or developers and see their influence on the environmental restructuring in one or two cities. Clearly, these studies would be helpful to supplement and quantify the argument put forward in this volume by providing generalizations of the empirical findings.

Globalization is indeed a major force of the current phase of modernity and, as we sought to demonstrate in this book, it is affecting the urban environment in a plurality of ways. Although there are several research approaches and techniques to explore how globalization is prompting environmental disruption and/or reform in different cities, what is important is not so much to stress shortcomings among the stakeholders in pursuing environmental care but above all to find entry points for solutions. Further research into this topic should therefore help enhance the argument of how – the mechanisms and extent to which – globalization, as a dominant and arguably irreversible trend in urban development, may be put to work to activate better local environments worldwide.

References

Abel, Chris (2000), *Architecture & Identity. Responses to Cultural and Technological Change*, Oxford: Architectural Press.

A Blueprint for Survival (1972), Harmondsworth: Penguin.

ABN AMRO Bank N.V. (2000a), *Annual Report*, Amsterdam: Press Relations Department.

—— (2000b), *Environment Report 1998–2000*, Amsterdam: ABN AMRO Bank N.V.

—— (2000c), *Portrait of a Building*, Amsterdam: ABN AMRO Corporate Communications.

—— (2001), *Annual Report 2001 ABN AMRO Holding N.V.*, Amsterdam: ABN AMRO Holding N.V.

—— (2002), *The Electric Energy Sector in Brazil*, internal report, ABN AMRO São Paulo.

Adams, Jan (1999), 'Foreign Direct Investment and the Environment: The Role of Voluntary Corporate Environmental Management', paper presented at the OECD conference on Foreign Direct Investment and the Environment, The Hague, the Netherlands, 28–29 January 1999.

Adams, W.M. (1990), *Green Development*, London: Routledge.

Albrow, Martin (1997), 'Travelling beyond Local Cultures. Socioscapes in a Global City', in Eade, John (ed.) (1997), *Living the Global City. Globalization as a Local Process,* London: Routledge, pp. 37–55.

—— Eade, J., Dürrschmidt, J., and Neil Washbourne (1997), 'The Impact of Globalization on Sociological Concepts – Community, Culture and Milieu', in Eade, John (ed.) (1997), *Living the Global City. Globalization as a Local Process*, London: Routledge, pp. 20–36.

Alexander, E.R. (1998), 'Amsterdam in the Red Queen's Country: Interorganizational Coordination and EU-Local Interaction in Spatial Planning and Policy', *European Planning Studies*, Vol. 6, No. 3, pp. 283–298.

AlSayyad, Nezar (1996), 'Culture, Identity, and Urbanism in a Changing World: A Historical Perspective on Colonialism, Nationalism, and Globalisation', in Cohen, M.A., Ruble, Blair A., Tulchin, Joseph S., and Allison M. Garland (eds), *Preparing for the Urban Future – Global Pressures and Local Forces*, Washington, D.C.: Woodrow Wilson Centre Special Studies, pp. 108–122.

Amsterdam Economic Development Department (2002), *Amsterdam Foreign Investment Office*, retrieved from http://www.ez.amsterdam on May 12 2002.

Amsterdam Physical Planning Department (2002), *Construction over the Ring Road*, retrieved from http://www.dro.amsterdam.nl on May 12 2002.

Anink, D., Boonstra, C. and Mak, J. (1996), *Handbook of Sustainable Building*, London: James & James Science Publishers.

Baker, N. and Koen Steemers (2000), *Energy and Environment in Architecture: A Technical Design Guide*, London: E&FN Spon.

Banham, Reyner (1969), *The Architecture of the Well-tempered Environment*, London: Architectural Press.

Battle, Guy (2003), 'The Air We Breath', in Gissen, David (ed.), *Big & Green: Toward Sustainable Architecture in the 21ˢᵗ Century*, New York: Princeton Architectural Press, pp. 36–45.

Beck, Ulrich (1992), *Risk Society. Towards a New Modernity*, London: Sage.

—— (2001), *World Risk Society*, London: Blackwell (1999, first edition).

Beijing Municipal Environmental Protection Bureau (2002a), *1998 Report on the State of the Environment in Beijing*, retrieved from http://www.bjepb.gov.cn/ English_homepage/breif_intro/brief_intro.htm on July 5 2002.

—— (2002b), *Brief Introduction*, retrieved from http://www.bjepb.gov.cn/English _homepage/breif_intro/brief_intro.htm on July 5 2002.

Beijing Standing Committee (2002), *The Organizational Set-up of the Standing Committee of Beijing Municipal People's Congress*, retrieved from http://www. bjrd.gov.cn/index_e.html on July 5 2002.

Benevolo, Leonardo (1963), *The Origins of the Modern Urbanism*, Paris: Dunot.

Bergs, J.A. and S. Renes, 'Sustainable Utility Building: a Matter of Sustainable Entrepreneurship', *Journal of Environmental Sciences*, No. 2, Year 15, pp. 71–78.

Bhatt, V., Casult, A., Covo, D., and Jésus Navarrete (1995), 'Les Projets de Reconstruction de Quartiers à Pékin: Le Cas de Huashi Xiejie', in Henriot, Christian (ed.) (1995), *Les Métropoles Chinoises au XXᵉ Siècle*, Paris: Editions Arguments.

Biswas, Ramesh Kumar (2000), 'An Approach to Chinese Urban Culture', in Kögel, E. and Ulf Meyer (eds), *The Chinese City. Between Tradition and Modernity*, Berlin: Jovis Verlagsburö, pp. 23–30.

Blair, A. R., Joseph S. Tulchin, and Allison M. Garland (1996), 'Introduction: Globalism and Local Realities – Five Paths to the Future', in Cohen, M.A., Ruble, B.A., Tulchin, J.S., and Allison M. Garland (eds), *Preparing for the Urban Future – Global Pressures and Local Forces*, Washington, D.C.: Woodrow Wilson Centre Special Studies, pp. 1–22.

Blowers, Andrew (1997), 'Environmental Policy: Ecological Modernization or the Risk Society?', *Urban Studies*, Vol. 34, Nos. 5–6, pp. 845–871.

Booman, O. and Roemer van Toorn (eds) (1994), *The Invisible in Architecture*, New York: Academy Editions.

Borja, J. and Manuel Castells (1997), *Local and Global Management of Cities in the Information Age*, London: Earthscan.

Bouman, A.H. (2000), 'Nike's European Head Office: a New Approach to Energy Efficiency in Office Buildings', *CADDET Energy Efficiency*, Special Issue on the Netherlands.

Brazil Ministry of Labour (2002), retrieved from http://www.mtb.gov.br/ on July 17 2002.

Brown, R., Carrie Webber, and Jon Koomey (2000), *Status and Future Directions of the Energy Star Program*, Proceedings of the 2000 ACEEE Summer Study.

Brundtland, H. (1987), *Our Common Future*, Oxford: Oxford University Press for the World Commission on Environment and Development.

Buttel, F.H. (2000a), 'Ecological Modernization as a Social Theory', *Geoforum*, Vol. 31, pp. 57–65.

—— (2000b), 'Classical Theory and Contemporary Environmental Sociology: some reflections on the antecedents and prospects for reflexive modernization theories in the study of environment and society', in Spaargaren, G., Mol, A.P.J., and Frederick H. Buttel (eds), *Environment and Global Modernity*, London: Sage, pp. 17–39.

Cao Lianqun (1993), 'An Exploration of the Thinking and Method of the Revision of Beijing's Master Planning', *China City Planning Review*, Vol. 9, Nos. 1, 2, 3, December 1993, pp. 7–9.

Carmona, M. and Jürgen Rosemann (eds) (2000), *Globalization, Urban Form & Governance*, Delft, the Netherlands: Delft University Press.

Castells, Manuel (1997), *The Urban Question: A Marxist Approach*, Cambridge, Mass.: MIT Press.

—— (1989), *The Informational City: Information Technology, Economic Restructuring, and the Urban-Regional Process*, London: Blackwell.

—— (1996), *The Rise of the Network Society*, Oxford: Blackwell.

—— (2000), 'European Cities, the Informational Society, and the Global Economy', in Deben, L., Heinemeijer, W., and Dick van der Vaart (eds), *Understanding Amsterdam: Essays on Economic Vitality, City Life and Urban Form*, Amsterdam: Het Spinhuis, pp. 1–18.

CB Richard Ellis (2001), *News January 2001*, retrieved from http://www.richard-ellis.co.uk/news on June 17 2002.

—— (2002a), *São Paulo & Rio de Janeiro Market Index 2002*, retrieved from http://www.cbre.com on June 17 2002.

—— (2002b), *Global Market Rents*, retrieved from http://www.cbre.com on August 12 2002.

—— (2002c), *People's Republic of China Market Index Brief*, retrieved from http://www.cbre.com on August 12 2002.

CBS (Centraal Bureau voor de Statistiek, the Netherlands) (1997), *Netherlands Official Statistics*, http://www.cbs.nl/en/products/articles/general/a-125/1997/nos97–4.pdf.

CETESB (Companhia de Tecnologia de Saneamento Ambiental) (1994), *Relatório de Qualidade do Ar no Estado de São Paulo-1993*, São Paulo: CETESB.

CG/LA Infrastructure (2001), *Snapshot of the Brazilian Electricity Marketplace – Part 2*, Washington D.C.: CG/LA.

Chang Sen-Dou (1998), 'Beijing: Perspectives on Preservation, Environment, and Development', *Cities*, Vol. 15, No. 1, pp. 13–25.

Chappells, H., Klintman, M., Lindèn, A., Shove, E., Spaaragaren, G., and Bas van Vliet (2000), *Domestic Consumption, Utility Services and the Environment*, unpublished report, Wageningen University.

Chinese Embassy to the United States of America (2001), *PRC Water: Waste a Lot, Have Not: The Problem is Policy not Technology*, retrieved from http://www.usembassy-china.org.cn/english/sandt/watercas.htm on September 4 2001.

Chung, C.J, Inaba, J., Koolhaas, R., and Sze Tsung Leong (eds) (2001), *Great Leap Forward*, Köln: Taschen.

Cohen, Michael A. (1996), 'The Hypothesis of Urban Convergence: are Cities in the North and South becoming more alike in the Age of Globalization?', in Cohen,

M.A., Ruble, B.A., Tulchin, J.S., and Allison M. Garland (eds), *Preparing for the Urban Future – Global Pressures and Local Forces*, Washington, D.C.: Woodrow Wilson Centre Special Studies, pp. 25–38.

Conlon, Joseph (1999), *Energy Efficient Improvements Enhance Value*, retrieved from http://albany.bcentral.com/albany/stories/1999/05/31/focus5.html on August 6 2001.

Cook, Jeffrey (2000), 'Evolution of American Office Architecture to 1950. Pollution vs. passive strategies to design the work environment', paper presented at the PLEA 2000 conference on Architecture, City, Environment, Cambridge, England, 2–5 July 2000.

Coombes, Anthony (1999), 'Mass and Void in the People's Republic', *2G International Architectural Review* No. 10, 1999/II, Barcelona: GG, pp. 112–119.

Cox, Susan (1985), 'No Tragedy of the Commons', *Environmental Ethics*, Spring, pp. 49–61.

Cunningham, W. and Barbara W. Saigo (1997), *Environmental Science – A Global Concern*, London: Wm. C. Brown Publishers.

D'Arcy, E. and Geoffrey Keogh (1999), 'The Property Market and Urban Competitiveness: A Review', *Urban Studies*, Vol. 36, Nos. 5–6, pp. 917–928.

Daniels, Klaus (1997), *The Technology of Ecological Building: Basic Principles and Measures, Examples and Ideas*, Berlin: Birkhauser.

Davies, C. and Ian Lambot (1997), *Commerzbank Frankfurt, Prototype for an Ecological High-Rise*, Surrey: Watermark/Birkhauser.

Der-Petrossian, B. and Erik Johansson (2000), 'Construction and Environment: Improving Energy Efficiency', *Building Issues*, Vol. 10, No. 2, Lund: Lund University, Housing Development & Management.

Dewulf, G., Krumm, P., and Hans de Jonge (eds) (2000), *Successful Corporate Real Estate*, Nieuwegein, the Netherlands: Arko Publishers.

Dianchun Jiang, Jean Jinghan Chen, and David Isaac (1998), 'The Effect of Foreign Investment on the Real Estate Industry in China', *Urban Studies*, Vol. 35, No. 11, pp. 2101–2110.

Dicken, Peter (1997), 'Transnational Corporations and Nation-States', *International Social Science Journal*, 151, March 1997, pp. 77–89.

Dijk, H. van and Paul Meurs (1998), 'Megalopolis adrift: São Paulo's structured calamity', *Archis*, No. 1, the Netherlands.

Dong Guangqi (1994), 'Retrospect and Prospect of the Protection and Reconstruction of Old Beijing', *China City Planning Review*, September 1994, pp. 12–16.

DTZ (2001), *Global Office Occupancy Costs Survey 2001*, New York: DTZ Research.

Duara, Prasenjit (1998), 'Transnationalism in the Era of Nation-States. China: 1900 – 1945', *Development and Change*, Vol. 29, No. 4, pp. 647–670.

Dunlap, Riley (2000), 'The Evolution of Environmental Sociology: A Brief History and Assessment of the American Experience', in Redclift, M. and Graham Woodgate (eds), *The International Handbook of Environmental Sociology*, Cheltenham: Edward Elgar, pp. 21–39.

Dürrschmidt, Jörg (1997), 'The Delinking of Locale and Milieu. On the Situatedness of extended Milieux in a Global Environment', in Eade, John (ed.) (1997), *Living the Global City. Globalization as a Local Process*, London: Routledge, pp. 56–72.

Dutch National Team (1998), 'Sustainable Building: Enhancing the Energy Performance Coefficient', *CADDET Energy Efficiency*, Newsletter No. 1, 1998.

Eade, John (1997), 'Reconstructing Places. Changing Images of Locality in Docklands and Spitalfields', in Eade, John (ed.), *Living the Global City. Globalization as a Local Process*, London: Routledge, pp. 127–145.

Edwards, Brian (1996), *Towards Sustainable Architecture, European Directives & Building Design*, Oxford: Butterworth Architecture Legal Series.

—— (1998), *Green Buildings Pay*, London: E&FN Spon.

Eletropaulo (Electric Energy Utility of São Paulo) (2002), retrieved from http://www.eletropaulo.com.br on July 9 2002.

Elmroth, Arne (1991), 'Building Technology and Energy Management', *Building in China*, Vol. 4, No. 4, pp. 26–30.

European Academy of the Urban Environment (1997), *Designing Ecological Settlements*, Berlin: Dietrich Reimer Verlag.

European Commission (1999), *Status Report on European Telework 1998*, retrieved from http://www.eto.org.uk/twork/tw98/index.htm on August 15 2002.

European Commission Thermie Project (1998a), *Design Standards for Energy Efficient Buildings*, Information Dossier, No. 6, March 1998, Brussels: The European Commission Directorate-General for Energy.

European Commission Thermie Project (1998b), *Radiant Cooling Systems and Applications*, Brussels: The European Commission Directorate-General for Energy.

EMPLASA (Metropolitan Planning Company of Greater São Paulo) (1990), *Sumário de Dados da Grande São Paulo*, São Paulo: EMPLASA.

—— (2000), *Por Dentro do Município de São Paulo*, São Paulo: EMPLASA (CD ROM).

—— (2002), retrieved from http://www.emplasa.sp.gov.br on July 7 2002.

ESCAP (2003), *Sustainable Development Strategy of Beijing*, retrieved from http://www.unescap.org/drpad/vc/conference/ex_cn_12_sds.htm on October 6 2003.

Fainstein, Susan (2000), 'The Egalitarian City: Images of Amsterdam', in Deben, L., Heinemeijer, W., and Dick van der Vaart (eds), *Understanding Amsterdam: Essays on Economic Vitality, City Life and Urban Form*, Amsterdam: Het Spinhuis, pp. 93–115.

Fan Yaobang (1994), 'Some Issues concerning the Layout of Beijing City', *China City Planning Review*, March 1994, pp. 12–17.

Foster and Partners (2002), *Commerzbank*, retrieved from http://www.fosterand-partners.com on May 18 2001.

Friedmann, John (1986), 'The World City Hypothesis', *Development and Change*, Vol. 17, pp. 69–83.

Frijns, J., Phung Thuy Phuong and Arthur P.J. Mol (2000), 'Ecological Modernization and Industrializing Economies: The Case of Viet Nam', in Mol, A.P.J. and David Sonnenberg (eds), *Ecological Modernization around the World. Perspectives and Critical Debates*, London: Frank Cass Publishers.

Fu-chen Lo and Yu-qing Xing (eds) (1999), *China's Sustainable Development Framework*, Tokyo: United Nations University, Institute of Advanced Studies.

Gaubatz, Piper (1999), 'China's Urban Transformation: Patterns and Processes of Morphological Change in Beijing, Shanghau and Guangzhou', *Urban Studies*, Vol. 36, No. 9, pp. 1495–1521.

184 Transnational Buildings in Local Environments

Gemeentewaterleidingen Amsterdam (2000), *Amsterdam Water Supply*, Amsterdam: GWA.

Gentry, Bradford (1999), 'Foreign Direct Investment and the Environment: Boon or Bane?', paper presented at the OECD conference on Foreign Direct Investment and the Environment, The Hague, the Netherlands, 28–29 January 1999.

Gibbs, David (2000), 'Ecological Modernization, Regional Economic Development and Regional Development Agencies', *Geoforum*, Vol. 31, pp. 9–19.

Giddens, Anthony (1990), *The Consequences of Modernity*, Cambridge: Polity.

——— (1991), *Modernity and Self-Identity. Self and Society in the Late Modern Age*, Cambridge: Polity.

——— (1994) 'Replies and Critiques. Risk, Trust, Reflexivity', in Beck, U., Giddens, A., and Scott Lash (eds), *Reflexive Modernization. Politics, Tradition and Aesthetics in the Modern Social Order*, Cambridge: Polity.

Girardet, Herbert (1997), 'Sustainable Cities. A Contradiction in Terms?', *Architectural Design (The Architecture of Ecology)*, New York: John Wiley & Son.

——— (2001), *Creating Sustainable Cities*, Bristol: J.W. Arrowsmith Ltd (1999, first edition).

Gissen, David (ed.) (2003), *Big & Green: Toward Sustainable Architecture in the 21st Century*, New York: Princeton Architectural Press.

Goldenman, Greta (1999), 'The Environmental Implications of Foreign Direct Investment: Policy and Institutional Issues', paper presented at the OECD conference on Foreign Direct Investment and the Environment, The Hague, the Netherlands, 28–29 January 1999.

Gouldson, A. and Joseph Murphy (1996), 'Ecological Modernization and the European Union', *Geoforum*, Vol. 27, No. 16, pp. 11–21.

Gu Chaolin, Qiu Youliang, and Ye Shunzhan (1997), 'The Change of Designated Cities in China before and after 1949', *China City Planning Review*, Vol. 13, No. 2, pp. 10–23.

Gu Chaolin and Christian Kesteloot (2001), 'Beijing's Socio-spatial Structure in Transition', *Trialog*, Vol. 68, pp. 17–24.

Guy, S., Marvin, S., and Timothy Moss (eds) (2001), *Urban Infrastructure in Transition*, London: Earthscan.

Guy, S. and Suzie Osborn (2001), 'Contesting Environmental Design: The Hybrid Green Building', in Guy, S., Simon Marvin, and Timothy Moss, *Urban Infrastructure in Transition*, London: Earthscan, pp. 87–102.

Haarman, H.R., E.N. van Leeuwen and M.A.R. de Haan (2000), 'Sustainable Building Policy in the Netherlands', *Journal of Environmental Sciences*, No. 2, Year 15, pp. 62–70.

Hajer, Martin (1995), *The Politics of Environmental Discourse – Ecological Modernization and the Policy Process*, Oxford: Clarendon Press.

Hal, A., Vries, G., and Joost Brouwers (2000), *Opting for Change. Sustainable Building in the Netherlands*, Boxtel, the Netherlands: Aeneas Technical Publishers.

Hamer, Andrew (1993), 'China Urban Land Management: Options for an Emerging Market Economy', *China City Planning Review*, March 1993, pp. 17–26.

Hannigan, John A. (1995), *Environmental Sociology: A Social Constructivist Perspective*, London: Routledge.

Hansjürgens, B. and Gertrude Lübbe-Wolff (2000), *Symbolische Umweltpolitik*, Frankfurt: Suhrkamp Verlag.

Hardt, M. and Antonio Negri (2000), *Empire*, London: Harvard University Press.

Harvey, David (1989), *The Condition of Postmodernity*, Oxford: Blackwell.

Hawkes, David (1996), *The Environmental Tradition – Studies in the Architecture of Environment*, London: E&FN Spon.

Heerwagen, Judith (2000), *Do Green Buildings Enhance the Well Being of Workers? Yes.*, retrieved from http://www.edcmag.com/archives/7–00–1.htm on May 7 2002.

Held, David (1995), *Democracy and the Global Order: From the Modern State to Cosmopolitan Governance*, Cambridge: Polity.

Held, D., McGrew, A., Goldblatt, D., and Jonathan Perraton (eds) (1999), *Global Transformations: Politics, Economics and Culture*, Cambridge: Polity.

Henriot, Christian (1995), *Les Métropoles Chinoises au XXe Siècle*, Paris: Editions Arguments.

Hirst, P. and Grahame Thompson (1996), 'Introduction: Globalization – a Necessary Myth?', *Globalization in Question*, Cambridge: Polity, pp. 1–16.

Hoa, Léon (1981), *Reconstruire la Chine. Trente ans d'urbanisme 1949–1979*, Paris: Editions du Moniteur.

Hofstede, Geert (1991), *Cultures and Organizations. The Software and the Mind*, London: McGraw-Hill.

Hogenboom, J., Mol, A.P.J., and Gert Spaargaren (1999), 'Dealing with Environmental Risks in Reflexive Modernity', in Maurie J. Cohen (ed.), *Risk in the Modern Age. Social Theory, Science and Environmental Decision-Making*, Basingstoke: Macmillan, pp. 83–107.

Hoogvelt, Ankie (2001), *Globalization and the Postcolonial World. The New Political Economy of Development*, Basingstoke: Palgrave (1997, first edition).

Hou Renzhi (1995), 'Views on three Milestones in the Construction of Beijing City', *China City Planning Review*, September 1995, pp. 26–32.

Hu Zhaoliang (1991), 'Expansion of City – Beijing. Causes and Coutermeasures', *China City Planning Review*, March 1991, pp. 63–71.

—— and Peter Foggin (1995), 'Chinese cities after Reform and Opening to the Outside World', *China City Planning Review*, March 1995, pp. 12–24.

Huang, Y.J., Zimmerman, M.B., Watson, R., and Shi Han (1999), A Joint US-China Demonstration Energy Efficient office Building, unpublished report, Lawrence Berkeley National Laboratory.

Huber, Joseph (1985), *Die Regenbogengesellschaft. Okologie und Sozialpolitik*, Frankfurt: Fisher Verlag.

—— (1991), 'Ecological Modernization: away from scarcity, soberness and bureaucracy', trans. Mol, A.P.J., G. Spaargaren, and A. Klapwijk (eds), *Technologie en Milieubeheer. Tussen sanering en ecologische modernisering*, Den Haag: SDU, pp. 167–183.

—— (2000), 'Towards Industrial Ecology: Sustainable Development as a Concept of Ecological Modernization', *Journal of Environmental Policy & Planning*, Vol. 2, pp. 269–285.

Ibay, Leticia V. (1999), 'The Impact of FDI on Environmental Standards: Pollution Havens and Pollution Halos', paper presented at the OECD conference on

'Foreign Direct Investment and the Environment', The Hague, the Netherlands, 28–29 January 1999.

Ibelings, Hans (1995), *20ᵗʰ Century Architecture in the Netherlands*, Rotterdam: NAI Publishers.

—— (1997), *Americanism. Dutch Architecture and the Transatlantic Model*, Rotterdam: NAI Publishers.

—— (1999), *20ᵗʰ Century Urban Design in the Netherlands*, Rotterdam: NAI Publishers.

IBM (1999), *Environmental Report*, retrieved from http://www.ibm.com on July 9 2001.

IBM (2000), *Mostra Fotográfica do Edifício Tutóia*, internal report, IBM São Paulo

Infra (2001), 'IBM Tutóia', *Infra Retrofit*, June 2001, São Paulo: Editora Talen.

ING Group (2000a), *Annual Report. Ten Years of Growth and Innovation*, Amsterdam: ING Groep B.V.

—— (2000b), *ING in Society 2000*, Amsterdam: ING Groep B.V.

IUCN (International Union for Conservation of Nature) (1980), *World Conservation Strategy: Living Resource Conservation for Sustainable Development*, Gland, Switzerland: IUCN, UNEP, WWF.

Jakubowski, Klaus (2000), 'The Basics of Chinese Land Law', in Kögel, E. and Ulf Meyer (eds), *The Chinese City. Between Tradition and Modernity*, Berlin: Jovis Verlagsburö, pp. 71–79.

Jänicke, Martin (1985), *Preventive Environmental Policy as Ecological Modernization and Structural Policy*, Berlin: WZB (IIUG-paper 85–2).

—— (1986), *Staatsversagen. Die Ohnmacht der Politik in der Industriegesellschaft*, München: Piper.

—— (1993), 'Über ökologische und politische Modernisierung', *ZfU* 2/93, pp. 159–175.

Jensen, Jesper Ole (2001), 'Green Buildings in an Infrastructure Perspective', in Guy, S., Marvin, S., and Timothy Moss, *Urban Infrastructure in Transition*, London: Earthscan, pp. 120–135.

Jianfei Zhu (1999), 'An Archaeology of Contemporary Chinese Architecture', *2G International Architectural Review* No. 10, 1999/II, Barcelona: GG, pp. 90–97.

Jing Zhengzhi (2000), 'Public Space Typologies', in Kögel, E. And Ulf Meyer (eds), *The Chinese City. Between Tradition and Modernity*, Berlin: Jovis Verlagsburö, pp. 57–62.

Jones, David L. (1998), *Architecture and the Environment*, London: Laurence King Publishing.

Jones Lang LaSalle (2002a), *Beijing Grade A Office Market – 1Q 2002*, internal report, Jones Lang LaSalle Beijing.

—— (2002b), *Environmental Legislation and Real Estate in China*, internal report, Jones Lang LaSalle Beijing

—— (2002c), *Beijing Property Index. The Market as of April 2002*, internal report, Jones Lang LaSalle Beijing

Kaimowitz, David (1996), 'The Political Economy of Environmental Policy Reform in Latin America', *Development and Change*, Vol. 27, No. 3, pp. 433–452.

Kahn, D. and Gerrit van der Plas (1999), 'City Profile: Amsterdam', *Cities*, Vol. 16, No. 5, pp. 371–381.

Ke Huangzhang (1993), 'A Great Across-the-Century Planning to Build Modernized Capital. The Revision of Beijing City Overall Plan', *China City Planning Review*, Vol. 9, Nos. 1, 2, 3, December 1993, pp. 2–6.

—— (1997), 'Beijing 1996–2010: A cross century development plan', *Ekistics*, Vol. 64, No. 385/386/387, pp. 189–97.

Kemme, Guus (1996), *Amsterdam Architecture. A Guide*, Bussum: THOTH Publishers.

King, Anthony D. (1991), *Culture, Globalization, and the World System*, London: Macmillan.

Kirkby, J., O'Keefe, P., and Lloyd Timberlake (eds) (1995), *The Earthscan Reader in Sustainable Development*, London: Earthscan.

Kloos, Maarten (ed.) (1995), *Amsterdam's High-Rise. Considerations, Problems and Realizations*, Amsterdam: Architectura & Natura Press.

Kloosterman, R. and Bart Lambregts (2001), 'Clustering of Economic Activities in Polycentric Urban Regions: The Case of the Randstad', *Urban Studies*, Vol. 38, No. 4, pp. 717–732.

Kögel, E. and Ulf Meyer (eds) (2000), *The Chinese City. Between Tradition and Modernity*, Berlin: Jovis Verlagsburö.

—— (2000), 'The Chinese City between Tradition and Modernity', in Kögel, E. and Ulf Meyer (eds), *The Chinese City. Between Tradition and Modernity*, Berlin: Jovis Verlagsburö, pp. 6–12.

Koster, Egbert (1998), *Architecture for Nature – IBN-DLO Wageningen*, Schuyt & Co., the Netherlands.

Koster, E. and Theo van Oeffelt (eds) (1997), *High-Rise in the Netherlands*, The Hague: NAI Publishers.

Kowarick, L. and Milton Campanario (1986), 'São Paulo: The Price of World City Status', *Development and Change*, Vol. 17, pp. 159–174.

Krut, R. and Harris Gleckman (1998), *ISO 14001 – A Missed Opportunity for Sustainable Global Industrial Development*, London: Earthscan Publications Ltd.

Leaf, Michael (1997), 'Urban Social Impacts of China's Economic Reforms', *Cities*, Vol. 14, No. 2, pp. v–vii.

LEED (2003), *Leadership in Energy and Environmental Design*, retrieved from http://www.usgbc.org/LEED/LEED_main.asp on June 12 2002.

Lefèbvre, Henri (2000), *Espace et Politique. Le Droit à la Ville II*, Paris: Anthropos.

Li Min (1997), 'Development of Green Space in Beijing', *Ekistics*, Vol. 64, No. 385/386/387, pp. 255–261.

Lin Zhenguo and Liu Yingchun (1995), 'Evaluation on the Factors Concerning the Urban Economic Performance', *China City Planning Review*, December 1995, pp. 12–18.

Lin Zhiqun (1991), 'The Urban Infrastructure of China (1949–1989)', *Building in China*, Vol. 4, No. 2, June 1991, pp. 2–52.

Liu Bomin (1991), 'On the Dynamic Model of the Development of the Urban Business Centre System', *China City Planning Review*, September 1991, pp. 35–42.

Liefferink, D. (1997), 'The Netherlands: a Net Exporter of Environmental Policy Concepts', in Andersen, M.S. and Duncan Liefferink (eds), *European Environmental Policy. The Pioneers*, Manchester: Manchester University Press.

Littlefair, P.J., M. Santamouris, S. Alvarez, A. Dupagne, D. Hall, J. Teller, J.F. Coronel, N. Papanikolaou (eds) (2000), *Environmental Site Layout Planning: Solar Access, Microclimate and Passive Cooling in Urban Areas*, London: BRE.

Lin, Nancy (2001), 'Architecture Shenzhen', in Chung, C.J, Jeffrey Inaba, Rem Koolhaas, Sze Tsung Leong (eds) (2001), *Great Leap Forward*, Köln: Taschen, pp. 156–263.

Low, Murray (1997), 'Representation Unbound: Globalization and Democracy', in Kevin Cox (ed.), *Spaces of Globalization*, New York: Guilford Press, pp. 240–280.

Luo Tingdong (1993), 'Water Resources in Beijing', *China City Planning Review*, Vol. 9, Nos. 1, 2, 3, December 1993, pp. 15–18.

Marshall, Gordon (1998), *Oxford Dictionary of Sociology*, Oxford: Oxford University Press (1994, first edition).

Mao Qizhi and Jin Ying (1997), 'Development Issues and Planning Strategies in the Beijing Metropolitan Region', *Ekistics*, Vol. 64, No. 385/386/387, pp. 203–210.

Mawakdiye, Alberto (1998), 'Edifícios Inadequados', *Techné*, year 5, No. 33, pp. 48–50, São Paulo: Pini.

McNeill, Donald (1999), 'Globalization and the European City', *Cities*, Vol. 16, No. 3, pp. 143–147.

Meel, Juriaan van (2000), *The European Office. Office Design and National Context*, Rotterdam: 010 Publishers.

Meikle, S. and Julian Walker (1999), 'The Changing Face of the Chinese City', *2G International Architectural Review*, No. 10, 1999/II, Barcelona: GG, pp. 98–105.

Meyer, Eric (2002), 'Pékin: Pour tout l'Or des Jeux', *Match en Chine*, No. 2 (numéro hors-serie de Paris Match), February–March 2002, pp. 26–31.

Miles, M. and A. Micheal Huberman (1994), *Qualitative Data Analysis. An Expanded Sourcebook*, London: Sage.

Milieudienst Amsterdam (1998), *Milieuverkenning Amsterdam 1998*, Amsterdam: Milieudienst.

MINEZ (Ministry of Economic Affairs, the Netherlands) (1999), *Action Programme: Energy Conservation 1999–2002*, The Hague: MINEZ.

Mol, Arthur P.J. (1995), *The Refinement of Production. Ecological Modernization Theory and the Chemical Industry*, Utrecht: Jan van Arkel.

—— (1996), 'Ecological Modernization and Institutional Reflexivity: Environmental Reform in Late Modern Age', *Environmental Politics*, Vol. 5, No. 2, pp. 302–323.

—— (2000a), 'The Environmental Movement in an Era of Ecological Modernization', *Geoforum*, Vol. 31, pp. 45–56.

—— (2000b), 'Globalization and Environment: Between Apocalypse-Blindness and Ecological Modernization', in Spaargaren, G., Mol, A.P.J and Frederick H. Buttel (eds), *Environment and Global Modernity*, London: Sage, pp. 121–145.

—— (2000c), 'Ecological Modernization: Industrial Transformations and Environmental Reform', in Redclift, M. and Graham Woodgate (eds), *The International Handbook of Environmental Sociology*, Cheltenham: Edward Elgar, pp. 138–149.

—— (2001), *Globalization and Environmental Reform. The Ecological Modernization of the Global Economy*, Cambridge, MA: MIT Press.

—— and Gert Spaargaren (1993), 'Environment, Modernity and the Risk-Society. The Apocalyptic Horizon of Environmental Reform', *International Sociology*, Vol. 8, No. 4, pp. 431–459.

—— and David Sonnenfeld (eds) (2000), *Ecological Modernization Around the World. Perspectives and Critical Debates*, London: Frank Cass Publishers.

Moll, H.C., K.J. Canters, P. Glasbergen and G. de Vries (2000), 'Sustainable Building in the Netherlands', *Journal of Environmental Sciences*, No. 2, year 15, pp. 55–61.

Moran (1996), 'Tools of Environmental Policy: Market instruments versus Command and Control', in R. Eckersley (ed.), *Markets, the State and the Environment. Towards Integration*, Houndsmill and London: Macmillan, pp. 73–85.

National Dubo Centrum (2000), *Sustainable Building: Frameworks for the Future*, Rotterdam: National Dubo Centrum.

Nederveen Pieterse, J. (1995), 'Globalization as Hybridization', in Lash, S., Featherstone, M., and Roland Robertson (eds), *Global Modernities*, London: Sage.

Netherlands National Team (2000), 'Aquifer Thermal Energy Storage in the Netherlands', *CADDET Energy Efficiency*, Special Issue on the Netherlands.

Newman, Paul (1996), 'Reducing Automobile Dependence', *Environment and Urbanization*, Vol. 8, No. 1, April 1996, pp. 67–93.

Nguyen, Phuc Qhoc (1999), *Industrial Solid Waste Prevention and Reduction*, unpublished MSc Thesis, Wageningen University.

Nijman, Jan (2000), 'The Global Movement in Urban Evolution: A Comparison of Amsterdam and Miami', in Deben, L., Heinemeijer, W., and Dick van der Vaart (eds), *Understanding Amsterdam: Essays on Economic Vitality, City Life and Urban Form*, Amsterdam: Het Spinhuis, pp. 19–57.

Novem (Netherlands Energy and Environmental Agency) (various years), *Novem: in Short*, Utrecht: Novem.

—— (1991), *Hoofdkantoor NMB – Postbankgroep*, Utrecht: Novem.

—— 1999), *Energiegebruik. ING Hoofdkantoor Bijlmerplein na Uitbreiding*, Utrecht: Novem.

—— (2000a), *EnergiePrestaties van Utiliteitsgebouwen*, Utrecht: Novem.

—— (2000b), *Inspiratiebron voor Duurzame Investeringen*, Utrecht: Novem.

—— (2000c), *Energieneutraal Bouwen*, Utrecht: Novem.

—— (2000d), *Energie-efficiënte Nieuwbouw van Utiliteitsbouwen. Wat kan Novem voor u betekenen?*, Utrecht: Novem.

Olgyay, Victor (1963), *Design with Climate – Bioclimatic Approach to Architectural Regionalism*, Princeton, New Jersey: Princeton University Press.

Passive Solar Industries Council (2003), *Build Better Buildings*, retrieved from www.getf.org/file/toolmanager/O16F10657.pdf on June 15 2001.

Pei Cobb Freed & Partners (2001), *ABN AMRO Bank Head Office*, retrieved from http://pcfandp.com/a/p/9304/s.html on June 4 2001.

People's Republic of China, State Council (1990), 'Provisional Regulations for Development and Management of Land Parcels by Foreign Investment', *Building in China*, Vol. 3, No. 4, pp. 2–5.

People's Republic of China (1997), *The Law on Energy Conservation of the People's Republic of China*, retrieved from http://eetd.lbl.gov/EA/partnership/China/chinaeelaw.htm on July 18 2002.

Phantumvanit, D. and Winai Liengcharernsit (1989), 'Coming to Terms with Bangkok's Environmental Problems', *Environment and Urbanization*, Vol. 1, No. 1, April 1989, pp. 31–39.

Philippi, Arlindo (1990), *Urban Management and the Environment: São Paulo City Environmental Profile*, unpublished PhD thesis, University of São Paulo.

Prefeitura do Município de São Paulo, Secretaria Municipal do Verde e do Meio Ambiente (1997), *Agenda Local 21. Compromisso do Município de São Paulo*, São Paulo: Prefeitura do Município de São Paulo, Secretaria Municipal do Verde e do Meio Ambiente.

—— (1998), *Do Global ao Local. Agenda Local 21. Compromisso do Município de São Paulo*, São Paulo: Prefeitura do Município de São Paulo, Secretaria Municipal do Verde e do Meio Ambiente.

Presas, Luciana Melchert Saguas (2001a), 'The Ecological Modernisation of the Building Industry. Policy Approaches to Higher Performance Buildings', paper presented at the PLEA 2001 conference on Passive and Low Energy Architecture, Florianópolis, Brazil, 31 October 2001.

—— (2001b), 'The Ecological Modernisation of the Building Industry. The Role of Stakeholders in the Construction of Sustainable Buildings', paper presented at the UICB 2001 conference on Housing Towards the Future, Beijing, China, 10 October 2001.

—— (2001c), 'The Environmental and Spatial Transformation of World Cities', *Habitat Debate*, Vol. 7, No. 4, December 2001, Nairobi: United Nations Centre for Human Settlements.

Ragon, M. (1986), *Histoire de l'Architecture et de l'Urbanisme Modernes – De Brasilia au Post-modernisme 1940–1991*, Paris: Collection Points.

Raymond, Santa (2001), 'Offices that Send the Right Signals', *Financial Times*, 29 May 2001.

Raymond, S. and Roger Cunliffe (2000), *Tomorrow's Office. Creating Effective and Humane Interiors*, London: E&FN Spon.

Redclift, Michael (2000), 'Environmental Social Theory for a Globalizing World Economy', in Spaargaren, G., Mol, A.P.J., and Frederick H. Buttel (eds), *Environment and Global Modernity*, London: Sage, pp. 151–162.

—— and Graham Woodgate (eds) (2000), *The International Handbook of Environmental Sociology*, Cheltenham: Edward Elgar.

Reijnders, L. and M.A.J. Huijbregt (2000), 'Tools for the Evaluation and Improvement of Buildings', *Journal of Environmental Sciences*, No. 2, Year 15, pp. 89–96.

Ribbeck, Eckhart (2001), 'Peking – vom Kaiserpalast zur Investoren Stadt', *Trialog*, Vol. 68, pp. 9–14.

Rienstra, Sytze and Piet Rietveld (1999), 'Spatial Economic Impacts of International Head Office Locations: a Case Study of Amsterdam South', *European Urban and Regional Studies*, Vol. 6, No. 1, pp. 85–89.

Rincón, Hugo R. (2000), 'São Paulo', in Romanos, Michael C. (ed.), *Spatial Transformations. Turning Points in the Evolution of Cities*, Cincinnati: University of Cincinnati, School of Planning, pp. 85–103.

Rinkevicius, Leonardas (2000), 'The Ideology of Ecological Modernization in "Double-Risk" Societies: a case study of Lithuanian environmental policy', in Spaargaren, G., Mol, A.P.J, and Frederick H. Buttel (eds), *Environment and Global Modernity*, London: Sage, pp. 163–185.

Ritzer, George (2000), *The McDonaldization of Society*, Pine Forge Press (third edition).

Roaf, S. and Mary Hancock (eds) (1992), *Energy Efficient Building: A Design Guide*, Oxford: Blackwell Scientific Publications.

Robertson, Roland (1991), 'Social Theory, Cultural Relativity and the Problem of Globality', in King, Anthony D. (ed.), *Culture Globalization and the World-System*, London: Macmillan.

—— (1992), *Globalization: Social Theory and Global Culture*, London: Sage.

Rocca, Jean-Louis (1995), 'Un Mal Nécessaire. Le Contrôle des 'Nouvelles Populations' dans la Municipalité de Pékin', in Henriot, Christian (ed.) (1995), *Les Métropoles Chinoises au XXᵉ Siècle*, Paris: Editions Arguments.

Rocco, Roberto (2000), 'São Paulo: Globalization, Governance and Urban Form', in Carmona, M. and Jürgen Rosemann (eds), *Globalization, Urban Form & Governance*, Delft, the Netherlands: Delft University Press.

Rogers, Richard (1997), *Cities for a Small Planet*, London: Faber and Faber.

Rolnik, Raquel (1997), *A Cidade e a Lei. Legislação, Política Urbana e Territórios na Cidade de São Paulo*, São Paulo: Fapesp, Studio Nobel.

Roo, Gerritt de (1999), *Environmental Conflicts in Compact Cities – Complexity, Decision making and Policy Approaches*, Gröningen, the Netherlands: University of Gröningen.

Roodman, D. M. and Nicholas Lenssen (1995), *A Building Revolution: How Ecology and Health Concerns are Transforming Construction*, Washington D.C.: Worldwatch Paper 124.

Roqué, Julie A. (1996), 'The Social Dimensions of Technological Change: Reshaping Cities and Urban Life', in Cohen, M.A., Ruble, B.A., Tulchin, J.S., and Allison M. Garland (eds), *Preparing for the Urban Future – Global Pressures and Local Forces*, Washington, D.C.: Woodrow Wilson Centre Special Studies, pp. 171–199.

Rosario, Louise (2001), 'Pain Barrier', *World Architecture*, Vol. 1000, October 2001.

Rosenfeld, Arthur H. (1999), 'The Art of Energy Efficiency: Protecting the Environment with Better Technology', *Annual Review Energy and Environment*, Vol. 24, pp. 33–82.

Rosenlund, Hans (2000), 'Climatic Design of Buildings Using Passive Techniques', *Building Issues*, Vol. 10, No. 1, Lund: Lund University, Housing Development & Management.

Ruano, Miguel (1999a), 'Urban Impressions', *2G International Architectural Review*, No. 10, 1999/II, Barcelona: GG, pp. 14–27.

—— (1999b), 'Strangers in … paradise?', *2G International Architectural Review*, No. 10, 1999/II, Barcelona: GG, pp. 30–87.

Rugman, Alan (1994), 'A Canadian Perspective on Nafta', *International Executive*, Vol. 36, No. 1, pp. 33–54.

SABESP (Water Utility Company of São Paylo) (2002), retrieved from http://www.sabesp.com.br on July 17 2002.

Santamouris, M. (2001), 'The Canyon Effect', in Santamouris, M. (ed.) (2001), *Energy and Climate in the Urban Built Environment*, London: James & James.

Sassen, Saskia (2001), *The Global City, New York, London, Tokyo*, Princeton, New Jersey: Princeton University Press (1991, first edition).

—— (1994), *Cities in a World Economy*, Thousand Oaks, CA: Pine Forge Press.

—— (1999), 'Hong Kong-Shanghai: Networking as Global Cities', *2G International Architectural Review*, No. 10, 1999/II, Barcelona: GG, pp. 106–111.

Savitch, H.V. (1996), 'Cities in a Global Era: A New Paradigm for the Next Millennium', in Cohen, M.A., Ruble, B.A., Tulchin, J.S., and Allison M. Garland (eds), *Preparing for the Urban Future – Global Pressures and Local Forces*, Washington, D.C.: Woodrow Wilson Centre Special Studies, pp. 39–65.

Schiller, Silvia de (2000a), 'Transformation of Urban Tissue and Environmental Impact: The Case of Buenos Aires', in Carmona, M. and Jürgen Rosemann (eds), *Globalization, Urban Form & Governance*, Delft, the Netherlands: Delft University Press.

—— (2000b), 'Sustainable Urban Form: Environment and Climate Responsive Design', in Carmona, M. and Jürgen Rosemann (eds), *Globalization, Urban Form & Governance*, Delft, the Netherlands: Delft University Press.

Schmid, Peter (1986), *Bio-logische Baukonstruktion – Wege zu einer integralen Bau- und Ausbautechnik*, Köln: Rudolf Müller.

Scholte, J.A. (1996), 'Beyond the buzzword: Towards a critical theory of globalization', in Kofman, E. and G. Youngs (eds), *Globalization*, London: Pinter.

Scholten, N.P.M., G. Huppes and Udo de Haes (2000), 'Environmental Analysis for Building Legislation Purposes. A Challenge to Science and Policy Making', *Journal of Environmental Sciences*, No. 2, Year 15, pp. 97–102.

Schteingart, M. (1989), 'The Environmental Problems Associated with Urban Development in Mexico City', *Environment and Urbanization*, Vol. 1, No. 1, April 1989, pp. 40–50.

Schwarz, Petra (2000), 'Sustainable Redevelopment in Chinese Cities', in Kögel, E. and Ulf Meyer (eds), *The Chinese City. Between Tradition and Modernity*, Berlin: Jovis Verlagsburö, pp. 63–70.

Seade (Fundação Sistema Nacional de Análise de Dados) (2000), *Investimentos Privados Anunciados no Estado de São Paulo*, retrieved from http://www.seade.gov.br on July 18.

—— (2002), *São Paulo: The Emerging Economies' Metropolis*, retrieved from http://www.seade.gov.br/negocios/english/snpct01i.html on July 20.

Secretaria do Verde e do Meio Ambiente do Município de São Paulo (1997), *Agenda 21 Local. Compromisso do Município de São Paulo*, São Paulo: Secretaria do Verde e do Meio Ambiente.

—— (1998), *Agenda 21 – do Global ao Local*, São Paulo: Secretaria do Verde e do Meio Ambiente.

Secretaria dos Transportes Urbanos do Município de São Paulo (2002), retrieved from http://www.stm.sp.gov.br on July 20.

Shen Yahong (1992), 'Enlightment from the Development of Ancient City Planning in China in the Ancient Times', *China City Planning Review*, March 1992, pp. 65–75.

Silva, Ricardo T. (2000a), 'Utilities Regulation and Urban Segregation. Research Notes on the Brazilian Context', in Carmona, M. and Jürgen Rosemann (eds), *Globalization, Urban Form & Governance*, Delft, the Netherlands: Delft University Press.

Silva, Ricardo T. (2000b), 'The Connectivity of Infrastructure Networks and the Urban Space of São Paulo in the 1990s', *International Journal of Urban and Regional Research*, Vol. 24, No. 1, pp. 139–164.

Simonis, Udo E. (1989), 'Ecological Modernization of Industrial Society: Three Strategic Elements', *International Social Science Journal*, 121, pp. 347–361.

Sinton, J. and David G. Fridley (2000), 'What goes up: recent trends in China's Energy Consumption', *Energy Policy*, March 2000.

—— Levine, M, Yang, F., and Jiang Lin (1999), *Status Report on Energy Efficiency Policy and Programs in China*, unpublished report, Lawrence Berkeley National Laboratory.

Smith, Michael Peter (2001), *Transnational Urbanism. Locating Globalization*, Oxford: Blackwell Publishers.

Smith, M., Whitelegg, J., and Nick Williams (1998), *Greening of the Built Environment*, London: Earthscan.

Soja, Edward (2000), 'The Stimulus of a Little Confusion: A Contemporary Comparison of Amsterdam and Los Angeles', in Deben, L., Heinemeijer, W., and Dick van der Vaart (eds), *Understanding Amsterdam: Essays on Economic Vitality, City Life and Urban Form*, Amsterdam: Het Spinhuis, pp. 117–141.

Spaargaren, Gert (1987), 'Environment and Society: Environmental Sociology in the Netherlands', The Netherlands', *Journal of Sociology*, Vol. 23, No. 1, pp. 54–72.

—— (1997), *The Ecological Modernization of Production and Consumption – Essays in Environmental Sociology*, unpublished PhD thesis, Wageningen University

—— (2000), 'Ecological Modernization Theory and the Changing Discourse on Environment and Modernity', in Spaargaren, G., Mol, A.P.J, and Frederick H. Buttel (eds), *Environment and Global Modernity*, London: Sage, pp. 41–71.

—— (2003), 'Ecological Modernization Theory and Domestic Consumption', unpublished paper, Wageningen University and Research Centre.

—— and Arthur P.J. Mol (1992), 'Sociology, Environment and Modernity. Ecological Modernization as a Theory of Social Change', *Society and Natural Resources*, Vol. 5, pp. 323–344.

Statham, Heathcote (1950), *A History of Architecture*, London: B.T. Batsford.

Steekelenburg, Ester van (1996), *An Emerging Land and Real Estate Market in the People's Republic of China*, unpublished MSc thesis, University of Amsterdam.

Sun Shiwen (1995), 'Economic Restructuring and the Further Development of Urban Planning', *China City Planning Review*, June 1995, pp. 2–6.

Tang Zhenggang (1994), 'Environmental Problems of Opening Cities in China During the Development of Internationalization', *China City Planning Review*, September 1994, pp. 30–34.

Taverne, Ed (1994), 'Randstad Holland: Horizons of a Diffuse City', *Archis*, July 1994.

TU Delft (Technical University Delft, Faculty of Architecture) (2002), *Architecture in the Netherlands; 1900 – 2000*, Rotterdam: NAI Publishers.

UNCHS (United Nations Centre for Human Settlements) (1999), *Cities in a Globalizing World*, retrieved from: http://www.urbanobservatory.org/swc1999/ on May 15 2001.

UNEP (United Nations Environmental Programme) (1996), 'The Construction Industry and the Environment', *United Nations Environmental Programme Review*, Vol. 19, No. 6.

Vale, B. and Robert Vale (1991), *Green Architecture. Design for a Sustainable Future*, London: Thames and Hudson.

Vaughan, Scott (2001), 'Reforming Environmental Policy', in Drabek, Zdenek (ed.), *Globalisation under Threat: the Stability of Trade Policy and Multilateral Agreements*, Cheltenham, UK: Edward Elgar Publishing Limited, pp. 147–171.

Verdú, Vicente (1999), 'The Chinese Castle', *2G International Architectural Review* No. 10, 1999/II, Barcelona: GG, pp. 4–13.

Vliet, Bas van (2002), *Greening the Grid. The Ecological Modernization of Network-bound Systems*, unpublished PhD thesis, Wageningen University.

VROM (Ministry of Housing, Spatial Planning and the Environment, the Netherlands) (1996), *Sustainable Building in the Netherlands, a National Package*, The Hague: VROM (Department for Information and International Relations).

—— (1998a), *Besluit Woon en Verblijfsgebouwen Milieubeheer*, The Hague: VROM.

—— (1998b), *National Environmental Policy Plan 3*, The Hague: VROM.

—— (1999a), *Sustainable Building: Quality and Amenity*, The Hague: VROM.

—— (1999b), *Sustainable Building Policy Programme 2000–2004. Firmly Embedding*, The Hague: VROM.

—— (1999c), *Sustainable Building Monitoring. Results of the Action Plans 1995–1999*, The Hague: VROM.

—— (2000), *Sustainable Building Regulation in the Netherlands: Towards Environmental Performance Standards for Buildings – a Description*, The Hague: VROM.

—— (various years), *Sustainable Building in the Netherlands, National Package*, The Hague: VROM.

—— (2001), *Fifth National Policy Document on Spatial Planning 2000/2020*, The Hague: VROM.

Wagner, S. and Karsten Sippel (2001), 'Traditionelle Bauformen in Peking', *Trialog*, Vol. 68, pp. 15–16.

Wallerstein, Immanuel (1990), 'Culture as the Ideological Battleground of the Modern World-System', *Theory, Culture & Society*, Vol. 7, pp. 31–55.

Wang Hui (2001), *PRC Cultural Studies and Cultural Criticism in the 1990s*, retrieved from http://www.lib.duke.edu/positions/issues/vol06issue01/hui_css.html on August 20.

Wang Tianxi (1989), 'National Style and Contextualism', *Building in China*, Vol. 2, No. 2, pp. 18–25.

Wang Xiaodong (2000), 'The Change of the City Concept', in Kögel, E. And Ulf Meyer (eds), *The Chinese City. Between Tradition and Modernity*, Berlin: Jovis Verlagsburö, pp. 17–22.

Waters, Malcolm (1995), *Globalization*, London: Routledge.

Watson, Donald (ed.) (1993), *The Energy Design Handbook*, The American Institute of Architects.

Weale, Albert (1992), *The New Politics of Pollution*, Manchester/New York: Manchester University Press.

—— (1993), 'Ecological Modernization and the Integration of European Environmental Policy', in Liefferink, J.D., Low, P.D., and Arthur P.J. Mol (eds) *European Integration and Environmental Policy*, London/New York: Belhaven.

Wei Gaochuan (2000), 'Public Space as a Stage', in Kögel, E. and Ulf Meyer (eds), *The Chinese City. Between Tradition and Modernity*, Berlin: Jovis Verlagsburö.

Wei Shiheng (1991), 'On City Chracteristics', *China City Planning Review*, March 1991, pp. 3–20.

Wever, Grace (1996), *Strategic Environmental Management: Using TQEM and ISO 14000 for Competitive Advantage*, London: John Wiley & Sons.

White, Leon (1967), 'The Historical Roots of our Environmental Crisis', *Science*, Vol. 155, pp. 1203–1207.

Wilson, A., Uncapher, J., McManigal, L., Lovins, L.H., Cureton, M., and William D. Browning (1998), *Green Development*, Rocky Mountain Institute, John Wiley & Sons, USA.

Wooley, T., Kimmins, S., Harrison, P. and Rob Harrison (1997), *Green Building Handbook*, Vols. 1 and 2, London: E&FN Spon.

World Architecture (1996), 'Special Report: Offices', *World Architecture*, Vol. 52.

—— (1997), 'Country Focus: Brazil', *World Architecture*, Vol. 59, pp. 46–71.

—— (1998), 'Special Report: Headquarters', *World Architecture*, Vol. 64.

—— (1998), 'Country Focus: The Netherlands', *World Architecture*, Vol. 69.

—— (1999), 'Sector Analysis: Energy Efficient Buildings', *World Architecture*, Vol. 74.

World Bank (1991), *The Environmental Profile of São Paulo*, Urban Management and the Environment series, Washington D.C.: The World Bank.

—— (1994a), *Infrastructure for Development*, Washington D.C.: World Bank.

—— (1994b), *Environmental Management Institutions & Organizations in Beijing*, City Working Paper No. MEIP/BEII1, Washington D.C.: The World Bank.

—— (1997), *Vehicular Air Pollution: Experiences from Seven Latin American Urban Centers*, World Bank technical paper no. WTP 373, Washington D.C.: The World Bank.

—— (1999a), *World Bank Development Report 1999/2000*, Oxford: Oxford University Press.

—— (1999b), *World Bank Development Report 1999/2000*, Oxford: Oxford Univ. Press.

Wu Jin (1993), 'The Historical Evolution of Chinese Urban Morphology', *China City Planning Review*, September 1993, pp. 36–51.

Wu Liangyong (1992), 'The Mega-Cities in China: Development, Problems and Prospect', *China City Planning Review*, Vol. 8, No. 2, June 1992, pp. 3–13.

—— (1992), 'The Mega-Cities in China: Development, Problems and Prospect' (continuation from Vol. 8 No. 2), *China City Planning Review*, September 1992, pp. 3–11.

—— (1997), 'Development Strategies for Beijing: The need for a holistic approach', *Ekistics*, Vol. 64, No. 385/386/387, pp. 198–202.

Wu Qingzhou (1994), 'Comprehensive System for Urban Flood Prevention in China and Counter-measures to Reduce Calamities', *China City Planning Review*, December 1994, pp. 26–29.

Wu Xumin (1993), 'Energy Supply Programme of Beijing', *China City Planning Review*, Vol. 9, Nos. 1, 2, 3, December 1993, pp. 20–22.

Ye Yaoxian (1991), 'Analysis of Some Structural Failures in China', *Building in China*, Vol. 4, No.1, March 1991, pp. 14–19.

Yeang, Ken (1994), *Bioclimatic Skyscrapers*, London: Artemis.

—— (1995), *Designing With Nature – The Ecological Basis for Architectural Design*, McGraw-Hill, New York.

—— (1996), *The Skyscraper Bioclimatically Considered*, London: Academy Editions.

Yin, Robert K. (1984), *Case Study Research. Design and Methods*, London: Sage.

Xu Anzhi (2000), 'Introduction', in Kögel, E. And Ulf Meyer (eds), *The Chinese City. Between Tradition and Modernity*, Berlin: Jovis Verlagsburö, pp. 13–16.

Xu Ronglie (1989), 'Construction Technology over the Last Forty Years in China', *Building in China*, Vol. 2, No. 3, pp. 10–17.

Zarsky, Lyuba (1999), 'Havens, Halos and Spaghetti: Untangling the Evidence about Foreign Direct Investment and the Environment', paper presented at the OECD conference on Foreign Direct Investment and the Environment, The Hague, the Netherlands, 28–29 January 1999.

Zhang Jinggan (1993), 'Two Strategic Diversions in the Urban Development of Beijing', *China City Planning Review*, Vol. 9, Nos. 1, 2, 3, December 1993, pp. 10–14.

Zhang Jingyi (1996), 'Legislation on Real Estate', *China City Planning Review*, Vol. 12, No. 2, pp. 46–52.

Zhang Yuanrui (1992), 'Reform and Development of China's Real Estate Industry', *China City Planning Review*, December 1992, pp. 54–59.

Zhao Baoshan (1991), 'Development Budget for Joint-venture Projects in the Beijing Region', *Building in China*, Vol. 4, No. 1, March 1991, pp. 2–13.

Zhao Bingshi (1997), 'Beijing: Urban Development and Planning', *Ekistics*, Vol. 64, No. 385/386/387, pp. 211–254.

Zhao Haiying (1997), 'Foreign Trade in the People's Republic of China: Past Performance and Future Challenges', *Asian Development Review*, Vol. 15, No. 1, pp. 88–110.

Zhao Shixiu (1994), 'Establishing an Operational Mechanism of Urban Planning in Line with the Socialist Market Economy', *China City Planning Review*, June 1994, pp. 15–17.

Zhou Ganzhi (1993), 'Policy Framework for the Development of Real Estate and the Real Estate Industry in China', *China City Planning Review*, March 1993, pp. 2–16.

—— (1994), 'In Search for a Healthy, Civilized and Sustainable Development', *China City Planning Review*, September 1994, pp. 2–4.

—— (1996), 'Transport in China's Megacities: Problems and Advice', *China City Planning Review*, Vol. 12, No. 1, pp. 8–12.

Zou Deci (1990), 'The Review and Prospect of Chinese Urban Planning from 1980s to 1990s', *China City Planning Review*, September 1990, pp. 3–16.

—— (1993), 'An Impact by the Leasing System of Urban Land upon Urban Development', *China City Planning Review*, March 1993, pp. 27–30.

—— (1995), 'The Introduction of Urban Development in China', *China City Planning Review*, March 1995, pp. 25–32.

Index

festive - have it might
as well be indoors
during session 3 ..?

(because so many
jokes about)

session ③ - if unhappy
with it - would
just do jobs rather
than anything
smaller scale.

You can have diff
conversations outside
s'times .

things being under
attack by the
practice !

points
bottomy
chunks

but remember
there can
be too
many people
s'times.

best not to
see others
outside -
disturbing

festive — have it might
as well be indoors
during section 3 ..?

(because so many
folks absent)

section ③ — if unhappy
with it — would
just 4 folks rather
than anything
smaller scale.

points
bothering
children

but wondered
if there can
be too
many people
i times.

best not to
see others
outside —
distracting

You can have diff
conversations outside
i times .

things being undo
altered by the
practice !